SECOND E

Generations at Work

SECOND EDITION

Generations at Work

Managing the Clash of Boomers, Gen Xers, and Gen Yers in the Workplace

Ron Zemke • Claire Raines • Bob Filipczak

AMACOM

American Management Association

New York • Atlanta • Brussels • Chicago • Mexico City
San Francisco • Shanghai • Tokyo • Washington, D.C.

Bulk discounts available. For details visit:
www.amacombooks.org/go/specialsales
Or contact special sales:
Phone: 800-250-5308
E-mail: specialsls@amanet.org
View all the AMACOM titles at: www.amacombooks.org
American Management Association: www.amanet.org

This publication is designed to provide accurate and authoritative information in regard to the subject matter covered. It is sold with the understanding that the publisher is not engaged in rendering legal, accounting, or other professional service. If legal advice or other expert assistance is required, the services of a competent professional person should be sought.

Library of Congress Cataloging-in-Publication Data

Zemke, Ron.
   Generations at work : managing the clash of boomers, Gen Xers, and Gen
   Yers in the workplace / Ron Zemke, Claire Raines, Bob Filipczak. — 2nd ed.
      p.   cm.
   Includes bibliographical references and index.
   ISBN-13: 978-0-8144-3233-4
   ISBN-10: 0-8144-3233-6
   1. Diversity in the workplace—United States.   2. Age groups—United
States.   3. Conflict of generations—United States.   4. Supervision of
employees.   I. Raines, Claire.   II. Filipczak, Bob.   III. Title.
   HF5549.5.M5Z45 2013
   658.30084—dc23   2012040281

About AMA
American Management Association (www.amanet.org) is a world leader in talent development, advancing the skills of individuals to drive business success. Our mission is to support the goals of individuals and organizations through a complete range of products and services, including classroom and virtual seminars, webcasts, webinars, podcasts, conferences, corporate and government solutions, business books and research. AMA's approach to improving performance combines experiential learning—learning through doing—with opportunities for ongoing professional growth at every step of one's career journey.

Printing number

10 9 8 7 6

*This second edition
is dedicated to the memory of
Ron Zemke*

Contents

PART 3
The Interviews

PART4
Articles

Introduction

The New Economic Reality and the Cross-Generational Workplace

It's been more than ten years since the first edition of *Generations at Work*. The world has changed profoundly and so have our personal circumstances. In 2004, we lost Ron Zemke, one of our original coauthors. He was the driving force that led to the first book. Ron was a brilliant writer, an even more brilliant presenter, and a great mind and mentor. We still can't stand in front of an audience without thinking of him and, every time we get a laugh from the group, it's because we are channeling Ron's spirit. In updating this book, there are phrases and paragraphs and whole pages of the original that are pure Ron, and it hurts to revise them. Just the act of deleting the words seems sacrilegious. Fortunately Ron was nothing if not irreverent, so the idea that we would attach religious potency to his writing would have him chasing us from his office with heavy projectiles—as we fled for the elevator on the eighteenth floor of Minneapolis' Foshay Tower.

Suffice it to say, the world we live in has changed. In some ways, it seems as if the earth has shifted on its axis. We find ourselves *near the end*—we use that phrase with great hope and determination—of a dramatic economic decline that has affected the entire world economy. Recent years have seen a sharp increase in oil and food prices, a precipitous drop in international trade, and low consumer confidence. The European Union (EU) is stretched to its limits as it decides whether to bail out the failing economies of Greece and Spain. Growth has slowed in the formerly booming economies of China and India. In the United

States, the number of foreclosures and personal bankruptcies has sky-rocketed. Hundreds of millions of people worldwide are unemployed. The poor economy has even affected birthrates; according to Demographic Intelligence, a company that produces quarterly birth forecasts, birthrates in the United States are at their lowest in 25 years, "in large part because unemployment and economic fear remain high" among twentysomethings.[1]

The first edition of this book focused on generational issues in the United States where, in 2000, we were experiencing our ninth year of economic expansion. For nine years running, the United States had added more than two million workers a year to its payrolls. The unemployment rate hovered around four percent. So it makes sense that our first edition emphasized recruitment and retention, labor shortages, and meeting the demands of workers who knew they were sorely needed. Those workers knew that, if their current positions didn't suit them to a tee, they could get a job just across the street.

Today, employees from every generation are going back to the basics and lowering their workplace expectations. Elizabeth Milligan, a recent college graduate, describes the shift: "I think the current economic crisis has changed things. I would have said a few years ago, 'We're really skilled. We're going to get jobs and we're going to do something interesting.' But we recognize that the economy is bad. If we can get a paycheck, we're pretty lucky. Today we're saying, 'We just need jobs.'"[2]

The shifting sands of the economy are playing havoc with the generational mix in virtually every organization. The Boomers—and even some members of the generation before them—aren't retiring as soon as everyone thought. As a result, Generation X is feeling as if it has been sentenced to an extended parole in middle management without much room for movement. And some Millennials will spend their early "working years" underemployed or even unemployed because the organizational pipes are clogged with more experienced Boomers and Xers.

Even though the current economic climate might make compromise on the part of employees and job seekers unavoidable, let's not be tempted to assume all those nagging differences among us will simply evaporate. While employees of all ages are surely less confident and emboldened than they were in 2000, history tells us that our tough economic times will be temporary. Job seekers might acknowledge that today they have to settle for less, and current employees might stay in their jobs a little longer, but that doesn't mean we will all perform at the highest levels—unless and until we create a workplace environment that respects and rewards workers of all ages. The cost to a business of replacing a disgruntled employee who is fortunate enough to find a greener pasture is approximately 2.5 times his or her annual salary. Now, more than ever, that's a cost few companies can afford.

In the first edition of *Generations at Work,* we made a case for a new crisis in the workplace that could be solved, or partially solved, by recognizing generational diversity. The work world was then at the beginning of an awakening about generational issues, and our primary objective was to convince readers that some common workplace complaints—lack of respect and inability to work as a team, for example—could, in many cases, be attributed to generational differences. We smiled to ourselves when you shared with us your "ahh haaaa" moments via email and after speeches and seminars. Awareness was raised. But in many cases, that's as far as it went. People got better at recognizing generational speed bumps—and even seeing how they affected work relationships and results—but they were often unsure how to navigate the speed bumps.

This edition is less about raising awareness, and more about problem solving. We look at causes of generational behavior and approaches that not only reduce conflict but actually make generational differences an organizational asset. In these turbulent economic times, it is even more critical that organizational leaders take steps that attract candidates with the right skills, engage every employee to bring out the best each has to offer, and create an environment that lowers anxiety, boosts morale, and increases productivity. With that as our goal, we invite you to read on and learn how to tap the potential of workers from all the generations.

The Generations

The generations vying with each other in today's workplace, as we depict them, are unique and a bit different than those commonly suggested by others. For instance, we define the Baby Boom generation as those born from 1943 to 1960. Others, particularly population demographers, define the Baby Boom as 1946 to 1964. Why the difference? We have factored in the "feel" as well as the "fact" of a generational cohort in our definitions. For instance, our research finds that people born between 1943 and 1960 have similar values and views as the "true" demographically defined Baby Boomers, those born between 1946 and 1964. Likewise, we date Generation X from 1960 rather than 1965. This again, comes from our research and conclusion that the 1960 to 1964 cohort act and think more like Generation Xers than any other group. In interviews and discussion groups, most members of that set of birth years adamantly refused to be labeled Boomers for any purpose. Our four generational groups therefore are:

1. **The Traditionalists: born before 1943**
Those who grew up in the wake of the Great Depression and World War II and faced the world with a can-do attitude.

2. **The Baby Boomers: born 1943 to 1960**
Those born during and after World War II and raised in an era of extreme optimism, opportunity, and progress.

3. **Generation Xers: born 1960 to 1980**
Those born after the blush of the Baby Boom who came of age deep in the shadows of the Boomers and the rise of the Asian tiger.

4. **Millennials: born 1980 to 2004**
Those born of the Baby Boomers and early Xers into a culture where children were cherished, nurtured, and protected.

Note that our generations overlap at their end points. If we wouldn't utterly confuse everyone, we would overlap them by three or four years. There are no hard stops or road signs indicating when one generation ends and another begins. Please note also that we are aware of the danger of stereotyping whether by generation or gender. To say that all Boomers strive for their greatest human potential or that all Xers are good project managers or that all Millennials are hard-working optimists would be a mischaracterization, even though those core traits tend to accurately describe the generation as a whole. The research we rely on describes a cohort of people that includes tens of millions, so whenever you take those generalizations and apply them to the guy in the next cubicle, you will run into problems. Rather than shoehorn your coworkers into the characteristics we describe for each generation, learn to identify the characteristics and see if some of them fit the coworkers who are driving you crazy—and then find creative ways to change your approach.

The most important thing to remember is that the specific markers of a generation's formative years *do* bind them together in exclusive ways. To say, for instance, that Millennials are more attuned to rock climbing and extreme sports than Boomers doesn't preclude the possibility of Grandmas who can ski a half pipe. It does suggest, however, that aside from the passion for snowboarding, she will still have fewer attitudes and experiences in common with the Millennial than would another Millennial. Those common ties are self-reinforcing and self-sustaining and lead to within-group cohesion.

How This Book Can Help

This book is divided into four parts. Part One, "Dynamics of the Multigenerational Workplace," digs into the generations, their histories, and how they arrived at the work characteristics that shaped them—before entering the workplace and then during their socialization into the work world. Without understanding where each generation got its ideas, you will be hobbled in your attempts to diagnose what's going on in your workplace. But this isn't Freudian analysis; it's just knowing enough history to be able to problem solve.

We've done everything in our power to give this new edition a global perspective. Chapters Two, Three, Four, and Five are told from an

American perspective. We outline the history of the eras that shaped the four generations in the United States. It's the history we as authors know best and can speak about with authority. If you're reading in Belgium or Bangalore, you may want to overlay your own history and adjust the timeline a bit. In any case, you will find helpful strategies, tools, and techniques that you can apply no matter where you live and work. And in Chapter Six, we tell you what we've learned about the generations in other parts of the world.

In Part Two, "Where Mixed Generations Work Well Together," we look at three companies where a mix of generations is treated as an asset rather than a liability. They represent a wonderful mosaic of the possible. Part Two is also chock full of tools. We introduce the ACORN imperatives and then provide best practices from a variety of organizations and industries. This section is designed to be a practical user-guide for today's day-to-day manager.

In keeping with the multigenerational approaches we endorse and support in our work, in this revision we don't just talk about the generations, we invite them to speak for themselves. We've been listening to workers, leaders, managers, mid-managers, and executives in interviews and focus groups, company offices, coffee shops, and college classrooms. In Part Three, "The Interviews" we hear from three executives who have put loads of time and effort into bridging generational gaps in their organizations—and from ten workers representing all the generations, who share their thoughts on everything from the worst boss to mandatory teambuilding sessions to retirement.

In Part Four, we've reprinted four of our best articles. They cover important issues from social media to mentoring—and how to chill when the boss is young enough to be your grandchild. Finally, we've included an appendix with an inventory you can use to evaluate the generational "friendliness" of your organization.

A Few Words About Our Research

Twentysome years ago, the three of us became interested in generational issues. We collected information separately and collectively that we used to write the first edition. Now, with another decade of experience under our belts, we are more certain than ever that helping people understand their own generational predilections and the generational eccentricities of others is a worthy calling.

As writers, consultants, speakers, and trainers, we have spent substantial time learning from those who are "in the trenches" facing intergenerational workplace issues on a daily basis. We have administered surveys and facilitated discussion sessions and focus groups to get a broad understanding of how the generations view themselves and each other. In addition to interviewing hundreds of managers and those who report to them, we have interviewed the leading experts on the sociology of generations. We have been part of think tanks and have been closely associated with two of the best minds in the history of generational studies—Neil Howe and Bill Strauss. Our findings are corroborated by the growing body of generational research conducted by organizations like the Higher Education Research Institute at the University of California at Los Angeles; Yankelovich Partners; the National Center for Educational Statistics; Northwestern Mutual Life Insurance Company; Harris Interactive; Pew Research; the Annenberg Foundation; and Zogby.

PART 1

Dynamics
of the
Multigenerational
Workplace

CHAPTER 1

A New Chapter in the Cross-Generational Workplace

"Every generation imagines itself to be more intelligent than the one that went before it, and wiser than the one that comes after it."
—GEORGE ORWELL

There is a problem in the workplace—a problem of values, ambitions, views, mind sets, demographics, and generations in conflict. The workplace we inhabit today is awash with the conflicting voices and views of the most age- and value-diverse workforce the world has known since our great-great-grandparents abandoned field and farm for factory and office. At no time in our history have so many and such different generations with such diversity been asked to work together shoulder to shoulder, side by side, cubicle to cubicle.

Sure, there have been multiple generations employed in the same organization before. But, by and large, they were sequestered from each other by organizational stratification and the structural topography of a manufacturing-oriented economy. Senior (older) employees, who were mostly white and male, worked in the head office or were in command positions in the manufacturing chain. Middle-aged employees tended to be in middle management or high-skill, seniority-protected trade jobs. The youngest, greenest, and physically strongest were on the factory floor or were camped out in specific trainee slots that they more or less quietly endured for significant periods—junior accountant, sales representative, teller, assistant manager. Their contacts were primarily horizontal, with people like themselves or, at most, one level up or down the chain of command. Generational "mixing" was rare and then significantly influenced by formality and protocol. Senior employees did not share their reasoning or ask for input for their decision-making. Juniors, when they had complaints or doubts, kept to themselves or at least to those on their own level, and then usually discussed them only "off premises."

In today's postindustrial info-centered work world, social and physical separations are no longer powerful barriers to generational mixing. Frequently, senior employees are older than senior employees were "back then," and the younger boss/older worker configuration is the new normal. The more horizontal, more spatially compact workplace has stirred the generations into a mix of much different proportions.

In this era when even the most profitable businesses are striving to run ever leaner and meaner, four very distinct generations are vying for position in a workplace of shrinking upward mobility. The old pecking order, hierarchy, and shorter work life spans that de facto kept a given generational cohort isolated from others no longer exist or they exist in a much less rigid, more permeable manner. Merit is overcoming time in grade, or any other variable, as the deciding factor in advancement. One outcome of this largely accidental generational blending is creativity, or at least it can be. People of different perspectives always have the potential to bring different thoughts and ideas to problem solving and future opportunity. An unfortunate outcome, one that mitigates against positive creative synergy, is intergenerational conflict: differences in values, views, and ways of working, talking, and thinking that set people in opposition to one another and challenge organizational best interests.

The sounds of generations in conflict are heard at the bar during after-work happy hours, across lunch tables, on *Facebook* walls, Tweets, and Tumblr blogs, and in text messages winging their way through every organization:

- "They have no work ethic. They just want everything handed to them."
- "You scheduled a meeting for 3 p.m. on a Friday? Get a life."

- "She wants to meet with senior managers regularly to get feedback on her performance. She just started."
- "If he asks us to write one more vision statement, I'm out of here."
- "You sent the meeting request by email? I check email once a week."
- "HR just got clearance so we can use *Facebook* at work. I don't have the heart to tell them we've been bouncing *Facebook*, YouTube, and Twitter off a proxy server for years."

More importantly and ominously, the gripes, complaints, and underlying fundamental differences are not always heard across the conference table or discussed and dealt with in any constructive fashion or forum. Like death and taxes, they are assumed to be immutable and irreparable, and, consequently, are never openly addressed. In the "old," rigid, highly regimented organization, they might not have mattered. In today's "new" organization, they can be devastating. They fester, cause tension, and lead to unnecessary, at times disabling, personal, departmental, and organizational conflict.

Bridging the Gaps

In truth, generation gaps are neither new nor forever insurmountable. The "Archie Bunker-Meat Head" differences of the 1960s divided many a family and society in general. The rancor between hawks and doves, flower children and traditionalists seemed destined to shake apart the United States forever. In the 1920s, the "flapper" era symbolized and chronicled by the likes of F. Scott Fitzgerald, was yet another period when the gulf between old and young seemed forever unbridgeable. Earlier still, in the immediate pre-Civil War period, the United States was rife with generational conflict. The realignment of political loyalties and political parties in the 1850s—with younger, more progressive Americans flocking to the then brand-new Republican Party—planted the seeds for the bloody domestic strife that was to follow. Earlier still—as any history book will confirm—Socrates of ancient Greece was slipped that hemlock highball not because of his annoying habit of answering a question with a question, but for riling up the *youth* of Athens and driving a wedge between them and their elders.

What is new and different is that the new generation gap is a four-way divide. There are four generations at odds in the workplace. In addition, unlike other eras, the power relations are not a simple, straightforward matter of the older generation having all the marbles—resources, power, and position—and the younger generation in revolt and anxious over access to, and control of, those resources. The once "natural" flow of resources, power, and responsibilities from older to younger arms has been dislocated by changes in life expectancy, increases in longevity and health, and disruption of a century-old trend toward negative population growth, as well as changes in lifestyle, technology, and knowledge base. A world that once seemed linear is no longer. Life for every generation has become increasingly nonlinear, unpredictable, and uncharitable.

In times of uncertainty and anxiety, differences between groups and sets of people, even generations, become tension producing and potential flash points. We increasingly live and work in a world of high stakes, winners and losers, high tensions, diminishing commonalities in values, and changing social contracts. And, ironically, we increasingly live and work in a world where the sheer numbers of us and the interdependent and virtual nature of the work we do often depend on and demand collaboration and compromise, not just independence and virtuosity. It means an explicit need exists for overcoming and understanding generational and communication differences to create positive ends for the organization and the individuals who inhabit it.

Demographic Imperatives

The legions of Ancient Rome were composed of ten cohorts each; cohesive units of 300 to 600 men who trained, ate, slept, fought, won, lost, lived, and died together. Their strength was their ability to think, act and, more importantly, to react as a unit. Though composed of individuals, training and socialization equipped them to behave as if of a single mind when called upon to do battle. Social demographers, students of the effects of population on society, use the term "cohort" to refer to people born in the same general span of time and who share key life experiences—from setting out for school for the first time together through reaching puberty at the same time to entering the workforce or university or marriage or middle age or their dotage at the same time.

Demographers like David K. Foot of the University of Toronto see demographics as critically influential in how we see ourselves as individuals and judge ourselves to be: "Most of us think of ourselves as individuals and underestimate how much we have in common with fellow members of our cohort."[1] To borrow an example from Foot, the 70-year old who is an avid rock climber is a unique individual.

> "Demographics are the single most important factor that nobody pays attention to, and when they do pay attention, they miss the point."
> —Peter Drucker

So is the 12-year-old opera lover. Just the same, says Foot, "The chances are good the young opera lover will rent his first apartment, buy his first car, get married at about the same age as his peers."[2] Both the timing and texture of most life events are highly, though perhaps not obviously, influenced by the backdrop of demographics. Members of a cohort who come of age in lean times or war years think and act differently than those born and raised to their majority in peace and plenty. In fact, an individual will often have more in common with members of his or her cohort than with family members belonging to different generations.

A word about stereotypes. We are all individuals; there are a multitude of ways each of us differs from all others in our generation, or even in our own family group. To be effective with other human beings, we must know them as individuals—their unique background, personality, preferences, and style. Nevertheless, knowing generational information is also tremendously valuable; it often explains the baffling and confusing differences behind our unspoken assumptions underneath our attitudes. The 65-year-old webmaster who does rap and mashup music doesn't fit the stereotype of the Boomer senior citizen, yet he was forever touched—along with all members of his cohort—growing up during the Summer of Love, Vietnam, and the 1960s counterculture.

How Generations Differ

In addition to the coincidence of birth, a generation is also defined by common tastes, attitudes, and experiences; a generational cohort is a product of its times and tastes. Those times encompass a myriad of circumstances—economic, social, sociological, and, of course, demographic. Particularly telling are a generation's defining moments: events that capture the attention and emotions of thousands—if not millions—of individuals at a formative stage in their lives. An old adage holds that "people resemble their times more than they resemble their parents." The first headlines to inspire and awe, to horrify and thrill, to send the imagination soaring or cause dark contemplation and heated conversation do much to shape the character of a generation. The music that members of a cohort hear, the heroes they respect and admire, the passions they agree or disagree about, and their common history shape and define a generation. And because generations share a place in history and have events, images, and experiences in common, they develop their own unique personalities. Not that every individual fits that generation's personality profile to an exact "fare thee well." Some embody it; some spend a lifetime trying to live it down. Either way, all members of a generation are deeply affected by the personality of their cohort group—their generation.

Generational commonalities cut across racial, ethnic, and economic differences. As unique as people's individual experiences may be, they share a place in history with their generation. Whether they were raised by neurosurgeons or a single mom, whether they grew up on "the Res" or in "the Hood" or on a military base, whether they wore designer jeans or hand-me-down shoes, they all share with their generation what was in the air around them—news events, music, national catastrophes, heroes, and heroic efforts.

Even immigrants to the United States have much in common with those in their generation who grew up in the United States. Although he

DEFINING EVENTS

1940s:
Hiroshima, Nagasaki
WWII Ends
UN Founded
Apartheid Begins
Israel Founded

1950s:
Korean War
TV in Every Home
Rock n Roll
Salk Polio Vaccine Introduced
Sputnik & Dawn of the Space Age

1960s:
Vietnam War
Birth Control Pill Introduced
Civil Rights Movement
Moon Landing
Woodstock
Cultural Revolution in China

1970s:
Global Energy Crisis
Oil Embargo
AIDS Identified
First PC's
Margaret Thatcher First British PM
Women's Rights Movement

1980s:
Challenger Explosion
Exxon Valdez Oil Spill
John Lennon Shot
Stock Markets Around the World
  Plunge
Chernobyl Nuclear Plant Disaster
Berlin Wall Comes Down
Uprising in Tiananmen Square

1990s:
Princess Diana Dies
Desert Storm
Apartheid Ends
Internet Hits its Stride
Popularity of Google, YouTube,
  Wikipedia

2000s:
Attack on the World Trade Center
War in Iraq
Tsunami Strikes SE Asia
Hurricane Katrina Hits New Orleans
War in Afghanistan
Great Recession Begins
The "i" Era Begins: iPod, iPad,
  iPhone
Rise of Social Media

grew up south of the United States/Mexico border, a 60-year-old Mexican immigrant in El Paso shares commonalities with his generational cohort born and raised in the United States. He, too, was touched by JFK and his early departure from this life. He dreamed of his favorite girl when Elvis sang "Love Me Tender" just like his cohorts up north. He was just as amazed as the rest of the world when a man took his first steps on the moon. Certainly the 22-year-old son of Taiwanese immigrants in Los Angeles is different in many ways from other Millennials, but he shares a whole set of sociology, trends, and heroes with his native-born counterparts. This is more true today than ever before, as we increasingly become a world community via the Internet.

Equally powerful in shaping the views and values of a generation are the first, nervous—sometimes traumatic—days in the labor market. A cohort that joins the workforce begging for jobs feels very differently about life and work from one that joins the workforce when jobs are going begging. The effort needed to bring in that first job makes a lasting mark. A first job that is a first choice and a steppingstone in a carefully planned career has a distinctly different feel and impact than a job that is a consolation, a disappointment, and a subsistence meal ticket.

The four generations that occupy today's workplace are clearly distinguishable by all these criteria—their demographics, their early life experiences, the headlines that defined their times, their heroes and music and sociology, and their early days in the workplace. Their differences can be a source of creative strength and a source of opportunity, or a source of stifling stress and unrelenting conflict. Understanding generational differences is critical to making them work *for* the organization and not against it. It is critical to creating harmony, mutual respect and joint effort, where today there is suspicion, mistrust and isolation (see Figure 1.1).

The Players

The four generations in the workplace span a remarkable slice of American and world history. Major wars, economic booms and busts, social upheavals, rocketing technological achievement, and the first steps beyond the boundaries of our planetary bounds are among the milestones that have directly and indirectly shaped the temper of their and our times. They and we have experienced directly and indirectly more significant history than perhaps any set of generations that have strode the face of the planet before us.

The four generations of today's workplace addressed here cover nearly eighty birth years. They are the *Traditionalists,* born before 1943; the *Baby Boomers,* born 1943 to 1960; the *Gen Xers,* born 1960 to 1980; and the *Millennials,* born 1980 to 2000. Each of these four generations,

Figure 1.1

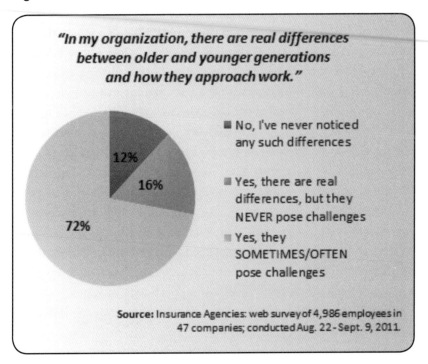

"*In my organization, there are real differences between older and younger generations and how they approach work.*"

- No, I've never noticed any such differences
- Yes, there are real differences, but they NEVER pose challenges
- Yes, they SOMETIMES/OFTEN pose challenges

12%
16%
72%

Source: Insurance Agencies: web survey of 4,986 employees in 47 companies; conducted Aug. 22 - Sept. 9, 2011.

Reprinted with permission from Life Course Associates

their formative forces, values, and views, their workplace aspirations and dreads, their hopes and fears, their delights and disappointments, will be addressed in separate chapters.

The thumbnail sketches that follow preview those in-depth treatments, and they should assist the reader in anticipating the broader context in which each exists and the conflicts and clashes that ensue from their differences.

The Traditionalists (born before 1943)

George and Dorothy are proud members of what Tom Brokaw calls the "Greatest Generation." Beboppers and Bobby Soxers, Rosie the Riveter, and "Don't Sit Under the Apple Tree with Anyone Else But Me" compose the heart of this cohort group. They were infants as World War II ended, and they grew up in its shadow. Born before the official arrival of the vaunted postwar Baby Boom, they are the last of the gray flannel suits, the corprocats. Think "traditional values," and you've got their number—civic pride, loyalty, respect for authority, and apple pie. They attend more symphonies than rock concerts, watch more plays than play in pick-up softball games, and eat more steak than tofu.

Only a handful of them are still working, but they built the foundation for the way business is conducted throughout the world today. They are the classic "keepers of the grail" of yesteryear. They are also an irreplaceable repository of lore and wisdom, practical wiliness, and more than a few critical organizational contacts. Though they are nearing the end of their work-a-day-world conscription, they are still, and yet, good soldiers and solid, no BS performers. And, oh yes, those Grey Panthers control a significant part of the optional spending economy, own billions of dollars of Sun Belt real estate, and are a staunch political force via AARP—and they still hold a few CEO slots in vaunted Fortune 500 companies.

The Baby Boomers (born 1943–1960)

Tom and Linda, the postwar babies, are graying, and many of their compatriots are looking forward to the unbearable lightness of fulfillment at the end of the tunnel. And they'd really rather not be seen as the "problem" in the workplace—though they frequently are. After all, they've been defining everyone else as "the problem" since "Don't trust anyone over 30" was the rule of cool. And to this day, they define the generational world as "pre-us" and "us" and "post-us" when they look to make sense of it. They've never met a problem they couldn't bluff, blunder, or power through—and then pronounce themselves master of. If it wasn't invented in the 1970s or 1980s, it can't have a decent ROI. That's the dark side.

At the same time, this is the cohort group that invented "Thank God, It's Monday!" and the 60-hour work week. Boomers are passionately concerned about participation and spirit in the workplace, about bringing heart and humanity to the office, and about creating a fair-and-level playing field for all. They are, after all, the civil rights, empowerment, and valuing diversity generation. Their energy, enthusiasm, and ability to become engrossed in causes has made the business of business worthy of many Hollywood epics. Their slogan "50 is the new 30" has inflated to "60 is the new 40," but we can probably expect those numbers, and the ratios, to be with us for some time. Stay tuned, they will redefine *old* and *cool* and *important* and *success* a half a dozen more times before they are done with the world they've sworn to change for the better.

The Gen Xers (born 1960–1980)

They are edgy, in your face, and have redefined what it means to have attitude. Li and Devon bring their cynicism and dark humor with them into middle management. Initially admired for being technologically adept, clever, resourceful, and willing to work in an Internet startup from dawn till dusk, they are now having kids. They have a deeply segmented, fragmented psyche. They brought rap and hip hop to fruition; now they're watching *Mad Men* and reviving the cocktail hour. They are a DIY cohort who live and breathe and calculate in terms of project management. Accustomed to little or no supervision, they are content to sit in a cube—though they will complain about it relentlessly—and get their work done. While Boomers consistently reach for their own true potential, Xers are interested in three hot meals and a bed.

Survivalists in their compounds in the wilds of Idaho have a lot in common with Xers. They have grown tired of the vision and mission statements their Boomer predecessors wrote; Xer business leaders publish manifestos rather than vision statements. Boomers are akin to Gandhi; Xers are more psychologically attuned to Martin Luther. They have always been clear about the meaning of the word "balance" in their lives: Work is work. And they work to live, not live to work. Protective parents, they will drop everything to attend to their children.

Xers as individuals are positive about their personal futures and pessimistic about their generation's future. It's a lottery mentality. They don't believe anyone is going to do better than their parents did, but they have the inside line on a lottery number they're sure will pay off. It's the kind of thinking that gives birth to entrepreneurs. Most futurists say the majority of entrepreneurs in the next decade will come from the ranks of this independent-minded cohort.

Most reject the *Generation X* label. Recently, over lunch with Keith, the conversation turned to generations. He said he didn't think any of the Generation X characteristics fit his personality. "So," we asked. "Do you think of yourself as a practical, street smart, skeptical person who works best alone, hates meetings, and delivers projects on time?" His eyes widened.

"Yeah, that's me exactly. Is that Generation X?"

It sure is.

The Millennials (born 1980–2000)

Call this Group 3.5.1, the newest version on the job market. Allison and Nick are among the smartest, cleverest, healthiest, most confident, most-wanted *Homo sapiens* to have ever walked the face of the earth. Their parents see themselves as devoted guardians who sacrificed to bring this new generation to adulthood. Think soccer moms and Little League dads, and nonstop rounds of swimming meets and karate classes and dancing lessons and computer camp. Millennials are an optimistic bunch, and what their parents think *is* important to them. In fact, they think their parents are cool. When you ask incoming college freshman who their heroes are, who they turn to for advice, who they talk to about their problems, and who their best friends are, one answer eclipses all the others: *my parents.* They express doubt about traditional racial and sexual categorizing, and they have *Facebook* friends all over the world who they can, and do, contact at any hour of the day or night. Barriers of time and space have a different, less absolute meaning for them. They aren't confused by the international dateline or perplexed by relativity.

Amidst this dawn of a generational and technological shift, those born with their iPod ear buds firmly attached aren't looking quite so strange. So let's move forward with wonder and enthusiasm as we welcome our Millennial colleagues to our offices, our board rooms, and our flat-screen TVs.

The Challenge

These four generations—Traditionalists, Boomers, Xers, and Millennials—have unique work ethics, different perspectives on work, distinct and preferred ways of managing and being managed, idiosyncratic styles, and unique ways of viewing such work-world issues as quality, service, and, well…just showing up for work.

Managing this melange of ages, faces, values, and views can be difficult duty. For one thing, few of us understand our own generation in context. Marshall McLuhan observed, "We don't know who discovered water, but it probably wasn't a fish." It is difficult to look at one's own life as part of a segment, trend, era—or generation. We each feel too unique and individual to be just another statistic. According to William Strauss and Neil Howe, authors of *Generations,* "people of all ages feel a disconnection with history. Many have difficulty placing their own thoughts and actions, even their own lives, in any larger story."[3] You could even call it diversity management at its most challenging, because the obvious markers of race and sex have less clear impact on the differences. And now, in the hypercompetitive global workplace, frustrated managers need to figure things out, and they need answers right now. Questions such as:

- How can I get my older employees to stay put until they've downloaded their knowledge and experience to their younger colleagues?
- How can I train my young employees to filter out the phrases older employees use—"in my day" or "before the Internet" or "we tried that years ago" and listen to the essence of what they're saying?

(text continues on page 26)

Table 1.1

	The Traditionalists	The Baby Boomers	The Gen Xers	The Millennials
Popular Names	George and Dorothy	Tom and Linda	Devon and Li	Nick and Allison
Generation	*The Traditionalists*	*The Baby Boomers*	*The Gen Xers*	*The Millennials*
Also known as…	Depression Babies The Greatest Generation GIs Matures WWII Generation	The Silent Generation Boomers The "Me" Generation	Xers Postboomers Twentysomethings Thirteeners Baby Busters	Generation Y The Net Generation The Digital Generation
Birth Years	Pre-1943	1943–1960	1960–1980	1980–2000
Defining Events and Trends	Patriotism Families The Great Depression WWII New Deal Korean War Golden Age of Radio Silver Screen Rise of Labor Unions	Prosperity Children in the Spotlight Television Suburbia Assassinations Vietnam Civil Rights Movement Cold War Women's Liberation The Space Race	Watergate Latchkey Kids Stagflation Single Parent Homes MTV AIDS Internet Challenger Disaster Fall of Berlin Wall Persian Gulf Glasnost, Perestroika	Social Media and Facebook Mobile Computing End of Apartheid It Takes a Village Reality TV Multiculturalism Tea Party Occupy Wall Street Tsunami in Southeast Asia

Visible Members	Harry Belafonte	Bill and Hillary Clinton	George Stephanopoulos	Paul Ryan
	George Bush	Steve Jobs	Douglas Coupland	Mark Zuckerberg
	Jimmy Carter	David Letterman	Kurt Cobain	Will and Kate
	Geraldine Ferraro	Oprah Winfrey	Michael Dell	Beyoncé
	Phil Donahue	Bill Gates	Larry Page	Dev Patel
	Sidney Poitier	Rush Limbaugh	Brad Pitt	LeBron James
	Lee Iacocca	P.J. O'Roark	Michael Jordan	Ksenia Sobchak
	Gloria Steinem	Mick Jagger	Matt Groening	Justin Bieber
	John Glenn	George W. Bush	Neil Stephenson	Taylor Swift
		Newt Gingrich	Barack Obama	Michael Phelps
				Chelsea Clinton
Visible Members/ Millennials Music of Their Early Years	Swing	Rock 'n' Roll	Disco	Alternative Rap
	Big Band	Acid Rock	Punk	SKA
	Glenn Miller	Elvis	Rap	Remix
	Duke Ellington	Beatles	Reggae	Jewel
	Benny Goodman	Rolling Stones	Elvis Costello	Puff Daddy
	Tommy Dorsey	Grateful Dead	Bee Gees	Alanis Morrisette
	Bing Crosby	Beach Boys	ABBA	Toni Braxton
	Kate Smith	Jimi Hendrix	Bon Jovi	Will Smith
	Ella Fitzgerald	Janis Joplin	Michael Jackson	Savage Garden
	Frank Sinatra	Bob Dylan	Guns N' Roses	Spice Girls
		Supremes	U2	Backstreet Boys
		Temptations	Prince	Coldplay
				Katy Perry
				Lil Wayne
				Rihanna

- The new machinist in Section 9 just called and she wants to meet with me regularly to discuss her performance and long-term career goals. I'm the CEO. I don't have time for that. Where's her manager?
- My director is so defeatist. Maybe my solution wouldn't work, but I'll put in the time to make it work. How can we know if we don't try it?

In Chapter 8 we will look at six cross-generationally friendly companies and their efforts to turn generational differences into generational dynamics—and we explore a plethora of best practices that help solve issues like those raised by the questions above.

What follows in the next four chapters is a more extensive look at the generational rifts that divide today's workplace, the conditions that cause and perpetuate them, and some ways of minimizing—if not extinguishing—them. We begin with a portrait of each generation, what we and others have learned about their preferences in managing and being managed, leading and working. Then we discuss the implications for helping generations survive and thrive together in today's hectic and high-tension cross-generational workplace.

CHAPTER 2

The Traditionalists

What Will the Colonel Do Now—Work? Retire? Consult?

Born Before 1943

"The difficult we do at once;
the impossible takes a bit longer."
—MOTTO OF THE SEABEES

They are the generation whose vision and hard work built the foundation of the world we live in today with all of its inherent challenges and paradoxes. Viewed as a body, their accomplishments are staggering, "I am in awe of them," writes Tom Brokaw in his book, *The Greatest Generation*.[1] They did indeed have "a rendezvous with destiny" as Franklin Roosevelt so aptly put it. They shook off the Great Depression and rejuvenated a failing economy. They fought a world war and hammered out a lasting peace. They built a durable global infrastructure of highways, bridges, and dams. They built a space program and landed a man on the moon. They conducted the world's first successful human heart transplant. They created miracle vaccines and wiped out polio, tetanus, tuberculosis, and whooping cough.

Their mindset has so dominated world culture that every other set of beliefs is weighed against theirs. When people argue that we need a return to "family values," they mean we need to go back to the morality of the Traditionalist generation. When managers say young employees today lack a work ethic, they mean they don't have the work ethic of the Traditionalists. When we say, "Parents aren't teaching values in the

> **THE TRADITIONALISTS**
>
> **Core Values**
>
> - Dedication
> - Sacrifice
> - Hard work
> - Conformity
> - Law and order
> - Respect for authority
> - Patience
> - Delayed reward
> - Duty before pleasure
> - Adherence to rules
> - Honor

home anymore," what we really mean is they're not teaching Traditionalist values. It's a perspective on the world so pervasive that a large percentage of all generations continue to embrace it today.

Born before 1943, they're variously labeled the Veterans, Matures, Silents, Loyalists, GI Joes, and Seniors. They account for a tiny percentage of today's global work population, where their numbers have shrunk dramatically. For the most part, they've moved into retirement, part-time work, grand- and great grand-parenthood, and Sun City. The powerful past heroes of the workplace—Lee Iacocca, Jack Welch, Mary Kay Ash, Lou Gerstner, Warren Buffet—are the classic "keepers of the grail" of the organizational history and founding tenets. They understood and were comfortable with alternative "big pictures." Those still working today are solid, reliable, no BS performers.

"Tempered by War, Disciplined by a Hard and Bitter Peace"

They grew up in hard times. If anyone has earned the right to tell those stories that begin, "I walked three miles to school, uphill both ways through the snow and wind . . . ," it's these folks. In 1929, the U.S. Stock Market crashed and the bottom fell out of the world economy. The 1930s ushered in a worldwide depression. In the United States, nine million people lost their life savings. Eighty-six thousand businesses closed their doors for good. More than 2,000 banks failed.

Millions of workers lost their jobs; in 1932, about 14 million people were unemployed—nearly one of every four workers. The sight of ragged and hungry people waiting in line for soup and sustenance became commonplace. President Herbert Hoover's efforts to turn the economy around failed. "Prosperity is just around the corner," he kept saying, but no one was convinced, and it wasn't to be so. The Dust Bowl added insult to injury. The farm economy was already reeling when the worst drought in U.S. history burned up 300,000 square miles of Great Plains crops, turned the soil into dust, and ended forever a way of life for millions. Hundreds of thousands who had tended the soil and fed a growing nation became rootless wanderers blown before the winds that blew away the very soil they had lived on and lived for.

It was a "do without" era, but a new generation of hardy scouts had gumption to get things done . . . to accomplish any worthy goal . . . to "bear any burden, pay any price." The Empire State Building was the very incarnation of the spirit of the times. The nation's conscience whispered, "Do it big," and, despite—or because of—the times, construction began on the tallest skyscraper in the world. It stood as a monument to grandness—the biggest, the tallest, the best that American enterprise could construct and that the grit of American labor could create.

THE TRADITIONALISTS

Seminal Events

1929	Worldwide economic crisis begins
1933	The Dust Bowl
1937	Germany invades Poland: World War II begins
1945	World War II ends: millions dead, injured, displaced
1945	Establishment of the United Nations
1945	First computer built
1946	Winston Churchill gives "Iron Curtain" speech
1947	*The Diary of Anne Frank*
1947	Nuremburg trials
1947	Marshall Plan to rebuild Western Europe
1948	Gandhi assassinated
1948	Apartheid begins
1948	State of Israel founded
1949	Korean War
1949	First nonstop flight around the world
1949	First organ transplant
1951	Color TV Introduced
1953	DNA discovered
1953	Hillary and Norgay climb Mount Everest

If Traditionalists seem tight with a dollar and somehow risk averse, it is the legacy of the days when a handful of change was all that stood between many a family and an empty larder, and not even banks were trustworthy. Likewise, they can be excused for preferring cash on hand to a portfolio of high-risk investments.

In March 1933, a new American leader was inaugurated. President Franklin Delano Roosevelt had promised in his campaign to put the nation back on track. Enlisting the youth of the country, he instituted the New Deal, which established the Farm Credit Act, the Civilian Conservation Corps, the Tennessee Valley Authority, and thirteen other major bills for creating a modern national infrastructure, preventing another stock market crash, creating new jobs, and restoring the economy. Largely successful, he helped people to feel involved by broadcasting what he called "fireside chats," and, most important to this generation, he restored confidence in government. He reinvented government, shaping it as "the solution" to catastrophic woes.

THE TRADITIONALISTS

Cultural Memorabilia

Kewpie dolls
Mickey Mouse
Flash Gordon
The Golden Era of Radio
Wheaties
Charlie McCarthy
Tarzan
Jukeboxes
Blondie
The Lone Ranger

The entertainment industry soothed the suffering psyches of children and their families, serving up a brief escape from the harsh realities of their lives. In 1939, 80 million people spent 15 cents each week to see not only a feature film, but a newsreel, cartoon, and short subject. According to FDR, it was a "splendid thing that for just 15 cents an American" could "go to a movie and forget his troubles." The silver screen raised their spirits by transporting them to Tara, Oz, and The Ritz. Garbo, Hepburn, Grant, Gable, Astaire, Rogers, and Tracy gave them glamour, glitz, and hope. It was also the golden era of radio. Nearly every home had a set, and when families sat down at the dinner table, the repast might not be a sumptuous meal, but it was accompanied by the magic of live shows—*The Shadow, The Lone Ranger,* and *Amos 'n' Andy* —along with the big-band sounds of Goodman, Ellington, and Miller. Kids escaped to comic books, and their greatest hero was Superman. He was powerful, masculine, and logical, with a "can-do" attitude. Always upbeat, he didn't let the bad times get him down. The message was to "ac-cen-tu-ate the positive."

In the late 1930s, Americans watched in horror as European parliamentarianism gave way to the tyranny of social democracy and totalitarianism; Hitler's troops marched into Austria, Czechoslovakia, Poland, Scandinavia, France, Romania, Bulgaria, Yugoslavia, and Greece. By July 1940, the only free European nation not in Hitler's grasp was England, where air raids became a regular phenomenon. Out of the troubles in Britain emerged one of the most colorful and dynamic heroes of an era that was to produce an abundance of bigger-than-life heroes—the new Prime Minister Winston Churchill. They were dark times, but Churchill stood for the same sense of determination that was and would continue to be an American and British generational hallmark. "I have nothing to offer but blood, toil, tears, and sweat," he proclaimed. He was fondly caricatured as a bulldog and was adored on both sides of the North Atlantic.

THE TRADITIONALISTS

Heroes

Superman
Franklin Delano Roosevelt
MacArthur, Patton, Montgomery, Halsey, and Eisenhower
Winston Churchill
Audie Murphy
Joe Foss
Babe Ruth
Joe DiMaggio

For Americans, time stood still at 7:49 AM local time on the morning of Sunday, December 7, 1941, when 183 Japanese carrier-based dive bombers and fighters attacked the U.S. Naval Base—and the bulk of the U.S. Pacific Fleet—at Pearl Harbor, Hawaii. As individuals in the Mountain and Pacific time zones awoke, and Midwesterners and Easterners returned from church, they joined family and neighbors around the kitchen table to listen with horror as events unfolded and were announced on the radio. The next day, President Roosevelt labeled it "a date which will live in infamy." He declared war and called on the well-practiced "can-do" spirit of the nation so that, "with the unbounding determination of our people, we will gain the inevitable triumph."

The new generation responded with gusto, inspired by a whole new set of real-life heroes—men whose wits, courage, and commitment were tested in Europe, Africa, and the South Pacific. Men like Bernard Montgomery, Lieutenant General Dwight Eisenhower, General Douglas MacArthur, General George S. Patton, Audie Murphy, and George Marshall were revered by the new generation of soldiers. Some said the initials GI stood for "galvanized iron," metal heated to unbearably high temperatures and molded into something strong and durable. Others thought GI stood for "general issue" or "government issue"; indeed, it was a time when conformity and obedience to central authority were considered a national necessity. "Loose lips sink ships" was the watchword of the day; it seemed there were Fascists everywhere looking for ways to destroy the world, even in the Saturday movie serials. President Roosevelt urged the young to discard the concept of "each individual for himself" and to embrace instead the concept of "a broad highway on which thousands of your fellow men and women are advancing with you." The civic mind believed that standardized things were the "best," "most modern," "advanced," and "efficient"—and the young generation marched in formation. It is fitting that Traditionalists wore uniforms more than any other generation, from their Boy Scout greens to their Civilian Conservation Corps (CCC) uniforms.

By late 1944, the Allied forces were beginning to break Hitler's iron will in the European theater and to thwart the Japanese in the South Pacific. While young men in their 20s fought for freedom on land, on sea, and in the air, the young women at home sacrificed and served as well. Rosie the Riveter and 15 million other American women answered the call for production, turning out ships, tanks, airplanes, and weapons at unprecedented rates. The war effort at home involved doing without—and this generation of women did it good naturedly, creatively, with flair. Living on rations, they "used it up, wore it out, made it do, or did without," conserving coffee, sugar, rubber, nylon, and gasoline. Finally, in 1945, peace had been earned—in Europe in May; in the Pacific in September. World War II was over, and a new era was about to begin—one in which the Traditionalist generation had earned high rank and set a tone of accomplishment they would pursue with vigor for the next 50 years.

The Sandwich Group: Today's Workplace Elders

When considering this generation, it's important to remember that its two halves were not created equal. Those born before 1930 set the pace, while their younger cohorts moved quietly into the parade. The older set were just the right age to answer the call to serve in World War II. They're the ones who fit comfortably and proudly into the sociology we've spoken of here.

On the other hand, the second-halfers—a few of whom are still working today—were not old enough to serve. They waited at home while the cohort ahead made big sacrifices to create a brighter future. Some of these second-halfers will tell you they hoped the war would go on and on, so that when their time came, they could prove themselves as worthy as their older brothers. But the war came to an abrupt halt in Hiroshima and Nagasaki and the younger group had to live in the shadow of all that their older brothers and sisters stood for and accomplished. Instead, they grew up in a postwar world—one that was digging itself out from the ravages of war and turning its collective attention to a different type of conflict, the Cold War, a continuous state of nearly unbearable political and military tension. They learned to walk on eggshells. Though many second-halfers did, in fact, serve—bravely and with distinction—in the Korean War, it has simply never "counted" in quite the same way as service in World War II.

They don't feel worthy of accepting the mantle the older cohort wears so proudly. Yet they can't identify completely with the Boomers who came along just behind them. In fact, they are positioned—both historically and demographically—in a trough between the two. Growing up in very different eras and separated by conflicting basic beliefs and values, the Traditionalist and the Boomer personalities sit in stark contrast to one another. The Sandwich Group rests in a trough between. Likewise, they are much fewer in number than those born a decade before or after them. The end result? The sandwich group grew up without a real sense of generational place, deeming themselves unworthy of Traditionalist status, unwilling to call themselves Boomers—only sensing they are "tweeners," whatever that may mean.

Many did, in fact, act as forerunners, pacesetters, and trendsetters for the boisterous generation just after them. Think of Ray Charles, Jane Fonda, and Gloria Steinem. They campaigned for John Kennedy, joined civil rights marches, and protested the war in Vietnam. In fact, the Sandwich group supplied all the major leaders of the modern civil rights movement, including Martin Luther King, César Chavez, and Russell Means. And it was from their ranks that the leaders of the feminist movement of the 1970s came.

Sociologically, they found themselves in between, as well. The country's mores around sexuality and marriage were shifting, and none felt the brunt of it as much as the second-halfers. As the Boomers mounted the soapbox to offer lip service to open marriage and free love, this group actually experimented—and then paid the price—in the shadows, getting sent off to the Florence Crittendon Home for Unwed Mothers to bear the baby the elders were ashamed to acknowledge.

But the second-halfers learned valuable skills in In-Between Land. Nobody can "get along" quite the way they do. Unlike the Boomers, they can watch a Borat rant without getting emotionally involved, easily and with humor. They are fair and impartial, with great communication skills and a deep belief in the power of dialogue. They don't mind being placed in the role of mediator. Torn as many are between Traditionalist and Boomer values and sensibilities, they are more comfortable with mediation than with direct, aggressive advocacy.

Today, they are transforming elderhood, forcing all the younger generations to redefine when "old" happens and what it looks like. After all, it was Gloria Steinem, a Sandwich Group member who, when she turned 50, grew so tired of hearing she didn't "look" 50 that she had a t-shirt made that read, "This *is* what 50 looks like." She's in her 70s now. "One day an army of gray-haired women," she says "may quietly take over the Earth!" You go.

Their Generational Personality

Traditionalists formed their view of the world in the shadow of hard times and the bright light of triumph that shone over them. They took up the challenge to rebuild war-torn Europe and the world economy— to build a foundation that would allow future generations to live in peace and prosperity—or so they truly believed. As they came of age, the world was in transition from a primarily Agrarian way of life to a manufacturing mindset.

Traditionalists like consistency and uniformity. Birdseye introduced frozen foods—comfortably consistent, uniform, standardized—in the 1930s. Manufacturing offered not only consistency but conveniences that made everyday life easier and more pleasant. Household objects— from dinnerware to dishwashers—took on a sleek new look. In 1934, nylon was developed; in 1935, the acrylics Lucite and Plexiglas burst onto the market; and in 1937, polyurethane and polystyrene promised to revolutionize equipment, housewares, and gadgets. No wonder the World War II era family friend in the 1960s movie *The Graduate* takes the fresh-faced young Boomer aside at his graduation celebration to whisper "just one word" into his ear—"plastics." A generational icon and symbol of triumph of man over the vagaries of nature.

Traditionalists like things on a grand scale. niftier, more new-fangled, bigger, better. The new technologies allowed people to become far more mobile; transportation quickly became faster, less expensive, more available. The New Deal had created a network of rails on which aerodynamically streamlined and affordable trains carried Mom, Dad, Sister, and Brother from Los Angeles to Tampa to see Aunt Tilly. But, by the end of the war and rationing, everyone pined to travel by car. Now that automobiles were mass produced and sold at prices that middle incomers could handle and were eager to commit to, the personal automobile became the symbol of freedom, prosperity, and accomplishment, the antithesis of mass transit, troop movement, schedules, and timed group transportation. Individuality was reasserting itself. Auto courts, motels, and service stations sprung up along brand new interstates to give these liberated drivers a place to rest their road weary heads and replace their fraying fan belts. In the late 1920s, Lindbergh had flown solo from New York to Paris, raising the bar on air travel. By 1932, Douglas Aircraft was producing planes designed for passengers instead of cargo. During the war, aircraft easily and routinely spanned the Atlantic and soared above the Himalayas. The nation was moving towards a bright future of bustling enterprise, and it was doing it on wings and wheels of manufactured steel. Some of their favorite films were giant epics like *The Bible*, the huge blockbuster *Gone With the Wind*, and the kaleidoscopic productions of Busby Berkeley.

Government has always played a big role in their lives, and they placed their faith in big institutions. One-third of all members of this generation are war veterans. The GI Bill helped them pay for college educations, and VA loans assisted them in buying their first homes. Never mind that the GI Bill was actually initiated to keep them out of the workforce while a peace-time economy developed or that the VA home loan program was a resuscitator for a housing industry that had gone comatose during the war. To Traditionalists, it felt like government was coming to their personal rescue and aid. And peacetime government grew to meet that perception of peacetime partner. Unprecedented numbers of the Traditionalist Generation worked in government jobs. Currently, Social Security and Medicare are paying the largest pensions and providing the most wide-ranging medical care in U.S. history to today's senior citizens. The circle is complete, cradle to grave.

Traditionalists are conformers. They learned from their Boy Scout leaders, President Roosevelt, and their drill sergeants to stay in line, be "a regular guy," and do "the right thing." They started young; the men married at 23, the women at 20—more than five years earlier than today's averages—and they started their families right away. The trumpet call to produce postwar Baby Boom babies was sounding, and 94 percent of all American women responded with an average of three plus children each. The roles of the sexes were crisp and clear, and both men and women accepted them without much question. "Gals" took very seriously their job of creating a wholesome and comfortable home for the mister and the kids. They'll tell you it was the best job they ever had—best working conditions, best pay, most rewarding. Their men were macho guys whose mettle had been tested and who now were busy building a better society. Men were men, modeled after John Wayne—left-brained, rational, with confidence in the scientific method: it's true if it can be proven so, with numbers, in black and white. They were taught clear rules about what topics were and were not appropriate for conversation—particularly in a "mixed" group that included "ladies."

They believe in logic, not magic. They prefer conversations that stay with "appropriate topics," and they often find their Baby Boom adult children prone to make conversation uncomfortable with talk of feelings and "too personal" information. They far prefer to watch violence on TV or in the movies than to be subjected to love scenes, especially those with graphic sexual content.

They are disciplined. Traditionalists get as frustrated as everybody else with things like general confusion, poor service, inconsistent leaders, and poor directions—but they're far more willing to put up with it than their younger cohorts. They'll suffer silently. The word "snafu"—"situation normal all fouled up"—grew out of their World War II experience and became a popular phrase of their formative era. When an order didn't make sense, the automatic response was, "Who knows? Some General made it up,"—but uttered quietly to close confidants. It would've been disloyal to say it aloud and in public. It was simply the way the world worked, and this generation didn't—and won't become irritated

—at least out loud—with glitches. One member of the generation says it this way, "Everything in life's a force-fit. All you need to keep things going is a big hammer and some shims."

They are past oriented and history absorbed. After all, they helped conquer the Evil Empire and a malevolent dictator to create a promising future. They feel the future is created by history; when it comes time to make a tough decision, their tendency is to look at the past to find precedents—What worked? What didn't? They make their decisions based on that data. This mode of operation lends predictability and stability to their world, a world that seems to have grown increasingly more chaotic.

It's true all generations become somewhat more focused on the past as they grow older, but for this generation, the past is an important part of their sociology. This is the final American generation to be part of what Alvin Toffler calls "the second wave," which centered on the development of commerce and industry, and was guided by traditions and history.[2] The late Clare Graves, an industrial psychologist who pioneered a body of work regarding personal values and their effects on the workplace, noted that, as we shifted into the Information Age, people became more future oriented.[3] But the Traditionalist generation was taught—and continues to believe—that the future is a product of history, that we have little control over destiny, and that we make our best decisions when we are guided by the lessons history offers.

They've always believed in law and order. The chaos of war and the thuggery of the Depression taught them the value of law. Depression era movies—like *Public Enemy Number One*—were a constant stream of morality plays, reinforcing the law-and-order message. Today, they are more likely than any other generation to favor stricter laws and longer jail terms. They have a much more definitive sense of right and wrong, of good and bad, than the generations to follow—who often view every question as having a field of correct answers. When Traditionalists went to school, they lost points for the wrong answer—and the teacher wasn't interested in how they solved the problem, just that they got it right.

They learned that divorce is wrong, and they've stuck with that notion; when the marriage was struggling, they hung in there, even if just for the kids, sometimes at high personal stakes. If life wasn't fun, "those were the breaks."

Their spending style is conservative. They have always saved and paid cash. Remember "layaway"? A gal saw something she really wanted in the department store, comparison shopped, pondered its purchase carefully, asked to have it "set back," made monthly installments, and then finally picked it up after she made her last payment. Of course, the Traditionalist generation buys American—they're the most fiercely materialistic and brand loyal cohort of consumers in the marketplace today. They tend to buy up inside a product line. For his first car, a guy just home from the war usually bought the lowest priced Chevy. Then, for his next couple of cars, he traded up inside the Chevy line. Maybe for his next car, he changed over to a Pontiac or an Olds. Then he upgraded in that brand. If he made it big, the ultimate purchase was a Cadillac if he'd started with a Chevy, or a Lincoln if he was a Ford man.

There's no denying it: the power and influence of this generation has begun to ebb. According to the National World War II Museum, an American veteran of World War II dies every 90 seconds; the Veterans Administration estimates that by 2036 none will be alive to recount their memories. Nevertheless, for nearly six decades, they were the only generation to support the winner of every U.S. election—from Franklin Roosevelt in 1930 to George Bush in 1988. Count on them exerting their strength in the political arena for at least another decade. Their influence in the workplace will likely remain for years to come; long after they've retired and even died off. Why? The hierarchical method of running business was uniquely suited to armies and manufacturing. It worked best to have the brains at the top, in the executive ranks, and the brawn on the bottom, on the front lines. Top management—the generals —made the important decisions and passed them down the chain of command, where they were carried out without comment, respectfully

THE TRADITIONALISTS

Markings	Conservative, somewhat "dressy" clothing: coats and ties and nylons, neatly trimmed hair, American cars, golf clubs, mixed drinks
Spending Style	Save and pay cash
What They Read	*Reader's Digest, USA Today, Time, The Wall Street Journal*
Their Humor	*The Better Half*

and thoroughly. Competition, the demand for speedy responsiveness, the Information Age, and the nature of workers themselves are, of course, challenging the old order. But, as much as we read about flattened organizations, empowerment, employee involvement, and democratic workplaces, the hard truth is that most operations are still, underneath it all, basically hierarchical. It's a tough change to make, a hard habit to break. Not only are managers having a hard time turning over information and decisions, but the average nonmanagerial employee is reluctant to get involved in many of the more challenging parts of management—like appraising the performance of fellow workers. And, when push comes to shove, most everyone likes to have someone to blame for the myriad of things that just aren't right—and bosses make perfect targets in the blame game. Thus the most enduring workplace legacy of the Traditionalist Generation is likely to be the old style command-and-control leadership they learned in war, modified for peacetime—particularly manufacturing—and believe in their hearts is the only sane way to organize work—and society.

Though World War II was the great annealing event of the leading edge of this generation's youth, its emotional impact and circumstance, its values-shaping power is largely lost on later generations. Boomers have always identified it as the defining event of their parents'—even some of their older brothers' and sisters'—lives. GenXers know it as an historical data point and textbook, multiple choice, pop quiz answer. Millennials know it from movies like *Inglorious Basterds*.

Most—not all, but most—of those who actually served in World War II are disinterested, if not unable to describe their experiences in any meaningful way. Those who try are often frustrated by their inability to characterize the experiences without oversimplifying or sounding like braggadocios. How do you describe an experience that was alternately frightening, exhilarating, humiliating, boring, frustrating and incomprehensible? Or make sense of the oft-heard GI Joe-ism, "I wouldn't trade the experience for a million dollars or do it over again for two."

So it is that Traditionalists have become indebted to Boomer Steven Spielberg for his 1998 film *Saving Private Ryan* and the portrayal of their experience in terms they could never summon. Whether it is true—as media critic Neal Gabler contends—that *Private Ryan* was "the bloody, heartfelt, cultural salve to the divisions and tumult that have riven this country throughout the postwar period," or simply entertainment, it told a story Traditionalists have difficulty conveying. It compellingly told the tale of one of the few times this country was united in a common, moral cause. And it previewed their later attitudes, feelings, and behaviors in the workplace. Given orders that sent them into frightening personal peril, they somehow survived and learned to accept and follow incomprehensible orders ever after. And, in turn, expect their own orders to be followed as they did without hesitation in much more dire circumstances.

George: A Regular Guy

Saturdays, you can find George, 79, on the golf course that runs through his retirement community in Oro Valley, Arizona, where he lives with his wife. Although he officially retired more than a decade ago, he spends most weekdays working at a pleasant building in Innovation Park, a 535-acre master planned business park less than five miles from his home. An engineer for nearly 50 years, he specializes in designing clean rooms, manufacturing environments that must have low levels of pollutants like dust, aerosol particles, microbes, and chemical vapors. George has promised his wife numerous times that he's quitting. It does look like he'll finish up on this current project by the end of next week—which is a good thing, because two grandchildren will be graduating from college, one in New Mexico and the other in Connecticut, and he and his wife want to be there to enjoy both events. Scheduling hasn't been an issue, though. He's an independent contractor and the company gives him great flexibility.

One of the defining events of George's life was the Korean War, although he rarely talks about it. After returning from the war, he married his best friend's little sister—Meg had turned into a real beauty while he'd been gone—completed his bachelor's degree, began his family, and completed a graduate degree from Stanford. After fifteen years with a large firm in Colorado, he was hired by the international technology company he retired from—and continues to work for today. It would be fair to say that George had two life partners: his job and his wife. He became known in the company as a proficient, no-nonsense guy who could be counted on to get the job done. George worked hard, putting in long days, and even an occasional weekend when a deadline loomed. It paid off: The investments he made with his profits will pay the couple's bills and finance a comfortable lifestyle for as long as they should live. Their portfolio took a hit in 2008, but they had invested conservatively, they waited out the market, and now their financial profile looks almost like it did before the plunge.

Today, George maintains his business acuity—although it's not as important to him as it once was. He gets the *Wall Street Journal* on his laptop at home, but these days he often just reads the Tucson newspaper that gets delivered to the house. He likes to do the crossword while he lingers over his coffee. George is active in Lions Club and attends his investment group's monthly breakfast. He reads AARP publications, and regularly forwards emails to his buddies about political issues that interest him. He carries an iPhone and gets a kick out of recommending new apps to friends and family. Technology has never intimidated him—after all, he's an engineer; he enjoys Skyping with his grandkids and following them on Facebook. He would tell you that the Internet and social media keep him young; as he sees it, his dotage will be very different than his parents'.

George enjoys his increasingly more leisurely lifestyle. When he started this clean room project, he planned to make it his last. But work is what he does. He enjoys the stimulation and the challenge. The younger engineers, he says, are good at CAD and other technologies, but they don't have experience in the field, something he has in spades. A few days ago someone mentioned a project he might be interested in that's coming up in about six months. He thinks that might be just about right.

Dorothy: A Tweener

It is 6:00 A.M., and Dorothy, 69, is leaving her home in the Chicago suburbs to drive to McCormick Place, the convention center where she has worked part-time for the past year. She retired from the corporate world four years ago when she was 65. Dorothy was ready to be finished with the corporate politics and demanding schedule, and she was looking forward to spending more time with the Urban League, a social justice organization where she has volunteered for years, and with her church. She planned to join a bridge group, take drawing classes, and spend more time just putzing around the house.

But a year ago, a financial planner forced her to face facts—that unless she could supplement her Social Security and investment income with some additional earnings, she would be out of funds within ten years. She had once thought retirement would mean living on a pension, but the pension plan at her company dried up long before she was ready for it. When she decided to retire, she hoped that if she watched her spending she could survive on Social Security and her investments. But the economic downturn hit her small portfolio hard and her cost of living expenses skyrocketed. And, truth be told, three years after the retirement party, she hadn't quite gotten around to the drawing class and she had played enough bridge for a lifetime. Maybe even more important, she missed using her personality to solve problems and win people over.

Dorothy grew up in a middle-class family that migrated to Chicago from the rural south a decade before she was born. She was raised on the south side with four brothers and sisters. Always an extrovert and a charmer, she pushed herself hard and earned a scholarship to college where she got a degree in liberal arts. After graduation, she took a service assistant position in the international division of a large New York City bank. In five years, she worked her way into the international correspondence room. And from there into the personnel department. All of which made her perfect recruitment bait for the Chicago bank where she would spend the last 20-some years of her career. Soon after returning to Chicago, she found herself caught up not only in the emerging civil rights movement, but the early women's movement as well. Those lessons became the foundation for her career and her life. Dorothy is a great communicator. She moves with ease into and out of distinctly different groups of people. She listens with heart and speaks in such a way that those around her stop what they're doing and focus on what she has to say.

Her job at McCormick Place has worked out well. Each week the center plays host to events from auto shows to gatherings of professional societies to major dog shows to the annual meeting of the National Restaurant Association. Her job is part time but, as it turns out, she can log pretty much as many hours as she wants. She often works in event registration, but she has also served as usher and information booth attendant. Working at the convention center is all about the customer, and her people skills matter. It helps, too, that she's always on time and she's never missed a day of work.

Dorothy doesn't really consider herself part of Tom Brokaw's *Greatest Generation.* Though she clearly isn't a Boomer, she doesn't identify with the Traditionalist personality either. She knows Glenn Miller and the jitterbug from the "old movies" and is surprised by the current swing-dancing fad, something she vaguely remembers her parents doing. She does exemplify the work ethic, loyalty, and discipline of her older cohorts, but she also has spoken up all her life for the Boomer tenets of participation, involvement, and fairness.

> ### THE TRADITIONALISTS
>
> **On the Job**
>
> **Assets**
>
> - Stable
> - Detail-oriented
> - Thorough
> - Loyal
> - Hard-working
>
> **Liabilities**
>
> - Inept with ambiguity and change
> - Reluctant to buck the system
> - Uncomfortable with conflict
> - Reticent when they disagree

George and Dorothy on the Job

George and Dorothy are part of the cohort of Americans whose childhoods took place in an era of hardship and struggle, strong nuclear families, and faith in big business and government.

They share a belief in the intrinsic value of work. Both grew up in times when most people were trained once for life. The question, "What are you going to be when you grow up?" was valid; people didn't re-answer it every few years. Members of their generation held just one to four jobs over a lifetime. Both George and Dorothy are hard working and loyal—and they honor history and the past.

Working with George and Dorothy is different than working with members of younger generations. They see the world of work in subtly different, but important, ways. Working for them or with them, selling to them, or influencing their opinions requires understanding them: who they are, what forces shaped them, what is important to them, and what they want now. Even if you aren't *of* their generation, they're worth your time—after all, their way of thinking laid the foundation for everything the workplace is today. If history holds any lessons of value for today, George and Dorothy are the living repositories of that wisdom.

Their Work Ethic

Good or bad, it's fair to say that many, if not most, managers hanker for associates with the Traditionalist work ethic—at least the part of it that includes loyalty, dependability, and stick-to-it-ism. As employees grow increasingly more sophisticated, demanding rights and privileges, managers of all generations become more and more nostalgic for people who believe in "an honest day's work for an honest day's pay" and who aren't big on "rocking the boat." Many of their parents lost their jobs during the Great Depression, and the whole family experienced hardships. As a result, members of this cohort don't take a job for granted; instead, they're grateful for it. In their view, work is noble and ennobling, something to be revered. Their lives have not been easy, but that's okay. They worked hard to get things accomplished, and that's how they wanted it.

Their work ethic was hugely influenced by the manufacturing economy—a perspective most Boomers and Gen Xers, who grew up in the postindustrial world, would never experience and never really understand. The Traditionalist Generation experienced uncertainty and insecurity during the years following the Great Depression. The postwar manufacturing boom their fathers worked in provided a certain security where there had been none before. They knew there were no guarantees; they knew that they too were, by and large, interchangeable parts. As they advanced in their careers and their corporations aged, these folks hung in there. When, long-time employees were "riffed," "re-engineered," "laid-off," and just plain put out to pasture during the economic downturn, the lesson was not lost on this generation. It confirmed much of what they knew—and feared all along.

Just as they are loyal consumers, they are loyal employees—up to a point. Due to the world war and its aftermath they are fiercely loyal to the United States and its products. They're the ones who responded with "Buy American" bumper stickers when, in the 1970s, the Japanese exported increasing numbers of automobiles into the U.S. market. Many would rather eat their shirts than drive a German or Japanese car—depending on the theater in which their brothers and cousins fought. They have long memories. So it is with work. They tend to view a job as something to have over the long haul. They figure the company has made sacrifices for them—and vice versa—and many have stayed all the years required for that gold watch. They created the strongest union movement in history, banding together to organize their coworkers to overcome unfair labor practices, tyrannical bosses, and inhumane working conditions. But bosses wanting "more for less" isn't seen as sinful or a breach of a social contract. It is "just the way of the world," just one darned thing after another. There's always another battle to be fought.

Traditionalist employees grew up valuing obedience over individualism on the job. Find an old *Reader's Digest* from the 1940s, and you'll see that following the leader was highly valued—and taught rigorously to America's children. Members of this cohort tend to feel confident in their own abilities, but they were taught to respect leaders and their institutions. As a result, you'll rarely find your older employees speaking out—loudly—against authority. This can be a welcome relief—or a troubling challenge. On one hand, it's great to have a good soldier who simply does what you ask without demanding your rationale. On the other, you may find when your older employees disagree, their paths of communication are rather circuitous and indirect. They carry with them the residue of a value that says "I don't get it, but the big boys must. That's why they're in charge."

Traditionalists tend to get satisfaction from the work itself (though that satisfaction tends to come of doing a job well, rather than from seeing extraordinary meaning in the work they do), and you won't find them focused—particularly at this stage in their careers—on climbing the corporate ladder. They'll leave that to their younger Boomer, Xer, and Millennial counterparts. They also tend to get far less stressed out than other employees. Perhaps because their lives are a less complex balancing act now—most of their kids left the nest quite some time ago—they feel less rushed. And, of course, they never had the "you-can-have-it-all" ethic so prevalent among the Boomers. They know that, in fact, you can't have it all—that duty comes before pleasure; that hard work and sacrifice pay off over the long haul; that success comes quietly without a lot of self-aggrandizing hype and lip service.

Where They Work

Attracted to security and stability, many went to work originally for big companies and government. Up until the last decade, manufacturing was particularly dependent on this generation of workers. Today, a few of the nation's senior business and government leaders are members of the Sandwich Group, serving as executives, senior officers, and board members.

They've been attracted away from big cities. Members of the Traditionalist generation always tended to live outside the metropolitan areas and, as they've aged, they have moved into rural areas, suburbs, and small towns. They tend to avoid the inner city, which feels chaotic and lawless to them, and disturbs their preference for law and order. Many members of this generation, too, have small-town roots; in their elder years, they want to recapture that lifestyle.

The few still working part time or on a contractual basis are consultants, writers, researchers, and tinkerers. Some have found that their empty nests have created new, less pressured employment

---

THE TRADITIONALISTS

Messages That Motivate

- "Your experience is respected here."
- "It's valuable to the rest of us to hear what has—and hasn't—worked in the past."
- "Your perseverance is valued and will be rewarded."

options for them. As they make the transition from semiretired to completely and truly retired, they find they are still needed—for their wisdom and experience, and for their work ethic.

The Workplace of the 1950s

To understand the Traditionalist associate or executive, it is helpful to keep in mind the workplace they first entered and that shaped their view of what "ought to be."

Division of Labor	Executives supplied the thinking, made decisions, and passed them down. Workers supplied the brawn, carried out the plans, and did most of the labor.
Rank and Status	Seniority and age correlated.
Structure	A clear, well-defined hierarchy. People knew where they stood.
Advancement	Employees moved up the ladder rung by rung through perseverance and hard work.
Relationships	Formal, almost military-like. Employees called those above them on the organization chart by their last name . . . with Mr. in front of it.
Authority	Call it respect, call it fear, call it a social norm—there was a clear distance between the boss and worker. They didn't often socialize.
Conversation	When people at more than one level were involved, conversations were limited to the work issue at hand; it was irregular to talk about one's personal life, especially about intimate issues like problems with the "Missus"—save over several drinks off premises—if then. Executives on the same level often discussed their golf swings, but that was about as far beyond the world of work as things went.
Boundaries	"Work life" and "family life" were separate and distinct.

Speaking Up   When it came to asserting an opinion about one's own career or a business issue, there were certain unwritten rules about what and how a junior member could say what he wanted to say. He was best served by making rather oblique references to the topic on his mind—and he was likely to get answers couched in third-party language: "The company thinks very highly of you. We haven't seen a way to move you along just yet, but management thinks if you're patient, there will be a place for you at the top."

Their Leadership Style

In leadership roles, Traditionalists tend toward a directive style, which was standard operating procedure in the workplace they first entered. In many ways, command-and-control leadership and executive decision-making was a good system—simple, clear, and evident, without all the complexities of getting the masses involved. It got things done, and produced legendary leaders like Patton, MacArthur, and Lombardi.

Prevailing leadership theories began to change in the 1960s with the advent of "T-groups," Theory X–Theory Y, job satisfaction concerns, and encounter groups. But, in truth, early attempts at participative management and employee involvement were less than successful, causing, more often than not, frustration and poor morale. Most Traditionalists have never seen a compelling reason to change their leadership style, though many have learned to talk the game quite well. After all, their generation accomplished far more than the big-mouthed, big-dreaming Boomers ever have or will—ask 'em.

If the Traditionalists in your organization are in leadership positions, expect them to take charge, delegate, and make the bulk of decisions themselves. If called on it, they may apologize—but not with much enthusiasm. Expect, also, to be a bit surprised at how well some employees respond to this management style. There are a surprising number of Boomers, Xers, and Millennials who like being able to leave their work at work at the end of the workday and appreciate a take-charge-style manager who allows them to do just that.

As Team Member

Don't count your Traditionalists out when you're forming teams. After all, they grew up working as a team, and they're civic minded. They watched the nation form teams that worked together to overcome hardships. They witnessed business and government come together during the New Deal to conquer the Depression. They saw the power of union membership and collective action make dramatic changes in workplace dynamics, and they have seen the impact of the collective actions of all shape and manner of special-interest groups. The early Traditionalists made Gray Pantherhood a potent set of political alliances.

It's just that teamwork has changed its look a bit in the last 15 years in business—with a new sense of equality throughout the team. During their tenure, Traditionalists worked on many teams—but under strong leaders who told them exactly what to do, how, and when. They learned to conform to the needs of large efforts—as soldiers, citizens, and factory workers.

Recently, as consultants, we've seen very strong teams where the majority of team members were of the Traditionalist Generation—or held a similar work ethic—and the team leader was willing to take a rather directive role.

On the other hand, we've seen such teams come apart when a younger team leader did not enforce rules, policy, and mutual agreements consistently, allowed the stress of continual change to affect the team, and failed to manage the generational differences of the team members.

A Word About Teams

All generations participate on teams of some sort. What sets the generations apart is the size, rules, and roles. For the Traditionalist Generation, the team was huge—the U.S. Army, for example, with command and control rules, with highly specialized roles and a strong central authority figure. For Boomers, the group is community-sized—"It Takes a Village"—interconnected like a commune, with shared leadership. The Xer team can be virtual rather than real and often involves no more than three people; it has the rules of a jazz improv group and no defined leadership. Millennials form huge civic-minded teams, much like the Traditionalist generation did, teams that include everyone.

Managing the Traditionalist

Managers of all ages tell us there are traits of the Traditionalist worker they absolutely treasure and that their oldest employees also offer some unique challenges. The ease and pleasantry with which they deal with customers and their dependability top the list of attributes. Conversely, we hear that Traditionalists sometimes buck the authority of younger managers, that they are occasionally overbearing when directing others —possibly because of their "one-right-answer" tendency, and that they often get stuck in the "We've-Never-Done-It-That-Way" school of thinking. Whether George, Dorothy, and their counterparts report to you or work on your level, their wisdom, talents, and skills are unassailable, though sometimes their "hard won" truths are dated and irrelevant. With employee retention at the top of the list of contemporary cost-containment measures, it is wise to do all you can to keep them motivated, productive, and employed—by your organization.

Always keep in mind the workplace they first joined; it laid the foundation for the way they think of work today. The workplace of the 1950s was made up mostly of men. Gender roles were stereotypical; most of the women who worked were nurses, secretaries, paper processors, light manufacturing drudges, or teachers. Corporate men wore white shirts—only—and arrived and departed with their hats on. They've seen the changes, adapted to and adopted them, but are not necessarily enamored of them. Their adaptations are of behavior—not attitude or heart. That, in and of itself, is important to remember: you can rely on them to change their behavior when requested and required. Do not expect their hearts to follow. Their attitudes and thoughts are their business—not yours.

If you're from a younger generation and managing a Traditionalist, it's worth learning from them about their background, experiences, work preferences, and personal needs. Go to lunch. Or breakfast. Or coffee. Break the paradigm, and earn their trust. It *will* take time. And don't expect to learn everything at one sitting. Respect their experience. But don't be intimidated by it. If you grew up in a home where you learned traditional values like respect for elders, that's great—but don't let that respect get in the way of effective management. Go ahead and respect your older employees, but also remember that you're the boss for good reason. Be honest. Say the hard stuff when it needs to be said.

> ### THE TRADITIONALISTS
>
> **What the Other Generations Say About Them**
>
> **Baby Boomers say...**
>
> - "They're dictatorial."
> - "They're rigid. They need to learn flexibility and adapt better to change."
> - "They are inhibited."
> - "They're technological dinosaurs."
> - "They are narrow-minded."
>
> **Gen Xers say...**
>
> - "They're too set in their ways."
> - "Jeez, learn how to text, man!"
> - "They too shall pass."
> - "They've got all the money."
>
> **Millennials say...**
>
> - "They are trustworthy."
> - "They are good leaders."
> - "They are brave."

Some Key Principles

Recruiting

1. Don't limit your consideration of older employees to full-time only. The "all-or-nothing" transition patterns of the past—straight out of full-time employment, then cold turkey into retirement—are far less popular than they used to be. A good portion of older workers are not interested in leaving the workforce entirely, and they welcome opportunities to share their lessons with others.

2. Be open minded and consider using older workers for part-time or project employment.
3. Messages that speak to family, home, patriotism, and traditional values touch the right buttons.
4. Let them know their age and experience will be considered assets—not liabilities. Phrases like "I could really use your help and experience on this project" ring the right bells.
5. Use clear enunciation and good grammar. Include "please" and "thank you," and avoid profanity like the plague.

Orienting

1. Take plenty of time to orient the Traditionalist employee—even if just a part timer. They're far less comfortable than younger generations with just jumping in and learning on the fly. They prefer to know what to expect, what the policies are, and who's who.
2. Bring them up to date on the history of the department and organization. They appreciate and relate to your company "story"; where the company came from, where it is trying to go. They like the "big picture," especially if it is wound around an interesting tale.
3. Emphasize long-term department and organization goals, and show them how they will be contributing to the long-term strategies.

Opportunities

1. Stress the long haul; communicate in terms of months and years—not weeks.
2. Keep in mind that if your customer base includes a good percentage of seniors your workforce should, too.
3. Keep gender roles in mind. Traditionalists grew up with clear distinctions between the roles of the sexes. And at no other stage of life do lifestyles of men and women differ so greatly as when they are in their 70s and 80s. Because men tend to marry when they are a bit older . . . because men die younger . . . and because widowers often remarry, it is likely that Traditionalist men are members of a couple; often the women are singles.

Developing

1. You are likely to need to train this group in technology. Traditionalists didn't learn about the computer in the two most common places: school and work. Those 70 and older tend to find technology intimidating and confusing. They appreciate logic, and the logic of technology isn't always obvious to them. Three in 10 own laptops. (In the Generation X cohort, it's six of 10. In the Millennial group, seven of 10.)[4]

2. Don't rush the training itself. Train in an atmosphere that is as free of stress as possible. Avoid situations where your older employees can "lose face"—where others are watching or waiting.

3. Some Traditionalists are uncomfortable learning from a "wired 20-year old." Find older trainers or teach your younger ones to speak the language of the Traditionalist.

4. Use large text in printed materials. The Traditionalists aren't the only ones who will appreciate the larger type. Boomers with sixtysomething eyesight will also be grateful.

5. A point of caution: don't stereotype all Traditionalists as technophobes. Once trained, lots of members of this cohort take well to new technology and continue their learning, many developing a fascination with it. Remember: They and their cohorts did invent the electromechanical and telephonic concept structures that make today's hi-tech possible. Computer technology didn't spring whole from the teeth of a Hydra or Steve Jobs' brain. Daytime presence on the Internet includes retired seniors who have taken to the World Wide Web, even social networking, with glee.

Motivating

Ask those who report to you what personally motivates them. Even amongst Traditionalists, personal preferences vary.

1. Use the personal touch. Handwrite a note. Traditionalists want to work in an atmosphere with living, breathing humans—not recorded messages and IMs. Remember that the "hurry-up-and-wait" many of them experienced in the military and in 1950s-style organizations

led to idle chatter and socialization being an acceptable way of corporate life; when your assigned tasks were completed, there was time to kill and it was best not to have independent initiative.

2. Remember that traditional perks were visual symbols of status—the executive washroom, company cars, and up-front parking places. While you probably won't be giving top performers their own restrooms, consider plaques and more traditional rewards for this cohort group. A photo of them with the CEO or an important visitor will likely find a place on their bookshelves or cubical wall.

Mentoring

It isn't true that you can't teach an old dog new tricks, but it can be a challenge. Some Traditionalists have a hard time accepting coaching from markedly younger colleagues. While your younger employees may be interested in advancing their careers, that motivation is likely to fall short with this group. They will be willing to learn new skills if you can prove the necessity for change—in terms of the corporate or department goals.

1. Consider finding a coach for your Traditionalist employees who is respected as a leader—possibly because of age and experience.
2. Coach tactfully. Be respectful. Ask permission to coach. Describe the performance issue and get agreement on the problem. Then suggest ways of improving behavior that focus on long-term goals.
3. Establish rapport by acknowledging the employee's background and experience.

This process is further explained in what Dr. Thomas Connellan calls the *Four-Step Coaching Conference.*[5] It is outlined in detail in the following example.

Step 1: Position the Discussion

The goal is to not take the employee by surprise and to give him or her the time to feel prepared—important to a Traditionalist.

> *"Mary, I'd like to sit down with you later today to talk about new account openings. I'd like to work with you to get back on track. What*

time would work best for you?" (And of course this would be done out of earshot of other employees.)

Step 2: The Discussion
During the discussion you should:
Put the employee at ease:

> *"Mary, I know you are working on meeting your sales goal. I want to meet with you to make sure that all that work is going to get you where you need to go."*

Describe the performance issue:

> *"As you know, the goal is four account openings a month. You are running between two and three through the first quarter. Does that square with your count?"*

*Get agreement on the problem:

> *"Would you agree that you need to find a way to improve on that record?"*

*Ask future-oriented, neutral questions:

> *"Is it possible to reach the four-account goal?"*
> *"What might you try to get your closing rate closer to the goal?"*
> *"How can I help you?"*

*Listen to and encourage employee ideas:

> *"That's a good thought. What else might you try?*

Step 3: Agree on a Course of Action
*After you and the employee have discussed a number of possible remedies, it is time to narrow the field and pick a course of action.

> *"Well, Mary, I think you've got some pretty good ideas here. Let's narrow them down to the one or two best and decide how to go forward from here."*

Step 4: Set a Follow-Up Date
A follow up commitment on your part says that you want to know that the problem is solved. It also communicates to the employee that your concern isn't simply the whim of the day, to be forgotten tomorrow.

"Mary, when would be a good time for us to meet again and see how the plan is working?"

Current and Future Issues

It is perhaps ironic that these "oldsters" have become a viable source of "new" labor. A handful of them—those able to wait out the market crash until their portfolios leveled out—were relatively unfazed by the economic downturn that began in 2007. According to the American Banking Association, older adults still own more than 75 percent of American assets and have $1.6 trillion in spending power.[6] But many of this generation were hit especially hard by the stock market plunge and the rising prices that immediately followed. This is the group that once planned to survive on small fixed incomes from Social Security or their pensions, but the rising costs of housing, food, and health care has made things especially difficult. Having learned to conserve during their youth, they will soldier on, making do and doing without—and taking jobs wherever they can find them. Then, too, their children and grandchildren continue to count on them for financial help—to pay for college educations and health care, to make down payments on homes and cars, and to pay for life's small indulgences. Today's grandparents buy one-fourth of all toys sold in this country.

They still wield a lot of clout. They contribute to causes they support, they let lobbyists know where they stand, and they vote. In the last U.S. Presidential election, voting was highly correlated with age: the older a voter was, the more likely it was that he or she voted. According to the U.S. Census Bureau, people 65 and older voted at an average rate of 70 percent. Don't expect them to fade into the background anytime soon. They will remain a powerful force for years to come.

The Future

When it comes to energy, productivity, and innovation, don't overlook this oldest generation. Sally Gordon, 101, has served as assistant sergeant-at-arms for the Nebraska Legislature for the last 26 years. Dr. Hedda Bolgar is a practicing psychoanalyst in Los Angeles at 102. Tao Porchan-Lynch, 91, teaches yoga in White Plains, New York. Japan's Tamae Watanabe, 73, recently became the oldest woman to climb Mount Everest. Kofi Annan, "the rock star of international relations" and currently the UN-Arab League envoy to Syria, is 70. Warren Buffet, 81; Betty White, 89; Larry King, 77; Barbara Walters, 81: all going strong.

Never in human history has our planet contained so many older people or so large a percentage of them. The fastest-growing segment of the world population is the oldest of the old—people 80 and older. Their growth rate is almost four times that for the total population. Mortality rates have fallen sharply this century; as a result, there are now 16 million Americans over the age of 75. And, average life expectancy is quickly approaching 80 years of age. Thus, more and more people will live 20 and 25 years after the usual retirement age. Actual retirement will become an unattainable luxury for some, and simply a too-boring alternative for others. Meanwhile, companies will continue to need experienced, qualified labor. For all these reasons, you simply can't afford to lose all your Traditionalist generation employees.

The problem is they have tended to leave the workplace earlier than any generation before them. The reasons are rather baffling, since some experts estimate that a full half of all retirees would really prefer to work. Perhaps they leave because of the dearth of incentives to keep them onboard, because it is the company norm to retire at a given age, or it may be that they are unaware of the need for their services. They simply may not have been asked to stay on. Or perhaps some over-eager Boomers and Xers grew tired of waiting for their next promotions, and viewed the Traditionalists as impediments to be pushed aside.

Innovative programs for keeping seniors in the workplace have emerged. The National Older Worker Career Center helps corporations

FACT AND FICTION ABOUT OLDER WORKERS

Myths	Facts
1. They can't learn.	1. They are willing students when the training is done right (respectfully, with low stress).
2. They aren't creative.	2. Seniors are "experimental innovators." They take an idea and pursue it with dogged determination, experimenting with small changes until the concept is perfected.
3. They don't want to work.	3. Many who are retired say they'd prefer to be working—at least part time.
4. They're not as productive as younger employees.	4. The U.S. Department of Health and Human Services reports that older workers are every bit as productive as younger ones. German researchers find *older* people tend to be more *productive* than their younger counterparts.
5. Customers don't respond well to older workers.	5. Many customers are older themselves and appreciate interacting with company representatives their own age. And verbal communication, critical to customer service, has been shown to improve with age.

and federal agencies to develop programs and options that appeal to workers 55 and older. (The National Older Worker Career Center is based in Washington, DC.) The U.S. Department of Labor has granted $250,000 to Green Thumb, a nonprofit organization that recruits low-income seniors to fill jobs as systems analysts and network administrators. The Massachusetts Manufacturing Extension Partnership and National Tooling and Machining Association have received a grant from the Commonwealth of Massachusetts to develop strategies for retaining older workers and studying the impact to local industries as these skilled laborers retire. But such programs are leading-edge exceptions. Those organizations that make their workplace Traditionalist-friendly will outdistance their competitors by capitalizing on the skills, talents, and experience of a pool of workers usually overlooked and undervalued.

More than just an untapped source of second-career labor, today's older workers offer us a laboratory. As the Traditionalist generation demonstrates, modern health care and the economy have conspired to make older workers an enduring and valuable resource. This trend is not a short-lived phenomenon. Baby Boomers, the next generation we'll talk about, will not only live longer than the generations ahead of them, but, because of their poor savings record and strong work ethic, it will likely be a chore to move them out of the workforce. In the United States, the number of workers 65 and older is predicted to soar by more than 80 percent in the next four years, according to the U.S. Bureau of Labor Statistics. What is learned from those Traditionalists who continue to work will form a valuable base of learning for the increasingly mixed-generation workplace of the next century.

CHAPTER 3

The Baby Boomers

Retirement Postponed

Born 1943 to 1960

"Boomers are now in their 'Grand Tweens,' shaping a new stage of life fueled by a renewed sense of purpose."
—GAIL SHEEHY

The Baby Boom was more than just a postwar—"Welcome home, Sailor!" —diapers on parade, nine-months-after-the-party-phenomenon. Much more. It was the beginning of a dramatic reversal of an American population trend. It was the beginning of the end of the country's rural, agrarian life style. It was the tumultuous and noisy dawn of a promising new day that had carried their parents' generation through blackouts, rationing, and the anxiety of separation. It was the beginning of a new world made possible by the sacrifices of hundreds of thousands in the annealing fires of the greatest, fiercest war ever fought.

In the first half of the 1940s, birthrates in the United States generally declined or remained about the same. Then, in 1946, almost precisely nine months after VJ day, a tsunami of babies broke across the fruited plain—and changed its physical and psychological geography forever. In 1957, midway through the tsunami, more children were born in the United States than ever before. Not only were more babies being born every minute—actually one every 17 minutes for 19 years—but thanks to the miracles of postwar medicine, more of them were surviving birth and babyhood, formerly the highest mortality segment of life span on the planet.

Healthier, more wanted, doted on, and cared for—the first generation when child rearing was a hobby and a pleasure and not an economic necessity and a biological inevitability—the Boom Babies were cherished by parents who had sacrificed and fought a war for the right to bear them, raise them, indulge them, and dream of a New Eden for them to live out their days in. By 1964, more than 76 million of these cherished, loved, coddled, hoped for, and doted upon children were walking, talking, crawling, toddling—and spitting up on the face of the planet, learning to flex their physical and psychological muscle and manifest destiny.

Technically, physically, temporally, the Boom Birth period began in 1946 and ended in 1964. But a generational cohort is defined as much by shared values, experiences, and worldviews as it is by zodiacal accident. A generation is defined by what it thinks, feels, and experiences together and not just by dates of birth. So, it is more accurate to define Baby Boomers as those born between 1943 and 1960. That added group, those born in the three years preceding the official "go" date—often referred to as the Silent Generation, are more like Boomers than the Traditionalist Generation in a number of ways and for many of the same reasons that Boomers are Boomers. Many of them started the trends "true" Boomers turned into generational milestones and Boomer icons. Without a Barbra Streisand would there be a Bette Midler? Without a Beach Boys would there be a Stones?

And without Boomers would the Sandwich slice—those born just prior to and during World War II have an identity at all? Think of them as the Lewis and Clarks of the Baby Boom era. And the subtracted

> "With the largest 50+ generation in history entering their mature years, life is about to get even better. The Boomers who make up part of this group are savvier about technology, about keeping fit, and about planning for retirement. Most important, they have been more engaged in social issues than many generations before them, simply by dint of their growing up mostly during the 1960s, a time of incredible social change around the world."
>
> —Bill Novelli, CEO of AARP

group—those born in the early 1960s—feel more affinity with the next generation, the Xers, who neither supported nor protested the Vietnam War and who don't remember the day of the assassination of a young president in a Dallas motorcade.

Their Generational Personality

The children of the 1940s and 1950s grew up in optimistic, positive times. For the United States, it was a time of expansion. The fertility boom coincided with the greatest economic expansion this country had ever experienced. The country was on a straight-up growth curve. With the only stable economy left after the destruction of World War II, the only imaginable obstacle to infinite expansion of American industry was imagination itself.

Boomers believe in growth and expansion. Americans of that era were fascinated by the lore and mythology of their last great frontier. The mythical, mystical Wild West was glorified on television and in Saturday movie matinees: Think Hopalong Cassidy, Daniel Boone, Davey Crockett, *Gunsmoke,* Roy Rogers, Dale Evans, and *Wagon Train.* According to the Boomer Institute, 75 million dollars were spent each year of the 1950s on cowboy outfits for little Boomers.[1] At the same time, they became broadly fascinated by the new frontier of space; "to boldly go where none had gone before;" think Buck Rogers, *Star Trek,* Tom Corbit, Captain Video and all those things that "Came from outer space!" Perhaps it was the lure of both simpler and possibly idyllic future times.

They are self-centered. They lived in nuclear families with a working dad and stay-at-home mom. Children were, for the first time in history, in the spotlight, representing as they did to the Traditionalist Generation, the symbol and fruit of their victories and the hopes for the future they fought to preserve. The American infrastructure was forced to expand rapidly to accommodate the Baby Boomers' needs. New hospitals, elementary

THE BABY BOOMERS

Seminal Events

1954	McCarthy HCUAA hearings begin
1955	Salk vaccine tested on public
1956	Rosa Parks refuses to move to the back of the bus in Montgomery, Alabama
1957	First nuclear power plant
1957	Russians launch Sputnik, Dawn of the Space Age
1957	Congress passes the Civil Rights Act
1960	Birth control pills introduced
1960	John Kennedy elected
1961	Kennedy establishes the Peace Corps
1962	Cuban missile crisis
1962	John Glenn circles the earth
1963	President Kennedy Assassinated
1965	United States sends ground combat troops to Vietnam
1966	National Organization for Women founded
1966	Cultural Revolution in China
1967	First heart transplant by Dr. Christiaan Barnard in South Africa
1968	Martin Luther King, Jr., and Robert Kennedy assassinated
1968	American Indian Movement founded
1969	Woodstock
1970	Women's liberation demonstrations

schools, and high schools. Health care and education became industrialized endeavors. Expectations for this new generation were so high that in 1967, *Time* magazine actually gave its coveted Man of the Year award to the whole generation, proclaiming them the people who would clean up our cities, end racial inequality, and find a cure for the common cold.

It was a heady, tumultuous, time. But it was not a golden age, as some would have us believe. Domestic violence was as prevalent then as now, but it went unreported. People with problems had few places to turn. Unhappiness was kept secret. Racism and sexism were the norm, and the handicapped were sometimes treated maliciously, the disabled often warehoused. The few gays who chose to come out of the closet became targets of derision and violence.

They tend to be optimistic. The overall feeling of optimism and promise they were raised to take for granted, to see as their birthright, had a tremendous impact on the developing psyches of the Baby Boomers. They continue today to look at the world in terms of its infinite possibilities — something to be shaped and played with, aggressively, not passively, as a spectator might. The planet was—and is—theirs to shape; an attitude as clear in the ways of Boomer Greens as it is in the means of Boomer Developers.

In school and at home, the Boomers learned about teamwork. There were so many of them—like puppies in a pile—that they had to collaborate and cooperate, sharing textbooks and sometimes desks. They were the first generation to be graded on their report cards for "shares materials with classmates" and "works with others." And everything they did was in the spotlight. They understood tacitly, perhaps simply assumed, that the purpose of the world they lived in was to actively serve their needs, wants and whims, a feeling they carried into adolescence and adulthood. They continue to be caught up in their own interests and priorities—some would say self-absorbed and perpetually spotlight conscious.

> ### THE BABY BOOMERS
>
> **Heroes**
>
> - Gandhi
> - Martin Luther King, Jr.
> - John and Jacqueline Kennedy
> - John Glenn

They have pursued their own personal gratification, often at a high price to themselves and others. If the marriage wasn't working out, they dumped it and looked for another. If they didn't like the job, they moved on. Caught in a shady deal? Apologize, shed a few tears, blame some circumstance, and move on. They turned resurrection—and self-forgiveness—into a high public art. William Jefferson Clinton, the first Boomer President of the United States turned public apology and the expectation of instant, soap-opera-like forgiveness into a political norm.

They have searched their souls—repeatedly, obsessively, recreationally. Surrounded as they were in childhood by the expansion of material wealth and economic growth, perhaps it is no surprise that Boomers in their late adolescence felt compelled to pursue the flipside—spirituality, the inner world, and the meaning of life. Case in point: Boomers in the 1960s were attracted not so much by high-energy drugs like crack and cocaine, but to introspective drugs like marijuana and LSD, touted to take its users on a journey within. In the 1970s, if a given Boomer wasn't studying transcendental meditation, she was at a Ram Dass lecture or her yoga class. A decade ago, Boomers devoured books on any topic remotely concerned with spirituality. Nearly half the books on the nonfiction best-seller lists had spiritual themes. Deepak Chopra, head of the Chopra Center for Well Being in La Jolla, California, with tapes, seminars, and 122 books on the interaction between mind, body, and spirit, became a spiritual symbol—and a multigazillionaire.

> **THE BABY BOOMERS**
>
> **Cultural Memorabilia**
>
> * *The Ed Sullivan Show*
> * Quonset huts
> * Fallout shelters
> * Poodle skirts and pop beads
> * Slinkies
> * TV dinners
> * *Laugh-In*
> * Hula hoops
> * *The Mod Squad*
> * Peace sign

Nor did the Boomers leave their fascination with spiritualism at home; in the 1990s, they brought it to the workplace. A whole collection of business books that link jobs and spirit—*Care of the Soul, The Road Less Traveled, The Heart Aroused*, were bestsellers amongst Boomer managers. Seminars, training programs, and retreats walked the fine line between religion and work—dangerously, according to some theologians and executives. "But spirit has everything to do with work," one Boomer responds. "Work would be meaningless without it."

The Boomers have always been cool. Just ask one. In fact, they changed the sociology of coolness. Historically, trendsetters have been people in their late teens and early twenties. In the 1920s, two young book publishers ignited the crossword craze, and a 15-year old from Baltimore started the flagpole-sitting trend that was copied from San Diego to Philadelphia. But in the 1950s, little kids, by simple presence, started the fads. The Boomers, when mere babies, took center stage and set the pace; passive though their participation was. For the first time ever, Madison Avenue recognized children as a market segment, and they pursued the Boom Kids directly via television. Commercials for cereals, snacks, and toys saturated the prime

> **THE BABY BOOMERS**
>
> **Core Values**
> * Optimism
> * Team orientation
> * Personal gratification
> * Health and wellness
> * Personal growth
> * Youth
> * Work
> * Involvement

kiddy viewing hours; in fact, defined kiddy viewing hours. Little Boomers could recognize the word "detergent" before they could read. Shortly thereafter, retailers found a new group of buyers: Baby Boom girls who were a little too big for children's sizes and a little too small for women's sizes. In response, clothing manufacturers invented "preteen" and "junior" sizes, and they sold like hotcakes. The Boomer Institute tells us, "they were the first teenage consumers to spend over $12 billion of their own money for such things as cosmetics, pimple creams, and hair products."[2] Today, their temples gray, they run half marathons on replacement knees, and they still want to be cool, "the continuously morphing" market everyone wants to click with. After all, they are the world, they are the children. And they'll never, never, grow up, grow old, or die.

The Legacy of Vietnam

There is no simple way to talk about what Vietnam meant—and means—to this generation. What we can say is that its effect has been profound and divisive. To begin with, the war was the primary cause of the generation gap between the Boomers and their parents. The U.S. intervention in Southeast Asia caused many young Americans to question the integrity of our leaders as never before. Feelings about the war divided many a family, even close siblings. Perhaps even more disturbing is the effect the war had within the generation. It caused a schism that may never be bridged—and is rarely talked about, present as it is, like an unwelcome guest at a party.

The Boomers' reactions to the unpopular war were as complex as the war itself. Some Boomers signed up or were drafted, went to Southeast Asia, and became proud soldiers like their Traditionalist fathers in World War II. But they fought, died, were wounded, and returned home without ever understanding how their actions contributed to the long-term goal—or even what that goal was. Many returned and turned bitter and skeptical of authority—particularly governmental authority. Others served in Vietnam, but far less willingly. Some young soldiers participated in a military counterculture of sorts, tuning in, turning on, and dropping out, smoking pot, and listening to Jimi Hendrix. Many witnessed unspeakable horrors, which would haunt them for a lifetime. Yet, when they returned from the war, it was not to a hero's welcome like

---

THE BABY BOOMERS

How They Differ from Their Parents

Traditionalists	Boomers
• Followed traditional roles (male/female, ethnic)	• Redefined roles; promoted equality
• Were loyal (to their marriages, to their companies)	• Left unfulfilling relationships to seek more fulfilling ones
• Were willing to be disciplined and patient, waiting for their rewards	• Sought immediate gratification
• Played by the rules	• Manipulated the rules to meet their own needs

their fathers before them. Often wounded both physically and emotionally, when they got off the airplane returning them to their hometowns, many were greeted by antiwar peers who spat at them and shouted epithets. They learned a bitter lesson: to be silent about the war and their experiences in it.

Neither were things simple for those who stayed home and never even entered the jungles and rice paddies of Vietnam. A small but vocal minority actively protested American involvement. Others wore the antiwar mantle inactively and silently—some simply because it was rather fashionable. Still others suffered in confusion, not knowing quite how to resolve issues of patriotism and loyalty, how to make sense of the headlines, and what to think of the decisions coming out of the Pentagon. Then there was a significant group of Boomers who took steps to keep themselves out of the war. Some joined the National Guard. Some signed up for college courses with professors who promised to give them As or Bs so they could keep their college deferments. Some filed as Conscientious Objectors and were able to serve in nonmilitary capacities. Some fled to Canada, Sweden, and other places. Some starved themselves to get below the acceptable weight for military service. Still others threw shovels through windows to prove they were not mentally fit to serve. Time does not, in fact, heal all wounds. The shadow of Vietnam and how it was viewed by whom, will likely always loom over this generation.

First Half/Second Half: The Boomer Dichotomy

To add to the complexity of understanding Boomers, there's the issue of older Boomers and younger Boomers. Certainly within any generation, there is a great deal of diversity. We would expect important differences between those people of the same generation who grew up poor and those who grew up affluent, between rural and urban, between Midwesterners and Westerners, Easterners and Southerners. A "Ya'll Come" Atlanta Boomer does seem different—on the surface—from a Northeast "Hey You'se Guys" Boomer. And every member of the Baby Boom Gen can say that there are aspects of his or her generation's personality they don't see reflected in themselves and their lives. This is particularly true for those in the second half of the generation—those born in the mid-to-late 1950s—many of whom find they simply "do not fit" the Boomer style as characterized in the popular press.

"Second-Halfers" find "First-Halfers" more idealistic, more likely to be workaholics, and more likely to have put career first, family second. In fact, demographers tell us that First-Halfers, those born in the 1940s, make more money and own more homes than second-half Boomers, those born between 1950 and 1960. The First-Halfers' world view was more affected by the 1950s; they felt a more integral and active part of the 1960s "scene"—free love, drugs, sex, rock 'n' roll, Vietnam, Women's lib—if not as active participants as least as very aware observers. For Second-Halfers, the 1950s were mostly a vague memory and the 1960s "movements" more an observed than participated in phenomenon—though individual exceptions do indeed abound.

But for all the qualifiers and exceptions—and Boomers are very firm about their sense of individuality and not being a part of a predictable, statistical group—Boomers are Boomers by virtue of one indelible fact: they experienced the same growing pains and forces, were preached to by the same geography-spanning media, and understood the impact these same said forces have had on others in their cohort group. To paraphrase Robert Heinlein, a literary hero for many Boomers, they "grok" one another. They may not—do not—agree with stands and opinions of every part of the cohort group, or exhibit the same behavior in the same situations—but they do, in their hearts, understand one another.

First-Half Boomers: The Economic Achievers

Every generation has a cadre or cohort of "achievers" who change the world around them. Some achieve in commerce, others in literature, music, religion, engineering, science, philosophy, and the fine arts. While all these areas of achievement set the tone and lead the way for a generation, it is commerce and the practical economics of the workplace that affect the most people. And every generation, indeed, has a subset of Economic Achievers—those who are more ambitious and more driven to succeed than most in their cohort. Concerned with raising fortunes rather than consciousness, Achievers are always on the lookout for opportunities to get ahead, ways to increase their status and prestige, and chances to gain control and power. Goal and result oriented, they often "get along to get ahead." "Standing out" from the crowd has high value to Boomers, the generation that has refined "famous for being famous" to an art form.

Since Baby Boomers have a Pavlovian-like tendency to be driven anyway, the Economic Achievers among them are particularly remarkable; a real crème de la crème of ambition and accomplishment. The popular press branded the achievement-oriented "yuppies," and, although they really aren't typical of their generation as a whole, they are responsible for many of the stereotypes commonly associated with Boomers: ruthlessness, Lexus SUVs, designer sunglasses, vacations in Bali, second homes in Aspen. There is a love/hate relationship with the Economic Achievers. Modern versions of the old Horatio Algier story about the clerk whose personal drive and hard work took him all the way to the bank presidency are told with both admiration—and resentment. These Economic Achievers were the brunt of many a joke:

> *The yuppie and his BMW were in a terrible wreck. "Oh, my Beemer, my Beemer," he whined. The first person to arrive shouted, "Ohmigod, he's lost his arm!" The yuppie began to whine with renewed vigor, "Oh, my Rolex, my Rolex."*

And few of us—regardless of our generational affiliation—want to admit that we might have "yuppie" Economic Achiever tendencies ourselves. Put Donald Trump, Ted Turner, Michael Eisner, and Debbie Fields into this subset—and you can discern the plusses and minuses for yourself.

Linda: Achiever Par Excellence

It is 6:00 P.M. and the sun is setting across the San Andreas Fault. It's been a long day. Linda is ready to leave her corner office with its sweeping view of the downtown skyline. Dressed in a blue Dior pantsuit, she is headed for the gym to meet with her personal trainer. A divorced career woman of 64, Linda paid a high price for her "luxurious" lifestyle, putting in more than three decades of 60-plus-hour weeks to the companies she has worked for. Child rearing—or even child having—went on permanent hold and was a great contributor to the demise of her marriage. She doesn't have much tolerance for people who don't work as many hours or who insist on a "personal life," whatever that is. She recently chewed out an employee at a staff meeting for not answering her cell phone while on vacation. Today Linda is Vice President of Operations for a corporation that owns 600 restaurants around the world.

In her company and in the food service industry, Linda is well respected. She started as a store manager-trainee right out of college and has climbed her way to where she is, one rung at a time. She is known for her professionalism, quick wit, and personal warmth. People would tell you, however, that you don't want to get in her way. Linda knows what she wants and is accustomed to getting it. Politically wise, she knows the ropes and is demanding when she feels she needs to be. Though some have bluntly branded her "ruthless" behind closed doors, Linda would simply shrug and respond that her responsibility is for keeping the corporation solvent—not soothing people's feelings. Ten years ago, she daydreamed of the retirement package that awaited her; now—in order to maintain the lifestyle she's grown accustomed to—she'll have to depend solely on her IRA, so she's going to be hard at it for at least another five years.

The Late Boomers: Laid Back and Cynical

There were more than three million more babies born in the second decade of the Baby Boom than the first. Demographically, late Boomers, 1950s babies, are the largest single Boomer segment. They don't identify much with the 1960s; they were too young to feel the rush. Many of them were and are turned off by yuppie-ism. They see the BMW—or the Lexus—as the car for older, greedier, more materialistic Boomers; affluent younger Boomers tend toward Volvo crossovers. They say they were never as driven as their older counterparts, that they've always made decisions based on family—in the broadest sense. They take pride that fathering roles shifted during the years that Boomers were parenting—that the older Boomers, especially the fathers, tended to spend less time with their kids while the younger Boomers shared parenting responsibilities more equally. They saw their parenting obligation as not just financial but emotional and involving.

The late Boomers, or second-halfers tend to feel different about work. They graduated from college and went to work during the Reagan era. They got the first taste of downsizing—large-scale layoffs—the country had experienced since the Great Depression. This made them more cynical and less gung ho about management and the early Boomer mantra that "The Business of America is Business." They know that economics are as blind as justice; good work habits and positive mental attitude are not always rewarded and, often are not enough to save a job, regardless of how well it has been done. When it comes to work attitude, they sometimes identify with Generation Xers who cite Dilbert as their cultural hero and workplace icon. "Oh, boy, here comes another consultant/fad/reform/reorganization/vision/plan. Same old dog food, different can. Duck! This too shall pass."

Tom: Boomer Marching to a Different Drummer

Tom is a 56-year-old employee of a major telecommunications corporation. A software designer, he has been in the industry for two decades and has changed companies three times in that time. He is actually back with his original company, a change he made recently to take advantage of that corporation's policy on flexible hours. The father of three teenagers, Tom shares every bit of the responsibility at home equally with his wife, Tracy, who manages a small print shop in a mall near their home.

While attending college in the late 1970s, Tom worked construction in the summers to pay for tuition. Military service was never a concern. The Vietnam War and conscription ended before he got to college, although he remembers the angst and strife his older brother went through. Tom's main concerns have always been around career and lifestyle – particularly the balance between the two.

Today he is a self-described "fix-it guy." Twelve years ago, he and Tracy designed a comfortable, functional house—the kind of home they wanted to raise their children in. They bought three acres of land on the outskirts of the city and did most of the construction themselves. Tom likes his job and works hard, but he is also devoted to his family; when the kids were little, he spent four nights a week escorting them to soccer games, music lessons, and dental appointments.

His admirers—and there are plenty—refer to Tom as a caring, sensitive, modern man. Others in his peer group—the more driven, career-oriented, upwardly mobile types—think of him as the worst sort of Alan Alda clone. But Tom, no less than Linda, sees himself as time pressed and struggling to keep everything together. In his case, keeping the important things in his life —family and career—together.

Tom and Linda in the Workplace

Linda and Tom represent and embody themes of their generational cohort: the desires, aspirations, and values that make them unique among the family of generations that now live and work together—or at least side-by-side—in the transgenerational workplace.

Linda and Tom, though different from one another, are much alike in that they are both a part of the cadre of sons and daughters of the optimistic post-World War II era. They prayed in school, gathered around the first television in the neighborhood to watch the Mickey Mouse Club, and ate TV dinners. They watched the iron curtain descend, marched on Washington, and watched Neil Armstrong's first steps on the moon on TV. They joined the Peace Corps and fought in Vietnam— or didn't. They benefited from a prosperous economy, tremendous medical advances, an explosion of scientific research, and a school system—overcrowded but in fine fettle.

Although they comprise only about 23% of the U.S. workforce today, their impact on the workplace has been unmistakably huge. And, as the oldest of their wave prepare to turn 70, they are more determined than ever to think of themselves as forever and ever

THE BABY BOOMERS

On the Job

Assets

- Service-oriented
- Driven
- Willing to "go the extra mile"
- Good at relationships
- Want to please
- Good team players

Liabilities

- Not naturally "budget minded"
- Uncomfortable with conflict
- Reluctant to go against peers
- May put process ahead of result
- Defensive in the face of feedback
- Judgmental of those who see things differently
- Self-centered

young. "Don't trust anyone over 30" has become "Age is a state of mind. You are only as old as you think you are."

Working with Tom and Linda is different—different from working with the Traditionalist Generation, the Xers, the Millennials, even from each other. To better understand Tom and Linda and to work successfully with the mishmash and milieu of the transgenerational workplace, we need to understand who they are, what influenced them, what motivates them now, how they relate to others in the workplace, how to get them to stay a few more years, or how to urge them on if that's what needs to happen.

The Boomers, especially the first wave, those born just after World War II—grew up wanting, needing desperately to prove themselves. Veteran dads and moms reminded them that theirs was a great destiny, paid for by unprecedented sacrifice. Grandparents warned of the ills of the depression and the chaos of despair that followed. These Boomers know well the landmine of possibilities that accompanies the prosperity dream. Therefore, work has held a singular importance in their lives. Their fathers had proved themselves worthy in World War II—"tempered by war, disciplined by a hard and bitter peace." The Baby Boomers—most of them—would have to be tested on the job. Business would be their war; the competitor their enemy. They would win or lose their personal battles on the warship called "work." They've tended to define themselves through their jobs and to achieve their identity by the work they perform. For this generation, "work ethic" and "worth ethic" are synonyms even as they toil through the sunset of their careers.

The drive to prove their worthiness created a work ethic that surprised many early observers. These pundits remember the youthful activists of the 1960s who had challenged the establishment and promised never to "sell out" to the corporation. Many of those observers assumed the Boomers would be slackers. But the activist Boomer had never been against hard work. And work hard they have in the corporate world. Driven and dedicated, they still labor to prove they are worthy of the expectations that were placed upon them practically since birth. While the fu-

---

THE BABY BOOMERS

Messages that Motivate

- "You're important to our success."
- "You're valued here."
- "Your contribution is unique and important."
- "You are a proven leader."
- "We would like you to mentor...."
- "Be all that you can be."
- "We need you."

turists were promising 30-hour work weeks, Boomers were regularly punching in for 50 or 60. And, for many, loving it, feeling fulfilled in their need to be needed and worthy.

Where They Work

Boomers have been drawn to all types of industries and organizations from small nonprofit associations to multinational corporations. The key factor in their job choices has been opportunity, not glitz, glamour, and security, although they are not averse to these secondary attributes and see them as great perks when they are part of the package. And don't forget—these are men and women who have made reading business books a craze—and business writers and entrepreneurs national heroes. They can find romance, drama, challenge, glamour, and personal fulfill-ment in bagel baking and widget winding. By and large, they liked school when they were kids—and they've never given it up. Training as an industry has burgeoned under their tutelage. Not only do they pur-sue learning at work, but swarms of them sign up for evening and week-end classes.

Boomers express a preference for work environments that are dem-ocratic, humane, and casual. They've carried their value for affiliation with them into the workplace where they've advocated teams and team building, consensus, quality circles, and participative management. They prefer a workplace where there is a lot of room for relationships. They are not, however, as good at sharing as they think they are. The slogan "all for one and one is me" isn't foreign to a sizable number. Some cynics suggest that teamwork and participation became fashionable when Boomers figured out that the road to the top of their trade, craft, or corporation was already fully occupied. So, in typical fashion, if they couldn't reach the goal—they changed it. If being number 1 was out of reach, they reached instead for leaderless work designs, where everyone was equal and being number 1, individually, was frowned upon. (Until the next chance to be "the star" emerged, of course.)

In the service industries, we see Baby Boomers continuing to flour-ish. Perhaps because of their strong need to prove themselves, Boomers tend to be very good at delivering service. They want to be liked—one on one. They've learned to read people; they've had to. They're great rapport builders. They'll do what it takes to make the customer happy; as long as it puts them in a good light with someone—anyone. Given their choice, they prefer to work for a manager (if they can't *be* the manager) who knows and cares for them personally. And they tend to perform best for managers who treat their employees as equals—managers who let them feel they are in charge of something or at least empowered to dabble in everything.

Their Leadership Style

When they are in leadership roles, their tendency is toward a collegial, consensual—sometimes benignly despotic—style. They are the ones who advocated turning the traditional corporate hierarchy upside down. Their motivations for their advocacy aside, they are genuinely passionate and concerned about participation and spirit in the workplace, about bringing heart and humanity to the office, and about creating a fair and level playing field for all. The civil rights movement of the 1960s had a profound impact on their generational personality, and fair treatment—whether it be of persons of color, gays, or those with disabilities—is something they're willing to take to the soapbox and speak out for. It is the Boomers, particularly the early Boomers, who were the first to embrace "soft leadership skills," the kind advertised in business classics like *Steward Leadership*, *Managing from the Heart*, and *Leadership Is an Art*.

But those who report to them have found all this to be rather deceiving, a little disingenuous, and a bit bewildering. The Boomers grew up, for the most part, with conservative parents and worked in their early careers for command-and-control-style supervisors. Boomer managers sometimes have a hard time actually practicing, day-in and day-out, the management style they profess. Many, for instance, truly believe they are managing participatively, when, in fact, they're just giving it lip service. Participative management requires great skill in understanding, listening, communicating, motivating, and delegating.

Many Boomer managers are lacking in these areas and are in need of development to acquire the leadership style they espouse. Many who are lacking these skills are not even aware of their ineffectiveness. When Scott Adams created Dilbert's pointy-haired, cliché-spouting boss, he was modeling and mocking a dark and very, very real side of Boomer leadership—management by buzzword.

As Team Member

Linda and Tom tend to be good team members. They've been taught teamwork skills since childhood, and they enjoy being on work teams. But, at times, Linda's need to prove herself overrides her commitment to do what's best for the team. The eight-year old who had to jump up and down in class screeching "Me! Me! Me!, Miss Smith. Ask me. Ask me!" lurks just below the adult veneer of many a Boomer—and sometimes, when the stakes are right, makes a guest appearance in Conference Room B.

Boomers can be political animals, especially when their turf is threatened. At times like these, those well-honed rapport skills are used to sell a plan for self-protection or territorial improvement or self-betterment masked as concern, the best interest of the common good, or helping someone overburdened or with too much to do already. The net result is frequently confusion, frustration, and misunderstanding on the team. Of course, most Boomers read each other's machinations well and clearly. They recognize blind ambition and self-promotion—though they often haven't a clue for actually dealing with the slick moves of their colleagues. For most Boomers the playground taught that there are but two responses, two "models" of conflict resolution: knuckling under or duking it out—flight or fight. By 12 years of age, most had sorted out the approach that worked for them. And they learned again in their initial forays into the work place whether they were pushers—or pushees.

Mid-course, however, the rules changed. Perhaps it was the civil rights, women's lib, and EEO movements. Perhaps it was Vietnam.

Perhaps, as some feminists contend, it might have been the arrival of large numbers of women in the workplace—in professional and managerial positions. Whatever the cause, the natural selection system of schoolyard and workplace was turned on its head and a "play nice" ethic was grafted to the Boomer adult psyche. As they climbed the corporate ladder and moved into management positions, work rules, company policies, and mandatory consciousness-raising seminars taught Boomers without exception that aggressiveness—duking it out—was unacceptable, and assertiveness—stating and restating your "needs" until you get what you want—was in favor. Bottom line for the Boomer: Many of them are not very good at calling out conflict—or dealing with it directly. There is a sizable subset of people with ulcers, high blood pressure, and tension headaches unable to express their fight or flight reaction—nature's way of saying, "You need to speak up!"—in an acceptable, authentic, or stress-relieving way.

Managing the Baby Boomer

Whether Linda and Tom are teammates or subordinates, their talents and needs are unique and special. They are members of the first generation where the question, "How do you want to be managed?" was relevant. Where the question, "How do you maintain and motivate the best and the brightest?" was strategically and tactically important to business.

The thing about Boomers is they'll make life hell if, in their view, you're mismanaging them. They won't suffer in silence, but they won't necessarily confront their issues directly either. Says generational expert, William Strauss, "The generation that was awful for productivity was Boomers. Everybody was scratching their heads saying, 'Gee, technology is getting better; how come productivity isn't improving?' Well they had young Boomer workers arguing with everybody about what to do."[3] They are used to *sharing* with their peers. They will make sure everybody knows if they're not happy with "da boss" and make "boss" a real four-letter word.

So how do Boomers want to be managed? How can you retain and motivate the best and brightest members of this generation without simply handing them the keys and saying "Okay, Smart Person, you drive." How can you get them on your side and make them positive about being on your team?

Some Key Principles

Recruiting

1. Assure them you know they've still got lots of good years.
2. Let them know their experience will be valued. Boomers have put in their time, and they want to know they'll get credit for, and respect for, their accomplishments.
3. Give them the change agent challenge: "You can really make a difference."
4. Stress that this is a warm, humane place to work, though still a dynamic environment.
5. Show them places where they can excel; what their track will be.
6. Show them how they can be stars.
7. Demonstrate that your company is not backwater; promote the leading-edge nature of your organization and your industry.

Orienting

1. Direct your discussion to the near future of the company. Boomers tend to be future oriented. Although the number of years remaining in their careers is shrinking, they like to see themselves in a larger, worthwhile context: "Come with us, Tom, and we'll dominate the world of self-sealing gaskets."
2. Focus on challenges. Boomers want to solve problems and turn things around: "We really need your talent here, Linda."

Opportunities

1. As with any employee from any generation, get to know each of your people as individuals. What is true for one may not be so for another.

This is especially important when managing Baby Boomers, who put a high value on personal relationship and unique, personalized treatment.

2. Assure a Boomer job candidate that the company is poised on the edge of greatness and just needs the candidate to make it happen.

3. Show them how they can use this opportunity to really make a difference.

4. Teach people the politics of information; give them the inside edge on your organization's know-how.

5. Stress that they'll learn a lot and improve the value of the organization tenfold.

Developing

1. Boomers often need development in strategic planning, budgeting, coaching skills, and all the "soft stuff."

2. Provide challenging work with horizontal movement that provides opportunities for them to learn and use their skills differently.

3. Watch for the Boomer with an "I know all that" chip on the shoulder. Many do, in fact, know a lot—intellectually, in a textbookish way. The problem is they're not doing it. You may be forced to quote (anonymous) complaints from the people they manage to get their buy in to changing something about their management style. Note the popularity of 360-degree management feedback schemes in the high Boomer workplace.

4. Provide Boomers with developmental experiences—assignments where you help them through and develop their skills. Give them projects they can cite. ("I brought in the Meyerson account."). Give them gold stars even if it was a team effort.

5. Look for lots of Meyerson accounts.

6. Encourage Boomer employees to read business books and tune in to training DVDs, CDs, podcasts, and webinars.

Motivating

In your leadership role, take time for conversation. Find opportunities to become better personally acquainted.

1. Try the personal approach. ("You're the only one who can really do this right.")
2. Give lots of public recognition.
3. Give them a chance to prove themselves and their worth.
4. Give them perks—a company car, an expense account, corner office, or more flexible schedule.
5. Assist them in gaining name recognition throughout the company.
6. Help get them quoted in an industry journal.
7. Get consensus. Boomers think they invented participative management, and they will be mightily offended if you don't involve them.
8. Reward their work ethic and long hours.

Mentoring

Boomers have always valued personal growth; they continue to be committed to lifelong learning and self-improvement. Even in the twilight of their careers they see themselves as "learners." Although Boomers can get defensive, coaching is their preferred style of development.

1. Coach tactfully.
2. If you're blaming, they're not listening.
3. Be nice. Be warm. Find opportunities for agreement and harmony.
4. Let them tell you how well the Meyerson account went. When they ask for input or you see an opportunity, coach for improved performance.
5. Ask questions to get to the issues.
6. Think of yourself as a friendly equal. Ask permission every step of the way. ("Would it be okay if we talked about your performance on the Meyerson job?")
7. The toughest coaching situations are those in which you think their performance is substandard, and they don't. Assure them they're doing well, but you think they could be achieving more.
8. Respect them, but not the way you would a Traditionalist. Please don't call a Boomer *Sir* or *Ma'am*. Respect them for their experience. Ask them; don't tell them.

Current and Future Issues

Today's Boomers are just hitting their stride. In fact, they've always been just hitting their stride. Now their stride is to prepare for retirement, a chance to return to their quest of becoming complete and totally enlightened humans. Sociologists tell us they are beginning their golden age in terms of position, productivity, and earnings—despite being at an age that previous generations have labeled "over the hill." Boomer Fernando Torres-Gil, Director of the UCLA Center for Policy Research on Aging, says they may well be the "100-ton electoral force" in the next two decades. "I am hopeful," he says "we will use our numbers to make change for the betterment of all generations." A.C. Nielson reports that Boomers are the biggest buyers of everything from toothpaste to financial services. The next decade will see them with increased freedom to enjoy recreation and leisure, even as they work longer than previous generations in order to rebuild their nest eggs.

On January 1, 2011, the oldest Baby Boomers turned 65—and every day for the next couple of decades another 10,000 or so will cross that threshold.[4] By 2020, 64 million seniors will be eligible for Medicare. Make no mistake about it, Boomers intend to approach these next years entirely differently than their parents did, pushing back the frontiers on what it means to be elderly. They look at Tina Turner and Mick Jagger and say to themselves "If they can still shake it, why not me?" With life expectancy approaching 80, most of them have more good years of health and productivity to look forward to. By virtue of their numbers, but also based on their positions and earnings, they are likely to remain an important segment of the labor force for another decade, maybe even two. They are ensconced in upper management and have taken over the executive offices and the boardroom. In the last 20 years, Baby Boomers have instituted most of the policies, procedures, and structures that govern organizations today. They still switch careers and start their own new businesses later in life than those in previous generations.

Boomers have been working to achieve a more balanced work life since they started having kids forty years ago. In the 1970s, the term

"I decided to try to simplify my own life, reduce my consumption of material goods, eat lower on the food chain, and work toward mitigating the damage I was causing the earth. This was a start. But I also realized that if Patagonia tried to be what it is not, if it tried to 'have it all,' it would die. The American Dream is to own your own business, grow it as quickly as you can until you can cash out, and retire to the golf courses of Leisure World. The business itself is the product. Long-term capital investments in employee training, on-site child care, pollution controls, and pleasant working facilities are all just negatives on the short-term ledger. When the company becomes the fatted calf, it's sold for a profit and its resources and holdings are often ravaged and broken apart, disrupting family ties and jeopardizing the long-term health of local economies. The notion of a business as a disposable entity carries over to all elements of society. As we at Patagonia strive to make a sustainable product (hoping to make a sustainable business for a sustainable planet), we find disposability to be our greatest nemesis."

—Yvonne Chouinard, Founder and CEO of Patagonia

"workaholic" was coined to describe their work ethic. In the first two decades after they joined the American workforce, the average time spent at work increased one full month per year. As the Boomers began their own child rearing (later in life because work came first), they began to question this grueling pace and to seek a more balanced life. One-third say they would quit altogether if they could live comfortably without their salaries; the absolute fact is that most can't. At the same time, they are interested in more free time even at the risk of less pay. They are blocking the upward path for "youngers"—and don't care.

They certainly would have plenty of things to do with more free time. Many are wrangling with issues surrounding care of elderly parents —even elderly spouses. The term "Sandwich Generation" gets a lot of traction with Boomers. They know what it means to be caretaking family members on both ends of the spectrum with all the financial burdens that come with it. When they imagined themselves as humans who have reached their highest potential, it's likely they didn't imagine family caretaking would be such a big part of it. They are quickly finding that "life is work and work is life" is no longer an effective motto. And many are reluctantly admitting that they just can't have it all.

Getting Old

Boomers have made an art form of turning the mundane and ordinary into trendy sources of soap-opera-style drama, and they continue that practice in the way they look at aging.

They have reengineered the process. The Boomers are making senior citizenship as trendy as cappuccino and personal trainers. And they are celebrating with tucks, lifts, colors, and pills. The Big Pharma is playing to the Boomer desire to extend their quality of life and stave off old age. With a lengthened life expectancy borne of medical advances, healthier life-styles, regular exercise, and low-fat diets, many Boomers can expect to live into their nineties (maybe even to one hundred)—making retirement just another milepost on their life's journey, not a signal for the downhill coast. Thus, they are marking it off as a major positive life event.

Just the same, for many, it's the first time they've looked into the face of Old Man Death—up close and personal—facing the fact that, alas, they might actually get old and die. There's no avoiding it: on the continuum from birth to death, they have certainly begun the trek down the back side, continuing to lengthen the span from birth and shortening up day-by-day the time remaining. While this glimpse of mortality is causing the Boomers to reexamine their priorities, it also gives them another opportunity to put a designer spin on yet another life phase.

The retirement reality check gives many Boomers very low grades for life-beyond-work—especially bottom line numbers for their retirement. Thus, there is renewed interest in flexible scheduling, which Boomers are using to pursue personal, even spiritual, interests while clinging to the security of work. Some have recommitted to family and personal relationships. Although they're feeling professionally experienced and comfortably competent, many have discovered they are not nearly as ambitious as they were in previous decades. Work is slowly slipping down their list of priorities, becoming less and less the focus of their lives. This reprioritizing will actually have a positive effect on the workplace, according to Columbia/HCA Healthcare, as aging Boomers cause it to become both more informal and more humane.

Meanwhile, the Boomers are determined to age like wine—slowly and with style. Marketing research shows they won't be giving up the Rolling Stones—or their pizza—any time soon. They intend to be fit, healthy, active, self-indulgent older people.

Boomer feminists are seeking to change perceptions of the older woman, reasserting her value and importance. In ancient times, elders held power and enjoyed status. Free from the responsibilities of child-care and the rigors of work life, they were the healers, the wise ones, the spiritual guides. As one woman said, "I want to be sixty in a completely different way than my mother was. I'm proud of my age, my strength, and my experience. I've just begun to be the person I worked for five decades to become."

Why Care?

Simple. Boomer bosses are going through a sensitive "life passage." Walk carefully around them. Avoid the temptation to treat them as the "elder states people" of your organization. They will laugh with you at pointed age jokes—but beware your next performance appraisal.

Retirement: "Hell, No, We Won't Go"

The workplace will be influenced by the Baby Boom generation until at least 2030. While the next two generations might like to move up the ladder, the Boomers are, for the most part, secure and securing them-selves in their positions—all the more so because of the economic downturn that has played havoc with their IRAs. Not only is their expe-rience impressive, but they are well connected with the decision-makers in their companies and the industries to which they belong. They have taken connecting to a fine art—internally and externally--and are much better at organizational politics than the Xers behind them. We think of the "man in the gray flannel suit" as a networker, but he couldn't hold a candle to the Boomers. They took the adage, "It's not *what* you know but *who* you know" and made it—if not a science—a form of high art.

THE BABY BOOMERS

Markings	Designer sunglasses, designer suits, designer bodies, vintage wines, whatever's trendy
Spending Style	Buy now, pay later—with plastic
What They Read	*Business Week, People*
Their Humor	*Doonesbury*

As the world economy recovers, more and more Boomers will inevitably retire. And, once again, the American culture will find itself transformed by the needs of this giant generation: living arrangements, retirement funds, weighty pensions, accessibility, and large print editions of newspapers and magazines. It still remains to be seen what impact, if

---

THE BABY BOOMERS

What the Other Generations Think About Them

Traditionalists say...

- "They talk about things they ought to keep private...like the details of their personal lives."
- "They are self-absorbed."

Gen Xers say...

- "They're self-righteous."
- "They're workaholics."
- "They're too political, always trying to figure out just what to say . . . to whom . . . and when."
- "They do a great job of talking the talk. But they don't walk the walk."
- "Get outta my face."
- "Lighten up; it's only a job."
- "What's the management fad this week?"
- "They're clueless."

Millennials say...

- "They're good mentors and role models."
- "They should lighten up."
- "I wish they would take time to answer my questions."

FACT AND FICTION ABOUT BABY BOOMERS

Myths		Facts	
1.	They're on their way out.	1.	The U.S. Census 2012 Statistical Abstract lists life expectancies for women at 80.8 years and men at 75.9 years. Boomers can expect longer, healthier work lives than any previous generation.
2.	They'll grow up.	2.	The average age of a Harley owner is 45, so that means half of all Hog drivers are Boomers.[5]
3.	They've always had it easy; they're assured of a comfortable retirement.	3.	According to AARP, one out of four older workers lost their entire retirement savings during the Great Recession.[6]
4.	They've quit learning.	4.	In a survey by Campus Continuum, more than half of respondents aged 55-75 said they were interested in lifelong learning and living in a college atmosphere.[7]
5.	Boomers are workaholics.	5.	The Baby Boomers have tended to work grueling hours for the past thirty years, but today many of them are committing to a slower pace. They recently lost the title "most stressed generation" to the Millennials.[8]

any, health care reform will have on retiring Boomers. Former Colorado Governor Richard Lamm said, "When the Baby Boomers start to retire, it will be equal to any demographic event that has happened to this country . . . as big an impact as the settlement of the West."

They have been in the spotlight of every phase of life they've passed through. The Boomers will re-define retirement, of course, just as they have adjusted every other phase of life to meet their needs.

CHAPTER 4

The Gen Xers

Survivalists in the Workplace

Born 1960 to 1980

"It's no wonder Xers are angst-ridden and rudderless. They feel America's greatness has passed. They got to the cocktail party twenty minutes too late and all that's left are those little weiners and a half-empty bottle of Zima."

—DENNIS MILLER

Generation X never really inherited the spotlight from the previous generation, the Boomers. It's a generation that no one ever much noticed, that didn't exactly register, until recently. That quasi-invisibility, born of living in the long shadow of "The Boom," was but the lull before the storm of identity building. As a generation, it has been defined by what it's not more than by what it is. Xers grew up like the middle child, passively resisting most of the characteristics the elder sibling embraced. The media and national attention turned away from children. The Boomers had the spotlight, were unlikely to let go of it, and have held onto it—for now and into the foreseeable future.

Again defined by what it is not, the X generation in the United States consists of a lot fewer people than the generation before it. While Boomers were topping the population charts—the birthrate in the United States climbed above four million per year for most of the Boom's two-decade run—Xers were the inevitable birthing recession after the boom, with a low in 1976 when only 3.2 million babies were born. That's 76 million Boomers vs. 51 million Xers. Xers grew up aware of the

Industrial Age, but became fully sentient in the beginning of Toffler's Information Age. Boomers' economic fortunes in their formative years were so stable as to be a nonissue, allowing them to tune in, turn on, and drop out. Summers of love, drugs, political protests, and rock concerts were Boomer economic luxuries the Xers would learn they could never afford.

Gen X's collective psyche was shaped by a survivor mentality that can, from the outside, seem cynical, extreme, and solitary. Critics worry that Xers don't have the right stuff, don't care about the larger picture, and are only concerned about themselves. This generation has developed an almost myopic concern with subsistence, both economic and

THE GEN XERS

Seminal Events

1970	Women's liberation protests and demonstrations
1972	Arab terrorists at Munich Olympics
1973	Watergate scandal
1973	Energy crisis hits the global economy
1976	Tandy and Apple market first personal computers
1978	Mass suicide in Jonestown, Guyana
1979	Three Mile Island nuclear reactor nears meltdown
1979	Margaret Thatcher becomes first female British Prime Minister
1979	U.S. corporations begin massive layoffs
1979	Iran holds 66 Americans hostage
1980	John Lennon shot and killed
1980	Ronald Reagan inaugurated
1981	AIDS identified
1986	Challenger disaster
1986	Chernobyl (Ukraine) nuclear power plant disaster
1987	Stock market plummets
1988	Terrorist bomb blows up Flight 103 over Lockerbie
1989	Exxon Valdez oil tanker spill
1989	Fall of Berlin wall

psychological. The question they always ask, either out loud or in their own heads, is "What does this have to do with my survival?" They sensed early that no one was going to hold their hands, so they learned to take care of themselves. That single question signals a very different agenda to colleagues of other generations. There was a time when emphasis on survival would have been seen as a moral shortcoming. Now, however, a survivor mentality is so vital to the workplace that it seems atavistic to hear executives droning on about organizational values and vision statements.

But don't let all that Generation X *is not* cause you to dismiss them out of hand. Employers and markets who ignore this group or write them off as cynical slackers unwilling to make a real contribution to the workforce will be buying a one-way ticket to business failure. In the past, there was a temptation to dismiss Generation X as outsiders, nomads who could work for an organization but never really be A players. But they have ascended the ranks of middle management—due in part to the declining workplace demographics of the Boomers. Gen Xers are settling in and moving up!

For the next two decades, Boomers and Xers will work together—and not always with the Boomers in senior positions. The Xers' technological acuity and project management capabilities are helping them reshape the workplace, and it doesn't hurt that the invisible hand of demographics is creating a vacuum of talent and experience with retiring Boomers. Xers' survival mentality can be a force that propels them into that vacuum where they become the new leaders of "new" organizations.

"I Survived the 1970s"

Where did this survivor mentality come from? Try growing up in the wake of Vietnam, the only war the United States ever lost, and you'll get a hint. Then, as you're beginning to become politically aware, watch a President of the United States go down in flames. Nixon's resignation, the first in U.S. history, was further exacerbated—in the hearts of the children of the 1970s—by his pardon from the acting President, Gerald

THE GEN XERS

Heroes

(none)

Ford, whose name had never appeared on the ballot. This was followed by an oil embargo that signaled to Xers that anyone with a grudge could kick sand in the face of this once-respected superpower and bring its standard of living to its knees. In the 1980s, when many twentysomethings joined the job market, the Japanese shadowboxed heavily over the U.S. economy, again leaving the industrial base ruined and precipitating storms of layoffs.

Generation X watched as America seemed to fail militarily, politically, diplomatically, and economically. When the Japanese talk about saving face, this group nods enthusiastically; they feel the pain. They grew up watching their country lose face often. All the young, impressionable, Xers could do was hunker down and learn how to survive in a world where everything was *not* going to be all right, where the happy endings of the movies were just shadows on the wall, where the American Dream looked like a running joke or, at best, a memory.

This cohort has resisted labels, even balking at the moniker "Generation X," the title of a book by one its defining writers, Douglas Coupland. They resist categorization because it is a tool of the media, with whom Xers have an uneasy relationship. It was the media that focused so heavily on the Boomers, placing them in the spotlight, then creating new categories for them about every five years: The "Beat Generation" became "Hippies" became "Yippies" became "Yuppies," and on and on. Now every time some clever reporter comes up with another cute name for whatever phase the Boomers seem to be going through, Xers sit back and roll their eyes. For Generation X to accept any label at all is to become a media object. The Boomers clung so willingly to whatever label the media painted them with that the Xers' knee-jerk reaction is total rejection of all labels.

Consequently, because it defines itself reactively, it is one of the more difficult generations to describe. Any description is necessarily rife with generalizations, and this group has a duck-and-cover mentality about categorization. Nonetheless, categorization is inevitable. Definitionally, the Xers are those born between 1960 and 1980. One of the best test questions to determine whether someone is an Xer or a late Boomer is to ask where they were when John F. Kennedy was shot. If they're not old enough to remember, yet don't consider the topic ancient history, they're probably part of Generation X. As with most generations, there isn't a hard-and-fast dividing line between late Boomers and early Xers.

Boomers grew up during the Cold War, where Armageddon was what they vicariously experienced when they crawled under their desks in school to practice "surviving a nuclear disaster." Generation X grew up during the economic wars of the 1970s and 1980s, where the battlefields lay in Flint, Michigan, and throughout the Rust Belt. It seemed, like the Cold War, ongoing and endless. Though we know it now to be the opening round of industrial globalization, it seemed at the time as if the U.S. economy had been overthrown. But an economic war is a whole new animal, and the casualties show up every time some megacorporation announces another 40,000 layoffs. Generation X grew up in this economic DMZ, and it's shaped some very interesting characteristics.

> **THE GEN XERS**
>
> **Cultural Memorabilia**
> * *The Brady Bunch*
> * Pet Rocks
> * Platform Shoes
> * *The Simpsons*
> * *Dynasty*
> * *ET: The Extra Terrestrial*
> * Cabbage Patch Dolls
> * Amy Carter

Their Generational Personality

They formed their view of the world in the 1970s—the post-Vietnam-Watergate-Oil Embargo-Disco era. It was a particularly unpopular time to be a child; they were some of the first babies whose mothers took pills to prevent them. They came of age in an era of fallen heroes, a struggling economy, soaring divorce rates, and the phenomenon of the latchkey child—the first generation of living lifestyle accessories. For their parents, it was what author Tom Wolfe called the "Me Decade"—a time to focus on and develop themselves—at the health club, in self-help groups, and at work. For their children, it was another matter; it was parent-free childhood. A time of figuring it out for yourself.

Gen Xers are self-reliant. If the tabloids were to characterize this co-hort, the headline might read, "Generation X: Raised by Wolves." They were the most attention-deprived, neglected group of kids in a long time. Parents were absent without leave for two reasons. First, nearly half of their parents' marriages ended in divorce. Generation X children lived and breathed in an environment of joint custody, visitation rights, and weekend fathers. While their parents' unraveling relationships dev-astated them, many of their assets as a generation—self-reliance, inde-pendence, and just plain old chutzpah—developed as a result of this absenteeism. Then too, this was the first generation of kids within the bounds of the two-income family. Women were going to work in in-creasing numbers, and the economy was making it dramatically more difficult for a family to sustain a reasonable standard of living with only one wage earner. This one-two punch created a new sociological trend: Latchkey Kids.

THE GEN XERS

Core Values

- Diversity
- Thinking globally
- Balance
- Technoliteracy
- Fun
- Informality
- Self-reliance
- Pragmatism

They want balance. In the eyes of Generation X, their parents devoted their lives to the Religion of Work, spending evenings and weekends at the office, bringing projects home, and expending all their energy and attention on work issues. It looked like workaholism to their kids, who couldn't help but notice that most adults based their self-worth on their professional success. When family friends came over for dinner, the adults spent their time discussing their jobs, and phone calls focused on problems with the boss. Kids regularly spent an extra hour or two in day care because a work deadline threatened. In the words of many an Xer, their parents "lived to work." Xers simply want to "work to live." Members of this cohort group are distressed by the high prices their parents paid for success—stress and health problems, divorce, drug and alcohol abuse. And it didn't look as if the companies to whom they had devoted all their time and energy appreciated their efforts. Layoffs were living proof.

So Generation Xers committed themselves to more balance in their own lives. They don't believe that you can have it all. Rather, they know that life is a series of tough choices, and the least loyal entity in their lives is their employer. They won't try to juggle all those roles—parent, employee, spouse—or, if they do, it won't be with the same unrealistic expectations. They know something has to give. On the job, they expect to leave at 5:00 P.M.; they don't intend to give up their weekends, and they will rarely volunteer to work overtime.

Says LanceW7850 on an online forum, "most of us don't have any particular problem with staying late; we just have a life outside of work. I've come in on weekends, stayed late, to get a project done. But I don't like to do it. Life wasn't meant to be spent at work; it was meant to be enjoyed with people you value. I married my wife so I could be with her. If managers estimated the job correctly in the first place, there'd be no need to stay."

They have a nontraditional orientation about time and space. Xers don't think much of work hours. It won't be surprising if, within the next few years, a whole new batch of executives rediscovers management by objective (MBO). It strikes a chord with Generation X's philosophy of work, "As long as I get my work done, what does it matter how and when I get it done?" They show up late, leave early, and are keeping their eye on what they think is the ball—getting the work done. If they do it at home, at odd hours, in the car on the cell phone, or while telecommuting, they think that's *their* business—not their supervisor's. They don't come close to understanding "line-of-sight" managing. Nor do they understand the idea of being carefully hired and matched to a job only to be watched like a jailed felon.

They like informality. Having grown up in a serious world with a bunch of self-reflective Boomers for parents and bosses, this generation of employees wants to see things lighten up. They take casual days seriously. We've seen Xer workers go to amazing lengths just to win a sticker that allowed them to wear jeans on a day other than Friday. And being able to go to work in jeans and a T-shirt on Friday, many assert, isn't just a perk. They say it actually makes them work harder and get more done. Anything that makes work less "corporate" resonates with a generation who feels betrayed by corporate interests, and some companies have recognized that the nature of the work doesn't really require the suit, tie, wing-tips, or nylons.

Their approach to authority is casual. Formal hierarchical relationships are lost on Gen Xers—who aren't so much against authority as simply unimpressed by it. They've seen authority figures—Nixon, Clinton, and often even their own parents—step off the pillar and into the gutter. They treat the company president with respect because their survival instincts inform their behavior, but they will not seek out a meeting with him or her. They just don't see approval from above as a good way to get things done.

Greg was a research scientist at a Fortune 500 company, and he had a new idea for a product. A good idea. So good in fact, that he was called into a meeting to present it. His technical expertise on the subject was unassailable, so he didn't even hesitate when the CEO and some other C's showed up to listen. After his presentation, they discussed his idea for a few minutes and authorized the money to add a new wing onto the factory to produce it—at which point Greg left the meeting. He hadn't networked his way into the meeting, and he didn't stick around for the networking opportunities afterward, something members of any other generation almost certainly would have done.

They are cynical. Little Gen Xers watched with great anticipation as Christa McAuliffe, the first schoolteacher in space, boarded the space shuttle *Challenger*. Within a few seconds, the whole undertaking blew up and turned to dust right in front of their eyes. While the Boomers were told, "You can be anything you want—even the President," Generation X was told, "Be careful out there. It's a dangerous world." And so they are careful and guarded in their personal and professional relationships, withholding their optimism and excitement for fear that things won't work out quite as planned. And Gen Xers grew up with lip service that often didn't seem to be supported by action. They have learned not to place their faith in others, to be careful with their loyalty and commitments, for fear of getting burned. That cynicism is never more evident than when you look at their sense of humor. *The Daily Show*, *The Colbert Report*, and *The Onion* all appeal to the cynicism of Generation X.

They continue to be technologically savvy. Xers learned to operate the microwave, program the VCR, and play video games when they were little tykes. Computer skills were every bit as fundamental in their elementary education as the 3Rs were to generations before them. A recent report by Pew Research indicates that Gen Xers surpass Millennials on *Facebook* and other social media platforms. Xers' identity is inexorably tied to their ability to use technology. The money and success many achieved during the dot.com rush of the late 1990s cemented a mantra into their generational psyche: technology equals success equals survival. Now, with technological change happening at a startlingly rapid clip and a new technoliterate generation breathing down their necks, some Xers are struggling to keep up. Staying current will continue to be a source of anxiety for them. The Boomers had a similar anxious response when they became the boss. They had spent much of their lives and much of their personal capital challenging authority. When they finally became the leaders, they were uncomfortable with the mantle. In the future, challenging Gen Xers' technological knowledge will raise their hackles. It's core to their identity.

They are attracted to the edge. Where Boomers saw their careers as great all-consuming melodramas, to Xers, the job is "just a job." Their sense of risk and adventure is very much expressed outside the workplace. The latchkey kids developed a lone wolf mentality, and extreme life experiences will always be on their radar. In fact, the term "edgy" is a positive to them, and anything described as edgy probably belongs to them. Although their disregard for personal safety has been tempered by having kids, it's not uncommon for an Xer's Monday morning coffee chat to include matter-of-fact recountings of rock climbing, mountain biking, and parachute jumping exploits done with friends traveling in packs. After all, the X-Games were named in their honor and exemplify their spirit of eccentricity and physical derring-do.

First-Halfers: "Please Sir, May I Have Some More?"

The first group of Gen Xers to hit the workplace were the wretched refuse, the workers no one wanted. Not only did they join the labor marketplace in the wake of millions of Boomers, but they also arrived at a time when the U.S. economy was in the throes of globalization—losing jobs hand over fist to far-off locales. "Downsizing" went from euphemism to anathema overnight, and college students who had been told that a degree would be a ticket to a good job discovered they were the butt of an expensive joke.

"What did the art history major say to the engineering student?"

"Paper or plastic, Sir?"

So while the hippies were morphing into the winner-take-all yuppies during the Reagan 1980s, the Xers—just entering the workplace—had some cruel different lessons to learn. It wasn't uncommon for a college graduate to be handed the "opportunity" to work for minimum wage at a coffee shop or bookstore. To take a grim view of it—and they did—not only did the Boomers steal the nation's collective attention, they also took all the jobs with interesting wages.

When the layoff craze struck like a radioactive lizard in downtown Tokyo, things got even worse. The parents many Gen Xers moved in with after college were taking it on the chin, watching high-paying careers turn into corporate redundancy. Don't think this generation didn't

THE GEN XERS

How Xers Differ From the Previous Generation

Boomers	Xers
• Fight against authority	• Aikido rebellion. Ask forgiveness rather than permission.
• Media darlings	• Mostly overlooked
• Workaholics	• Work toward goals and objectives, not just putting in time
• Political	• Politics never solved anything, and usually made it worse.
• Political at work	• Corporate politics wastes time we could spend finishing the work and getting out of here.
• Nostalgia for the 1960s	• Ironic nostalgia for the 1970s and 1980s.

notice. Their consequent resentment of corporate America has manifested itself in a variety of ways. The Boomers may not have trusted anyone over 30, but the Xers didn't trust anyone in the Fortune 500.

In any case, the first half of Generation X joined the workforce in the era when the phrase "there is no job security anymore" was used so often as to become cliché. The job contract had been torn up and redrafted by corporations to fit the new "downsized," no stability employment model. Every once in a while, someone will ask, "Whatever happened to loyalty?" Most Xers will respond, "We're in charge of our own careers. The company won't take care of us, and we're quite capable of taking care of ourselves." Of course, since Gen X came of job-holding age during the age of downsizing, their predilection for survival clued them in: Everyone better look out for themselves. Thus was born a whole generation of corporate nomads, jumping from one entry-level job to another. It has been a generation almost unique in its ability to persevere in the redefined environment. You'll never hear them gripe about company loyalty; it's as foreign to them as buggy whips are to Boomers.

The only ticket that got them anywhere in the new economy was their own skills, and the best way to develop those was through real experience in real jobs, not with college degrees or book smarts. The current normal is for everyone coming out of college to have two or three internships in their portfolio, but that surge in internships began with Generation X's fanatical devotion to real, nontheoretical work experience.

Second-Halfers: The Gold Collar Workers

The second half of Generation X arrived in the workplace just as it experienced another major swing of the pendulum. A labor shortage hit full stride in 1997, and a significant proportion of the Gen X workforce was positioned to cash in. With the explosion of Information Technology (IT) as a function of every company—and now an industry unto itself—anyone who knew anything about computer technology could negotiate a pretty impressive starting salary. Most companies needed qualified computer technicians and programmers, but qualified techies didn't come ready made, fully formed from the ranks of Generation X in quite the way employers expected. Consequently, companies in many cases settled for whatever they could get—people without a fear of computers—and trained them, either formally or on the job. Say what you want about Gen Xers, people frequently do, but they're not afraid of technology. Companies recognized that, if they couldn't get a qualified person for their IT needs, a confident person was the next best thing. Back then, the rush to get a company up on the Web punched the ticket of many a college grad, even if they were sociology majors.

Management guru Robert Kelley called the trained ones *gold-collar workers*: highly desirable technically trained college graduates who were rare and commanded formidable starting salaries. Companies offered finder's fees to employees who recruited IT professionals, and those who were thus recruited commanded signing bonuses as high as $400,000. And it wasn't just the money. For these gold collar workers, the job market was so rosy they could make a variety of unusual demands of their employers: being allowed to bring pets to work, to stock the lunchroom fridge with beer, to follow any schedule that suited their whim. They required, and got, those perks from employers desperate for their skills.

The economic reality would turn bleak a decade later—with first-halfers and second-halfers alike thinking of the late 90s and the dotcom bubble as *the good old days* while they scrambled to hold onto their jobs. But their attitudes about work would be forever imprinted by the era in which they arrived. Whereas early Xers had entered a workplace that was glutted and underpaying, rife only with jobs for bag boys and baristas, the second half Xers with advanced skills found themselves embraced by a labor market with between 100,000 and 400,000 unfilled technology positions. For the first time since the rush for engineers and MBA's in the eighties, job seekers were in the driver's seat. The economics of the workplace for the second-half Xers were starkly different than those their earlier cohorts perceived to be their lot.

Devon: Economic Orphan

Devon graduated from a small Eastern college in 1985 with a degree in psychology and a minor in anthropology. He went looking for a job, hoping to land an entry-level position in a corporation and work his way up into a decent-paying job. He had dreams of his own apartment, a nice car, and an enjoyable nightlife with friends. After a nine-month search, however, he ended up with two part-time jobs: at a coffee shop in the mornings and at The Gap at night. These two jobs would cover his school loans but not much else. The dream of having his own apartment became dimmer, and it looked like living with his parents was going to be a long-term solution to his financial difficulties. He couldn't afford a car, so he biked to work. Any spare income seemed to get absorbed by printing up resumes and sending them, en masse, to hundreds of employers. He "forgot" to take any computer classes in college and regretted it every time he searched the want ads. In fact, it looked like he "forgot" to get any marketable skills, and he began to look for opportunities to acquire some kind of skill a company would pay for.

He finally decided the only way to get those skills was to take a job with a nonprofit that would give him a chance to prove himself without "3 to 5 years of previous experience." A low paying job in a homeless shelter actually paid off. It gave him work he felt was meaningful, let him mix with others his age, and gave him some modest exposure to computer technology. The organization was open to all kinds of ideas, as long as the person attached to the idea was willing to do the work. Some of the other staff members were his age, and they often went out after work, forging a small circle of friends. He even found a girlfriend. Best of all, the organization had a bunch of old computers people had donated, and during quiet times, he began to experiment with them. He often ran into trouble because the software—sometimes donated, sometimes illegally copied—was much too sophisticated for the equipment. He therefore found himself digging in the guts of the computers, opening them up and fooling around with the hardware.

Devon saved a little money. When his folks kicked in a thousand dollars, he bought himself a '79 Corolla and continued to pay down his student loans. When some coworkers proposed renting a three-bedroom place together, he jumped at the chance. It meant a considerable financial strain, but he continued to hope for a better job. Eventually he found a company that valued what he could do with computers. He moved deeper into the mainstream workforce by getting a series of IT certifications. Over the last 12 years, Devon worked his way into middle management, and a series of Boomer retirements at his current employer has left him just a few steps away from the coveted CIO position. He's looking at an online MBA degree to fuel that final jump to the C suite.

Devon's liberal arts degree coupled with his 1980s entry into the workplace added up to penny pinching, struggling to survive, and soul searching, a tough start to a slow-growth career. And a tone that colored his view of what is possible for him now and in the future. Fortunately, his DIY sensibilities and his Xer survival mindset got him through some tough times. The dotcom bust put him out of work for almost a year. But he was climbing into upper management when the Great Recession hit, so barring an abrupt M&A, he's safer than he's ever been.

Li: Gold Collar Employee

Li's is a happier story since it begins in the 1990s and includes a background in computer science. When Li was in college, the World Wide Web was just coming into its own. What she knew about the Internet, which wasn't a lot, was about to change in dramatic ways, and she went along for the ride. She didn't buy into the line about how valuable a liberal arts education would be, so she added a computer science minor to her English major. Her final paper for her degree was a demonstration of how someone with access to the World Wide Web could assemble—in less than an hour—a graduate thesis on James Joyce's *Ulysses* cutting and pasting from other works on the subject. She performed this feat live in front of three professors in 15 minutes, earning looks of horror from the assembled academics and an "A" on the project. After an extensive review of her previous papers, they gave her a diploma and wished her luck in her future endeavors. They needn't have bothered. Never have so few been wanted by so many.

While she was a below-average programmer, she understood computer networks like nobody's business. The job offers from two prestigious consulting firms during her junior year were certainly flattering, but she was holding out for a job in Silicon Valley. The organizations with the job offers, for their part, were offended by her brazenness and kept her resume in their "active recruitment" file. Until near the end of her senior year, she had been undecided if she wanted to work for a startup in Silicon Valley or strike out on her own with some venture capital—she had a friend who had a great idea for a Web-based company. Trouble was, she didn't know anything about venture capital and had heard her share of horror stories. She wasn't interested enough in the world of high finance to learn what she needed to know, so she took a job at a small Mountain View, California, company that was working on networking 3D computer animation. The money wasn't great, but the stock options would prove to be lucrative enough for her to set up her own company in a few years. And half the time she didn't need to leave home to go to work. She could set up her office anywhere she liked, as long as she came into headquarters a couple of times a month for some face time with the execs, most of whom were Xers themselves.

So she rented a loft in the warehouse district and spent her small signing bonus outfitting her office with an espresso machine, refrigerator, pool table, two old couches, and a very fast Internet connection. Her friends came to the office to see her, and she worked whatever hours she pleased. Her personal and professional lives completely merged, and it was hard to know when she was working and when she was goofing off. To afford her extravagant lifestyle, she did a little network consulting on the side. She didn't really think of her job with the animation company as full time, so the consulting helped to fill in the gaps when she was idle.

Eventually, she and the friend with the great software idea went looking for some venture capital. They got it, and when the company began to feel *corporate,* Li sold her share for a healthy amount—and got out. She soon started another company, but it didn't pan out. Embarked on a career as a serial entrepreneur, she soon took on the role of angel investor. Today Li works part time at the local university teaching classes and organizing competitions for young people who want to try their hands at startups.

Devon and Li in the Workplace

While it's true that Devon and Li have different skill sets and income levels, their primary difference is history. Li came to the workplace with high expectations that came to fruition. Devon barely survived his baptism by fire—learning bitter lessons about promises, hope, and disappointment. When the Great Recession hit, Devon was more psychologically ready for it than Li. There aren't a lot of starry-eyed second-half gold-collar workers left. Like their orphaned predecessors, their cynicism tempered their optimism about the future. All Xers know that their economic mistresses can grow bored and fickle at the drop of the next earnings statement. Most of them now have mortgages, families, and responsibilities, so the option of chucking it all and living with their parents is no longer viable. When their work is rewarding, gold-collar Xers are a bit more willing than their older peers to work long hours and devote their free time to their jobs. Devon and his peers will probably never make that commitment. It smacks too much of the Boomers in the C suite. Devon knows there will always be too much work and "having a life" has become gospel to him and his friends.

But Li and Devon still want many of the same things: atypical corporations where hours are flexible; independence is encouraged; fun and humor are incorporated into the work; and casual dress is an everyday standard, not just a Friday treat. They

---

THE GEN XERS

On the Job

Assets

- Adaptability
- Technoliteracy
- Independence
- Creativity
- Willingness to buck the system

Liabilities

- Skeptical
- Impatient
- Distrustful of authority
- Inept at office politics
- Less attracted to leadership

also, for the most part, share their disdain for Boomer bosses. Like many younger generations observing the absurdities of those elders in charge, Xers see most of what the Boomers have done as self-absorbed, overly ideological, and chock full of arrogant self-importance. They see much of Boomer work behavior as being beside the point. There is a natural tension between these two groups, as there is every time two generations work in close proximity.

If Xers embrace any management trend, it would have to be technology, particularly the networked work environment. That, to them, looks like salvation, a way to become more productive, less geographically limited, and, frankly, different from the generation before. Since Generation X has pinned its hopes on making its mark in the workplace on networked computers, they are now facing the prospect of no longer being the smartest person in the room regarding technology. And that scares them. The Millennial generation has already begun to challenge Generation X and its own sense of self. In some conversations, aging Xers are starting to sound down right curmudgeonly when faced with the new kids on the block—who seem to live and breathe in the social media soup.

One other skill has bubbled to the top as a real strength for Generation X. In the late 1990s *project management* became a vital skill to include on your resume; today it is needed by organizations everywhere. A project without a good project manager is destined to languish and die on the vine. Project managers, for their part, are always looking for that one project that will catapult them to the top of the heap and mark them for promotion. It's a skill that taps into the survival mechanism deep in the Xer psyche, while still appealing to their DIY mentality. It takes someone with a strong sense of determination and the willingness to nag people to get work done. Most projects aren't spelled out step-by-step: the project manager has to figure out how to take the project from start to successful completion. And that's the kind of stuff Xers love to figure out. A significant portion of Generation X was attracted to computer programming for the very same reason. Those who didn't acquire those skills became project managers. Both paths require the same personality. People who are good at project managing like to figure out new processes and implement them on the fly. They are seat-of-the-pants—or skirts—problem solvers. Teamwork is fine—and often necessary, but Xer project managers like to spend their time with Gantt charts and timelines. Think back to the latchkey kids of the 1970s and 1980s. Those scrappy street-smart kids with a penchant for survival are the project managers of today.

Their Work Ethic

Generation X didn't get labeled "slackers" for nothing. When Xers first arrived in the workplace, the Boomers complained about their work ethic, or lack thereof. And that's not all misperception. Xers have an attitude toward work that is as different from that of previous generations as anything we've seen before. Previous generations, maybe back to the beginning of history, equated work with survival. The Boomers put a new spin on that, turning it into "work equals self-fulfillment." But Generation X learned that work is no guarantee of survival, that corporations can throw you out of your job without warning, logic, or even an apology, and that work is often mindless, dull, and exhausting.

They're not likely to change their perception. Just as a child's early years determine his or her personality, early work experiences permanently shape workers' attitudes about corporate culture. The prevailing Xer attitude that all work is "just a job" is unlikely to change, tempered only by the fact that they now also have "just a mortgage" and "just some kids" who probably need "just some college."

But Generation X workers can be motivated to do work—good work. Flexible hours, an informal work environment, and just the right amount of supervision are great places to start. If you're searching for the Generation X work ethic, don't look through the traditional lens. You won't find it. If you want to tap into it, give them a lot to do and some freedom regarding how the work gets done. You'll probably be surprised how much these "slackers" can accomplish and still walk out the door at 5:00 P.M.

Where They Work

It's true that many members of Generation X have gone into technology. And while it's true that Apple is populated primarily by Xers and Silicon Valley is a bastion for them, the truth is, Generation X hasn't produced more than its share of computer scientists and engineers. In fact, this generation hasn't kept up with previous generations in its production of academically trained computer scientists. What surveys and research don't uncover is that most Xers learned computer "science" via trial and error. If a kid struggles for ten hours trying to get Doom to work on his network so he and three others can play death matches late into the night, he tends to learn some things of transferable value along the way, just like Boomer car mechanics did. In actuality, there are Xers in all areas of almost every organization. The most visible ones work as successful project managers, shepherding ideas from start to finish and then doing it all over again.

There's also a strain of Generation X workers who have gone into a very special sector of the economy: their own. A lot of Xers opted so far out of the corporate milieu that they decided to start their own businesses. According to a study by The Center for Work Life Policy, nearly 40% of Gen X men and 25% of Gen X women aspire to be entrepreneurs.[1] Two reasons: a deep distrust in a corporate America that has let them down through two recessions and a tech bust. Boomers too struck off on their own, but usually in the wake of layoffs or midlife crises. Xer entrepreneurs, by contrast, jumped into their own businesses right out of college— or after just a few years in the corporate world. The dotcom startup surge of the late 1990s is still in the collective Gen X memory bank. That strong sense of self-reliance developed during their formative years. "Having your own

> ### THE GEN XERS
>
> **Messages That Motivate**
>
> - "I don't care how you get it done."
> - "I'm not going to micromanage you."
> - "There aren't a lot of meetings here."
> - "Our team has a good sense of humor."

business means not worrying about what some head guy in Dallas thinks," says Sky Eacrett, a Redlands, California, tile store manager. "No matter how much money you make for them you are still just an X. And you can be X-ed off. With my own business, I could come in at 7 A.M. and leave at noon to play golf."[2] They usually don't; but the option is what's important.

Futurists predict that Generation X will be the primary source for new entrepreneurs for the next few decades. Their core characteristics—risk tolerance, survival mentality, lack of regard for rules and authority, DIY thinking—are the very traits embodied in most successful business founders. So if your organization needs more entrepreneurial thinking in the ranks, your current crop of Xers may well have just what you're looking for.

Their Leadership Style

With steadily increasing global competition, few things in the workplace have changed more dramatically in the last decade than leadership. The old chain-of-command system has proven tremendously burdensome; it simply takes too long to get the paperwork, the decision, and the product through the hierarchy and bureaucracy. Even Boomers will admit that they often succeed *despite* or outside of "the bureaucracy." Sophisticated and demanding customers expect their needs to be met right now. The new leader, then, must be skilled at supporting and developing a responsive, competent team of people who can change direction, or projects, on a dime.

Generation X is uniquely qualified for the job. They've never really been "good soldiers." They had an egalitarian rather than a hierarchical relationship with their parents; they went to school in a system that encouraged diverse viewpoints; and, in their first jobs, they usually worked for Boomer bosses, who espoused participation and involvement, although they often didn't practice what they preached. They thrive on change; many learned as kids to adapt to a new bedroom, home, and neighborhood on weekends. They are used to challenging and being challenged. Whereas the little Boomers were graded for "works well with others," little Xers were graded for their ability to challenge others' thinking. They were encouraged to disagree with things they read, to debate classmates, and to "Never just do what an adult asks. Always ask, 'Why?'"

They tend to be drawn to leadership for more altruistic reasons than the generation before them. For the Boomers, there's sort of a juju about authority. Although many of them distrust authority, they've lusted after leadership roles, seeking to prove their status, prestige, and general worthiness by climbing the ladder. Generation Xers don't equate magic and leadership.

> Gen Xer Greg Felt writes the fishing report in Salida, Colorado. He was born four months after the end of the baby boom:
>
> "It's like I'm a kid with a big brother and our parents left for the night and he threw a huge party at our house. Now it's morning and a total mess. The house is a total disaster, and I've been conditioned to think that it is now my problem—that I have to clean up the whole thing myself."[4]

Those in leadership roles tend to choose them, and be chosen for them, because they are competent and have good leadership skills. It's a job, just a job.

It is said that information equals power. Insomuch as this is true, Xers should be wielding more and more power because they're far more adept than the older generations at accessing information—on the Internet, via email, and through the company's information system.

Generation X managers tend to be fair, competent, and straightforward leaders. Their inclination is to create a conglomeration of circles of people into "campus cultures," complete with recreational opportunities. If there's one area where Xer leaders are not as strong as their Boomer counterparts, it's in the people skills arena. Xers tend to be honest, sometimes brutally so, and this can be devastating to a young employee in the midst of his or her first performance appraisal. A certain amount of tact on the part of the leader can go a long way toward employee retention.

The Boomers would tell you that they, themselves, are also better at corporate politics—knowing just how to say exactly the right thing to the penultimate person at precisely the right time. Xers would say they're not interested in that "political stuff." They see the 20 percent of their generation who are politically adept as corporate stooges.

As Team Members

In their personal lives, the *Friends* ethic is cherished—a group of friends hanging together working and playing as a unit. A "team" but without the explicit Boomer rules or the Traditionalist sense of duty. But as more and more Gen Xers move into the executive suite, a serious backlash against the concept of teamwork may occur—simply because Boomers are so team happy and Xers tend to reject Boomer metaphors and baggage. Of course, Generation Xers are on all kinds of teams right now, although most of them are convinced they could get the work done more effectively on their own. If they must be on a team, they prefer small ones of three or four people. Big groups—like the ones Millennials are drawn to—are less efficient, as they see it. Their independent nature comes from their upbringing. Unsupervised by parents for the most part, they navigated their way through life and got rather good at it. Even their sports tend toward the solitary. Take, for example, snowboarding, mountain biking, roller blading, and rock climbing. You'll often see Xers doing these activities in groups, but they could just as well be doing them alone.

If you want an interesting view of Xer teamwork, take a look at the way many software companies write code. Huge programming projects are often assembled by many teams of software developers, each piece taken by a separate team that must coordinate its programming to meet the goals of that distinct section of an application. But programming is, by its nature, a solitary effort. One programmer's code can look very different than another's, even if they both are doing precisely the same thing. Each has a style, and we're told that a project manager can tell which piece of a program was written by which team member by the style alone. A team leader's ability to piece all of these individually conceived programs together into a working piece of software is critical. This team system is a good match with the Gen X mindset.

In contrast, if this kind of project were set up by Boomers, it would likely consist of the whole team working in a shared space with no walls, so they could converse, collaborate, and generally do the project like a "community team." In the Gen X model, software developers each have their own office, complete with walls and doors, and they write code in solitude. They get together as a team from time to time to check on progress and work out particularly gnarly problems as a group, but most of their time is spent working alone, with only minor supervision. That model—virtual teamwork—is the norm in most software companies. Much of the communication among team members is handled by email.

This style of communication and collaboration still incorporates phone conversations, face-to-face meetings, and conferences; it just obviates some of these and extends the usefulness of others. Its main dynamic is its asynchronous nature. Not since the advent of the newspaper has asynchronous work taken such leaps ahead. Take an example from an early email discussion group called "The Well." During the Russian crisis when Gorbachev fell and Yeltsin faced off the tanks, one participant on The Well was talking to his daughter, who was in Red Square at the time, and he was reporting to others in the chat room what she was seeing. He was getting the news to them faster than CNN, which his wife was watching in the next room. He was way ahead of her. Not only could he get the facts, but he could ask questions of the "reporter" and get responses, something no other audience had ever been able to do. This was years before the Internet came into common use. This form of asynchronous communication is faster than other methods, is more grass roots, creates a permanent record that people can go back to, and is more interactive.

Managing Generation X

If you're ready to create a fun, flexible, nonmicromanaged work atmosphere where Xers have a variety of projects to engage them and minimal corporate politics to confound them, you'll have Generation X beating down the door to go to work for you and working hard to stay.

Let's face it: Most jobs are a mixture of intrinsically motivating tasks and drudgery. There's no evidence that Xers expect work to be totally engaging and completely meaningful. They are not naïve; they learned self-sufficiency early and never expected the world to be a bowl of cherries. As long as you don't pretend that some meaningless task is really important, they will respect you for your frankness and honesty.

Just the same, managers of Gen Xers, particularly those on the front lines, need to be clear in communicating that some repetitive tasks are simply part of the job and that quality outcomes require some checking. Even tasks requiring only modest skills have enough nuances that to be done well can't necessarily be automated. They require real human judgment, acquired through experience. Many Gen Xers recognize that in sports you've got to practice, practice, practice to develop skill and experience; sometimes they don't translate that lesson to work. Helping with that translation is critical to creating a productive Gen X coterie in your company.

Some Key Principles

Recruiting

1. Include the phrase "we want you to have a life" at least three times during the interview.
2. Convince them that in your company ideas are evaluated purely on merit, not by the person's years of experience.
3. Don't try the "change agent" routine on them. Xers have a sixth sense about business BS, and a lot of the jargon that gets tossed around in business qualifies. Instead, tell them that your company and industry is going through a lot of change. Leave it at that. To an Xer, change means opportunity--opportunities to move up or broaden the scope of their skills.
4. Warm and humane treatment—so important to Boomers—doesn't cut it with Xers. Instead, make it a fun, relaxed place to work.
5. Stress that your company wants to be a technological innovator and needs workers who aren't afraid of technology to make that happen. If your company blocks *Facebook* at work, it will turn off Millennials, but it will raise red flags for Xers, too.
6. Say the phrase "hands-off supervision" at least three times in the interview. Stress that you'll need them to manage a lot of projects at the same time—that you're looking for a good juggler.

Orienting

1. They're not afraid to ask questions, so make it easy for them by giving them a list of who to get in touch with for more information on a wide variety of subjects.
2. Include the phrase "we want you to have a life" at least three times during orientation.
3. Xers hate corporate politics but recognize that Boomers have a gift

for it. Let them know, as their boss, that you will "take point" on political maneuvers so the Xer can relax and concentrate on the job.

Opportunities

Companies come and companies go. Nothing is static. Everything changes, and keeping your eye on the ball, for Generation X, means looking out for number one. A lot of rah-rah about contributing to the organization and the greatness of team efforts and "all for one and one for all" rings hollow with this group. Yes, they like being treated as individuals and getting personal attention, but there's a fine line for them between good managing and micromanaging.

1. That's why it's best to err on the side of freedom. Plenty of elbow-room will appeal to your Gen X workforce and give them a favorable impression of your workplace. Because they are self-reliant, it's important to be there when they need questions answered—but also know when to back off and let them figure it out themselves.
2. Stress the dramatic changes your company is going through, with an eye to helping them develop all kinds of new skills. These are the corporate nomads, so if you have a large enough organization, you can let them roam from tribe to tribe without ever really losing them. For this cohort, moving sideways often is just as good as moving up. Frankly, many of them have given up on moving up.
3. An important message to send to this group is that ongoing training is an important part of their duties. Let them know they will be going through training on a lot of different systems continuously, as well as some professional development at outside conferences.

Developing

The nice thing about Xers is they are virtually self-developing. Their early years gave them the ability to learn quickly and develop skills on their own. Whereas many employees won't pick up a self-study computer course online, this generation will. They may not go through it in the order you want them to, but they will learn the important material.

That's the key to these workers: give them lots of resources so they can learn how to do their jobs and give the resources to them in a variety of media. Books, computer programs, podcasts, video and even face-to-face instruction all have their appeal to these employees, so make as many of them available—not mandatory—as possible.

1. Encourage and allow Xers to direct their own learning. They have a nontraditional orientation to time and place; they believe as long as the learning gets done, it's not important where or when.
2. Consider nongroup-meeting training formats: online training, videos, and electronic performance support programs that answer their questions as they work.
3. If they must show up for a training program for days on end at precisely the same time each morning, explain the rationale and get their buy-in—contractually and early on.
4. If you're the front-of-the-room trainer, get right into the material and demonstrate your expertise. Don't spend lots of time up front building relationship.
5. Give Xers opportunities to sample and learn by doing through activities like case studies and role play.

Motivating

1. Most Xers enjoy lots of simultaneous tasks and projects, work they can juggle. Giving them lots of projects, allowing them to prioritize them in their own way, gives workers the feeling they have more control over their work. Positive reaction to this feeling shows up on job satisfaction surveys, employee morale charts, and incentive reports again and again. Generation X is no exception—in fact, they may be the poster children for a self-managing workforce.
2. Like everyone else, Generation X employees need constructive feedback to become more effective. Some have even suggested they need it more than other employees. Since Xers yearned for their absentee parents' attention, positive feedback, sincerely offered, can be the difference between keeping them and losing them to competitors.

They will respond to negative comments better than the next generation, but they will want to know how to take action on their feedback. Anything that asks them to change their attitudes will be a tough nut to crack.

3. A little freedom goes a long way to keeping these workers satisfied. Give them time to pursue other interests, even have fun, at work. Google actually encourages its programmers to play games at work for about 15 minutes in the morning and 15 minutes in the afternoon—for fun and to learn about the latest and greatest software available.[3]

4. Likewise, 3M has a longstanding policy that allows employees to use 15 percent of their work time on their own projects. That's been a source of innovation for the company and is popular with employees from all generations.

5. One job perk Xers really appreciate is leading-edge technology. They think having the best computer equipment in their cubicles is as good as a corner office with a window and door. Give them two monitors.

6. Don't block sites like *Facebook*, YouTube, and other social media sites; they're instrumental to Gen Xers' lives. If you want them to use online access responsibly, tell them so and outline the organization's policy.

7. Review your overall employee motivation package. Xers may not be all that anxious to get perks, but they resent it when others get visible, expensive recognition. It smacks of the worst kind of corporate politics, the old boy network gone haywire, and it's likely to send Xer employees running for the exits.

Mentoring

Mentors can be important to this group, especially now. A mentor can give them the inside track on organizational politics. Xers rue politics, but they are beginning to realize they need at least rudimentary political skills to get ahead—and they're woefully aware of that gap in their skills. Look for opportunities to match directors and executives with those

Gen Xers who are poised to move into upper management and executive positions. Call it succession planning.

1. Pitch office politics as a way to get around the rules; that's something Xers love.
2. Make them feel like insiders as quickly as possible through access to promotional fast tracks (if you've got any) and particularly important meetings. Xers generally loathe meetings, but their street smarts tell them being invited to a meeting with the CEO or other C-level executives is a big deal—not for networking opportunities but for information.
3. Coach Gen X employees to take responsibility for their own issues by asking them questions like, "How do you plan to go about solving this?" and, "How do you think you might best approach this topic in the next staff meeting?"

Current and Future Issues

Over the next decade, Generation X will take charge of the workplace. There are a lot fewer baristas and a lot more gold-collar professionals— and middle and upper management Xers—who are earning good salaries. As opportunities accelerate proportionately to the Great Boomer Exodus—and the world economy emerges from the doldrums—Generation X can finally expect to settle into the C-Suite.

They are already planning for a retirement without social security; their self-reliance radar tells them that a sizable retirement nest egg will be a necessity. Look for IRAs and 401(k) plans to swell with funds contributed by this group. Rising costs of college for their children, however, will put some of these retirement plans on hold for a while. In fact, the Great Recession has put a lot of their plans on hold, They are staring down the business end of a major, years-long recession. Their survival mentality is causing them to stay put, wherever they are, no matter how bad the job is. But even the generation known for its skepticism is hopeful that things will soon be better. Gen X has weathered other recessions and downturns, giving them the confidence that they can handle whatever the economy dishes out.

The Future: Hell No, Please Don't Go

As much as the Xers "have issues" with the Boomers, they also don't want to see them leave. Boomers—because they like to work and because their nest eggs shriveled up in the last few years—are working into their late sixties and seventies. Boomers like the idea of living longer, more productive lives. Xers are interested in anything that will keep the glut of Boomers from going quietly into retirement. The longer the Boomers keep working, the more they will contribute to Social Security—and the long-term economic survival of Gen X. The prospect of they, the few Xers, taking care of them, the 76 million Boomers via Medicare and Social Security, frightens Generation X more than just about anything. So keeping Boomers working well into their geriatric years looks darn good.

Late-career Boomers who find themselves reporting to Gen X bosses may have to make a lot of adjustments. It may not be pretty, if those managers choose to manage in new ways based only on their own generational preferences. Some may become tyrannical. It's more likely, though, that they will design a newfangled hands-off, pragmatic, virtual management system with strong strains of project management throughout.

THE GEN XERS	
Markings	nose rings, navel rings, functional clothing, tattoos, ironic kitsch
Spending Style	cautious, conservative
What They Read	*Spin, Wired,* blogs
Their Humor	*Dilbert, The Daily Show, The Onion, The Colbert Report*

FACT AND FICTION ABOUT GEN XERS

Myths	Facts
They're materialistic.	Many are struggling to make ends meet. Economists tell us this is the first U.S. generation that probably won't be able to replicate or improve on their parents' lifestyle. They worry they won't have enough money to pay for a home and their children's education. They want to get out of debt. So money is important to them, but they scorn material wealth and status items.
They're whiners.	Gen Xers face some rather daunting challenges—skyrocketing healthcare costs and the rising cost of education for their children—yet most are philosophical about the problems they're inheriting.
They have a "you owe me" attitude.	No more so than any other generation.
They're not willing to work hard.	In interviews, Gen Xers consistently tell us they *are* willing to work hard. They don't want to be taken advantage of, though. Many believe it's unfair to expect a 70-hour week for 40 hours of pay. And, as a generation, they're committed to having a life beyond work.
They're selfish.	Gen Xers often put family and friends above their own personal needs. They're protective parents who will do whatever it takes when it comes to the kids.

CHAPTER 5

The Millennials

Be Careful What You Ask For

Born 1980 to 2000

"I know we were supposed to bequeath to the next generation a world better than the one we were handed. But we broke it. It just kinda got away from us. But here's the good news. You fix this thing—and I believe you can—you're the next great generation."

—JON STEWART[1]

They're the first generation to grow up immersed in digital media. Two-thirds of them used computers before the age of five. They are connected 24/7 to friends, parents, information, and entertainment. The global economic downturn has affected them worse than any other generation, yet they remain optimistic and energetic. Accustomed to being the center of attention, they have high expectations and clear goals. They are willing to work hard and expect to have the support they need to achieve. They have older parents and were brought up in smaller families. One in three is the product of divorce. One in four has at least one college-educated parent. Citizens of the world, they are the most racially and ethnically diverse generation in history. They're alternatively known as Generation Y, The Net Generation, and the Digital Generation. But in 1997 they chose their own name when Peter Jennings surveyed them online for *ABC News Tonight*—and the clear winner was *Millennial*. Whatever we call them, they will be the most carefully studied of all the cohort groups yet.

Born between 1980 and 2000, they are the fawned-upon, coddled, and confident offspring of the most age-diverse group of parents ever—ranging from adolescents to middle aged people, Xers to Boomers. One-third were born to single, unwed moms; hordes of others to Boomers who postponed having children until their forties, and even more to Gen Xers who pledged to make parenting a top priority. Remember the jokes about the parents who quibbled over which composer—Mozart or Bach—to pipe into their preborn's warm and watery environment? And how soon after their second birthdays to enroll their little ones in their first LSAT prep course? Well, Millennials are those kids come of age, starting their tours of college campuses, finding their first jobs, getting their first promotions—even getting laid off, outsourced, and redeployed. If Generation X was "the lost generation," this is "the found generation," with parents not only escorting but advocating for them.

If ever there were an ominous chasm between generations, it's the one between the Millennials and the Boomers. They have contrasting views on a plethora of topics from politics to religion, from immigration to gay marriage, from school funding to the military. TV virtually created the Baby Boom generation. Boomers were marked forever by the early black-and-white shows they watched after school; then, as young adults, they watched all their generational events on TV—JFK's funeral, Woodstock, Vietnam, civil rights demonstrations, the moon landing. The impact of the digital age on the Millennial Generation will be immeasurably greater. When Millennials were growing up, kids were the authority—for the first time in history. They knew far more than their parents about one of the basics. There weren't just three Rs anymore—as in reading, writing, and 'rithmetic. Suddenly, there was a fourth basic: digital technology—and it was as natural as breathing for Millennial kids. So much so they didn't even marvel at it much. Sure, in the past there had been things that kids were better at and knew more about than their parents, but not one so all-encompassing as digital technology. It changed the basic dynamic of families. Of course, parents knew more about most things, but during the Millennials' formative years, as never before, kids actually knew more about technology, and they taught and coached their parents. Boomer—even Xer—parents learned as fast as they could. But it's a little like learning a language. When you're a child, language acquisition is as easy as blinking. When you're an adult, it seems far less natural. It takes a lot more effort, so much effort that most adults choose simply not to add another language to their repertoire.

The torch is clearly passing—from old to new—from those "my way or the highway" Baby Boomers to later-day Boomers who popped onto the scene after the turbulent 1960s —from technophobes to people of all ages and in all sectors willing to embrace and capitalize on what technology offers. By some estimates, 82 million people are now AATK (always at the keyboard) sending text messages to family and friends. Amid this dawn of a generational and technological shift, those born with their iPod ear buds firmly attached aren't looking quite so strange. So let's move forward with wonder and enthusiasm as we welcome our Millennial colleagues to our offices, our board rooms, and our flat-screen TVs.

THE MILLENNIALS

Core Values

- Optimism
- Civic duty
- Confidence
- Achievement
- Sociability
- Diversity

Power in Numbers

Millennials now comprise a third of the population in the United States and nearly a quarter of the world population. The last 80 years in the United States have seen dramatic ebbs and flows in birth rates. From 1932 to 1946, the rate of live births averaged 2.5 million per year—and birth rates remained fairly steady, neither rising nor falling dramatically from year to year. Then, precisely nine months after the end of World War II, birth rates soared. The Baby Boom generation was named for its size: during the peak ten boom years, 1954 to 1964, over four million tykes came kicking and screaming into the delivery room every year.

When it was time to deliver little Gen Xers into the world, birth rates fell dramatically, dropping below four million again—and staying low for another 23 years. The Millennials then rolled in on another generational tsunami. Beginning in 1980, birth rates began to increase steadily—and a wave of immigrant children added to the burgeoning new generation. During the 1980s and 1990s, large numbers of children immigrated to the United States; a record average of nearly 8 percent of new immigrants were children—nearly twice the proportion of foreign-born children who had arrived on American shores when Boomers and Gen Xers were kids. By 2000, the Millennial Generation totaled over 87 million, making them an amazing 31 million souls larger than Gen X and a full 11 million more than the Boomers.

In every way, the Millennial Generation in the United States is more racially and ethnically diverse than any other generation in history. According to the Census Bureau, one in three reports being a member of a racial or ethnic minority. For their parents at that age, it was one in ten. In addition to being ethnically diverse, they are economically diverse, part of the largest economic divide in over a century. As the middle class has shrunk, Millennials have found themselves living at the extremes of rich and poor.

From Beanie Babies to Beepers

For the first time since the post-World War II era, it was "in" again to be a child when Millennials were coming of age. According to Landon Jones, author of *Great Expectations,* in the 1950s and 1960s, "Children were the whole point. Americans enshrined them. European visitors joked knowingly about how well American parents obeyed their children. American parents seemed to be making their kids their religion."[2] Then, in the 1970s, children lost popularity. The Gen X babies were some of the first whose parents had taken pills to prevent or at least to delay. As a matter of fact, the 1970s were actually the most anti-child decade the country had known, say Neil Howe and Bill Strauss in their

THE MILLENNIALS

Seminal Events

- Berlin Wall falls
- Cold War ends
- Oklahoma City bombing
- 9/11
- Columbine
- War on Terror—Iraq and Afghanistan
- The Great Recession
- Occupy Wall Street

book, *13th Gen.*[3] But in the 1980s, a "Baby-on-Board" sign in the station wagon's rear window signaled the return of a national concern for, and interest in, children.

Gen Xers complained that their two-career parents never had enough time for them, and they vowed that when they became parents themselves they would find more time for their own kids. Those Xer parents did just that and were joined by a whole cadre of Boomer parents who witnessed the result of their generation's benign neglect of Gen X children. The concept of "quality time" became obsolete—it didn't work—and parents recommitted to families. Then, too, a 50-year trend to exert less and less control over children's lives had made a U-turn. Howe and Strauss say that not since the early 1900s had "older generations moved so quickly to assert greater adult dominion over the world of childhood—and to implant civic virtue in a new crop of youngsters."[4]

THE MILLENNIALS

Cultural Memorabilia

- *Teenage Mutant Ninja Turtles*
- Tomagotchi and other virtual pets
- *Transformers*
- Beanie Babies
- *Nemo*
- *Harry Potter*
- *Shrek*

So kids became all the rage. Ninety percent of fathers attended their children's births. Las Vegas went "family." Donna Karan, Nicole Miller, Abercrombie & Fitch, and The Gap introduced new lines of clothing especially for wee ones. For $1,000 per month a child-care center in Denver cradled kids in amenities and tutored them in "arts, sciences, math, music and more."[5] Reading lessons began at eleven months. By age two, some spoke two languages. Club Med, flying in the face of its sybaritic swinging singles' image of the 1970s, reported its family villages accounted for nearly half of annual sales. TV programs for kids under six went from three basic

> ### THE MILLENNIALS
>
> **Heroes**
>
> - Captain Scully
> - Their parents
> - Passengers on Flight 93
> - Firefighters at Ground Zero
> - Bill Gates

choices—*Mr. Rogers, Sesame Street,* and *Captain Kangaroo*—to more than 50 options. Children were reading and being read to again; sales of children's books quadrupled from 1987 to 1997.[6]

Structured, Scheduled Lives

Millennials were the busiest generation of children we've ever seen. Parents and teachers micromanaged their lives, leaving them with little free time. When older Millennials were in high school, they carried Daytimers®. Today they listen for alerts on their cell phones, signaling their upcoming appointments.

In his 1996 presidential campaign, Bob Dole coined the term "soccer mom"; it soon described a whole sociological phenomenon comprised of the hectic lifestyle of moms—and dads, definitely dads—shuttling kids back and forth from football practice to violin lessons to math tutoring to ballet classes to chess club to karate. Two and three decades before, kids had "hung out" and played with buddies on the vacant lot on the corner, or they had taken off for parts unknown on their bicycles. When Millennials were kids, there was no vacant lot, and if there had been, it wouldn't have been deemed safe by their parents. Riding your bike to parts unknown simply wasn't a good idea anymore. "Commercial playgrounds" from Discovery Zone to Chuck E. Cheese to Dave & Busters provided safe areas in which kids could recreate. Some infants were in day care by the time they were six weeks old, dropped off in the predawn hours by parents on their way to work. Kids lived high-stress, fast-paced lives. Their amusements were far more dependent on their parents, primarily for transportation and funding, than for any generation before them. They knew they had to be careful; it was becoming an increasingly dangerous world.

Terrorism

On April 19, 1995, when the youngest Millennials were 15, the Alfred P. Murrah Federal Building in Oklahoma City was felled by a terrorist bomb. One hundred sixty eight lives were lost, including 19 children under the age of six. Four years and one day later, two high school seniors stormed into the school cafeteria of Columbine High School in Littleton, Colorado, killing 12 students and a teacher, and injuring 24 others. Then there was the moment that would become like D-Day was for the GI Generation or November 22 for the Baby Boomers. It was the morning of September 11, 2001. Nineteen terrorists hijacked four passenger jets. They flew two into the World Trade Center in New York and one into the Pentagon in Arlington, Virginia. On the fourth, passengers banded together to crash the airliner they were traveling on into a field near Shanksville, Pennsylvania. With nearly three thousand people dead, it was the worst act of terrorism ever perpetrated on U.S. soil.

What happened culturally in the aftermath of these—and other violent and horrific events—exemplifies the ways in which a generational personality is formed. Following the attacks, the approval rating for President George W. Bush soared to 90 percent. People everywhere marveled at the courage and wherewithal exemplified by passengers on Flight 93 who had banded together to prevent the plane they were traveling on from becoming a fourth terrorist weapon. The reaction across the nation—and, in fact, in many parts of the world—was to renew the focus on home and family. Millennials saw the violence—along with natural disasters like the Tsunami in Southeast Asia and Hurricane Katrina in New Orleans—as a call for civic engagement and collective action.

Sociologists describe Millennials as the most civic-minded cohort since the World War II generation. They were the first group of high school students for whom community service became a key to college admissions—and even in some cases, a requirement for high school graduation. Volunteer rates among high school students doubled. "Community service is part of their DNA," says Matt Kuhn in his doctoral dissertation about school leadership and generations.[7] *Keeping up with the Joneses* transformed into *helping the Joneses.* Youth voter registration rose, and in the 2008 U.S. Presidential election, young people turned out to vote in unprecedented numbers. Millennials are recognized as playing a major role in electing the nation's first black President. They have founded a variety of youth-driven activist organizations like Occupy Wall Street and have built grassroots movements to advance various social and political causes. They worry about the future—not just locally, but globally—and engage in collective acts to improve the government, the political system, and the environment.

Handled With Care

Perhaps because the world seemed so menacing and perhaps because this generation of children was so *wanted,* parents sheltered their children from the woes of the world. The nation became obsessed with child safety. This is a generation that was protected on so many levels that writers at *The Onion*—the Xer voice of sarcasm—quoted the *What About the Children Foundation* whenever they wanted to poke fun at American excesses. Parents monitored their kids electronically with a spectrum of devices from GPS units that could be locked onto children's wrists—to black boxes that tracked their teen drivers. New regulations prohibited parents from leaving the hospital without a certified baby carrier. Parents and coaches alike required their little players to wear helmets when they biked, skied, played hockey, or ran onto the football field. Bullying became the new cigarette, and school districts developed zero tolerance policies. The old days of, "Stand up for yourself"—an oft-heart adage when Traditionalists raised their children—were replaced by rules, policies, and parents committed to keeping their kids safe.

Protective parents paced alongside the soccer field, stood in the wings at dance recitals, and stayed up to the wee hours quizzing their children on possible spelling bee words. They're called Helicopter Parents—parents who hover over their children not only to keep them safe but to make sure they get every opportunity and advantage. When little Gen Xers were students, the biggest challenge for teachers was classroom discipline. With Millennials, it was "parent management"— keeping parents from interfering in the classroom, curriculum, and grading system.

Parents as BFFs

Millennials were raised with a kinder, gentler parenting style. Spankings were labeled *child abuse*; parents were encouraged to negotiate with their children. The relationship between parent and child became more egalitarian, less hierarchical. More like best friends, actually: there to counsel, support, and assist. This is a generation that *likes* its parents. In turn, the parents are interested in their offsprings' lives, even their adult lives. For the past 16 years, Millennials have been reporting for their first job assignments—sometimes with a parent in tow. "Sure, Gen Xers can laugh about it," says Ryan Healy, Co-Founder of Brazen Careerist, an online community and career center for Millennials, "but we respect our parents. Don't be surprised to see Gen Y employees giving their parents a tour of the office and calling up mom and dad for a little advice on their lunch break. It's not about being babied or refusing to grow. It's about a level of mutual respect that Gen Y has for our parents and our parents have for us. My mother is coming to visit in a couple of weeks, and guess what our plan for the day is? A tour of the office and a couple of hours of work for each of us before we go out and do the tourist thing."[8]

Girls Rule

While young Boomer women in the 1970s became involved in the Women's Movement, Millennial girls in the 1990s were actively involved in a new, more informal, but more far-reaching "girl's movement." When the Boomers were girls, 1 in 27 participated in team sports in high school. Social pressure and the reality of "Title IX" made that number one in three according to the January/February 1998 issue of *American Enterprise*[9] Take Our Daughters to Work Day grew increasingly popular in the 1990s, exposing hundreds of thousands of young women to career possibilities. In April 2011, the U.S. Census reported that, for the first time, women surpassed men in both bachelor's and advanced degrees.

Technology

"For them, technology is as natural as air," says Frank Gregorsky, social historian at the Discovery Institute, a Seattle think tank. They were weaned on video games, they did their term papers in full video, and they could troubleshoot the computer at home and then teach their parents how to set up their *Facebook* pages. Their connectedness gave them a new orientation in space and time. When they were kids, they had pen pals in Singapore and Senegal, and they learned to see the world as global, connected, and 'round the clock.

> "Now all of a sudden I've discovered this whole way of a civil society existing by simply being able to talk back and forth with each other by way of cyberspace. It's a revelation to me and I love it."
>
> —Daniel Schorr, National Public Radio Senior News Analyst, when he was 92

Hammered by the Downturn

As Millennials began their careers, they confronted massive layoffs and rising unemployment: the longest, deepest slump to hit the global economy in more than 80 years. People from all generations have suffered, but the situation has taken its highest toll on Millennials. They are less established in their working lives, and they struggle to find and keep jobs. The large size of their generation means they must compete against their peers for the few jobs available. According to the Bureau of Labor Statistics, one-half of all 16- to 24-year olds are unemployed—the largest share since 1948. The earnings gap between old and young has never been greater. While the average income of older Americans has remained essentially the same for the last decade, income for households headed by Millennials has dropped 11 percent.[10] The wealth gap is greater than at any point since the Federal Reserve Board started keeping track. So, too, for home ownership. As a result, Millennials have become less picky about the jobs they'll accept and they've lowered their expectations for finding the *perfect* job, but they haven't given up. They remain hopeful. One of their strongest assets is their resilient optimism.

Partly as a result of the downtown, many dream of starting their own businesses. According to global consumer research firm CEB Iconoculture, 35 percent of Millennials with jobs have also started their own business on the side. For many of them, it's the only way they can pay the bills. "I'm optimistic for our future," says Adam, 28, of Charlotte, North Carolina. "But I've watched the government bail out rich bankers while thousands of people lost their homes. I've been worked to the bone by a company that took advantage of the downturn to squeeze out more of its workers. I will not count on them. Last month, I broke off and now I work for myself."[11]

Their Generational Personality

Like all of us, Millennials were shaped by their times. Several key trends of the 1990s and 2000s—most notably, the focus on children, and the rise of digital technology and the Internet—had and will continue to have a profound effect on their generational personality. Their early experiences created the filters through which they see the world, and those filters directly impact the manner by which they will navigate the world of work.

They are resiliently optimistic. They were raised knowing they were wanted, sought-after, needed, indispensable. In Canada, they're sometimes called the Sunshine Generation. They admire integrity, they think

> In a recent survey, 92 percent of Millennials say a company's success should be measured by more than profit, and over 50% say they think businesses will have a greater impact than any other societal segment—including government—on solving the world's biggest challenges."
>
> —The Daily Stat, March 5, 2012, *Harvard Business Review*

education is cool, and they see their parents as role models. They believe in the future and see themselves as leaders and advocates of change. Millennials are much more likely to say that life is good—and will stay that way—than older generations, who believe that life is worsening. Rasmussen Reports recently released the findings of a survey asking voters whether America's best days are yet to come. Forty-two percent of Millennials said they were optimistic about the future—as opposed to only 15 percent of Baby Boomers and Traditionalists.[12]

They are digital natives. A digital native—the term was coined by game designer Marc Prensky—is someone who grew up with computers, video games, the Internet, cell phones, and MP3 players. They think and process information fundamentally differently from the generations before them. Digital immigrants, according to Prensky, are those of us who grew up before the digital age and learned, later in life, how to use its tools and toys. He compares these older generations to immigrants coming to a new country where they have to learn a second language. They always retain an "accent," he says, "a foot in the past." Digital immigrants, for example, read the manual instead of assuming they'll learn by doing. They print documents to edit them and invite colleagues into their offices to watch amusing videos instead of forwarding them.

> In 1966, when Baby Boomers were in college, 60 percent of them rated themselves above average on the "drive to achieve." Forty years later when Millennials were freshmen, 73 percent of them reported they had a strong desire to achieve.
>
> —*The American Freshman: Forty Year Trends,* Higher Education Research Institute, 2007

"We grew up with the Internet and on the Internet," says Polish Writer Piotr Czerski. "This is what makes us different; this is what makes the crucial, although surprising from your point of view, difference: we do not 'surf' and the Internet to us is not a 'place' . . . We do not use the Internet, we live on the Internet and along it."[13]

They are collaborative. They were taught to solve problems as a group. "For Millennials, says educator Matt Kuhn, "collaborative learning became as popular as independent study was for Baby Boomers or open classrooms for Gen Xers."[14] Denver Advertising Executive Cathey Finlon sees Millennials working more fluidly and with a great deal more teamwork than previous generations. "For 25 years I've watched people come and go in the agency. Millennials are the quickest. They increase your velocity."

> "My goal in life is to feel like I've been successful and have made an impact on the world around me. I think a lot of people my age are looking for that. If you can tie into those goals and explain that what you're teaching, the job skills we're learning, the job we're doing, tie into those goals, you've got us hooked."
>
> —Patrick, 25

They view themselves as more collectively powerful than older generations, citing the 2008 U.S. election and the Arab Spring movement in the Middle East as evidence. They are able to work together to define a clear collective mission and ambitious goals—and then send a text, IM, or *Facebook* message to rally their peers. Their reliance on and skill with technology are largely seen as the driving force behind the recent revolution in American political campaigning. Creating new websites and using existing ones like YouTube, MySpace, and *Facebook*, they have raised money, furthered issues, and supported get-out-the-vote efforts.

They're goal and achievement oriented. When they were kids, schools went back to the basics, set standards, and held teachers and student accountable through the No Child Left Behind Act. Kids were taught to be outer-driven, ideal-following team players. They felt pressure, not just from parents, but from themselves to get good grades and build impressive portfolios to enhance their college prospects.

"For my generation," says 20-year-old Megan Emme, a program director in the nonprofit sector, "it was very much: 'Okay, you've got to get straight As and excel on the standardized tests. You've gotta jump through hoops so you can get into college and get a job. I think it comes from fear. Millennials are scared that if you don't get it right the first time, everything is just going to collapse. There is a whole lot of pressure that has been put on us from a very young age to do well.'"

They are diverse. Those who grew up in the past two decades have had more daily interaction with other ethnicities and cultures than ever before. Unlike the Boomers who grew up in fairly homogeneous settings, the new crop of young adults had much greater exposure to—and casual acceptance of—multiculturalism, a diversity of races, religions, and backgrounds. Thirty-seven percent of kindergartners in 1997 were nonwhite, according to an article in the *Wall Street Journal*.[15] If they attended school in New York City, Los Angeles, or Chicago, Millennials could have been exposed to as many as 100 languages among their schoolmates. Data from UCLA's Higher Education Research Institute shows that interracial interaction among college freshmen has reached a record high and continues to increase. The Census Bureau tells us that ethnic "minorities" as an aggregate will become the majority within the Millennials' lifetime.

They were taught to see the world globally. "The first true cohort of "global citizens," they have been told by parents and teachers that they can make a difference in the world. It makes sense, then, that a number of surveys have found Millennials to be the most tolerant of all generations. According to David Leonhardt of *The New York Times*, "The increase in diversity in this country—the influx of immigrants, the fact that gays and lesbians are much more a part of mainstream life—younger Americans see this as an enormous positive."[16]

Reared without absolutes, diversity of thought was another important part of their upbringing. It was perfectly acceptable in elementary school classrooms for there to be more than one right answer. They came of age in families that agreed to disagree. Sixty-four percent of parents said they were better at openly discussing tough issues than their own parents had been. Moms and dads encouraged children to have their own opinions. One young mother we know refused even to divulge to her 11- and 12-year-old children who she voted for in Presidential elections, seeking at all cost to avoid superimposing her political agenda on theirs.

They are confident. They have been told they're special—that they carry the potential for greatness—since they were little tykes. A survey of high school seniors contrasted twelfth-graders' attitudes in 2008 with twelfth-graders' attitudes in 1975. The more recent crop was much more confident. They were certain they would be excellent "employees, mates, and parents."[17] Overall, the survey showed the 2008 seniors to be far more self-satisfied than the 1975 seniors. Throughout Millennials' development, their parents and teachers have encouraged them every step of the way. "A lot of us don't know what it's like to fail," says 24-year-old Lacy. "People started caring about our self esteem in sixth grade, and that's when everyone started getting a trophy."

Millennials' strong self-esteem is sometimes labeled *arrogant* or *entitled* by their older colleagues. A friend of ours who works in a small consulting firm says, "The majority of our consultants are Millennials, and many seem to feel entitled. Our company provides some nice amenities like coffee, water, and soda. And we've always ordered whatever office supplies anyone wants. So now we have six different kinds of pens. We have a kitchen where our support staff provides hospitality service—coffee and continental breakfast—for clients. The staff uses the same kitchen, but we're supposed to bus our own stuff. The Millennials—not all, but most—consistently leave their stuff all over the place. They seem to think cleaning up is beneath them, that it's the responsibility of the workers they consider to be below them: the support staff. I find it offensive." Another friend says it more succinctly: "I think they're entitled, spoiled brats." Call it confidence, call it entitlement, arrogance, or narcissism, Millennials will find this generational characteristic to be a double-edged sword. It can be a major turn-off for their older colleagues, but they will need to believe in themselves mightily to face the challenges ahead.

Allison: Dreams Deferred

Recently, Allison has wondered if the folks who encouraged her to go to college—parents, friends, and counselors—were being entirely honest about her prospects. Or, maybe they didn't really know. Whatever the case, before the ink had dried on her diploma, she began receiving *payment due* notices for her college loan. But she was optimistic; she had a job and the beginnings, she hoped, of a career. She was nearly ready to move out of her parents' house and forge out on her own. Then, the economy fell apart, and every marketing budget in the city was cut. Now she's out of work, and the lenders don't seem to care. And while her parents are eligible for all kinds of debt forgiveness under bankruptcy laws—she checked—her loans don't qualify.

In the meantime, there aren't a lot of marketing jobs out there for a 29-year-old college grad with only a BA, no matter how prestigious the school. She has lost count of the cover letters she's written and resumes she has emailed. Her three company internships didn't help either, since all those companies have cut jobs and shrunk down to skeleton crews.

So she decided to volunteer at the local Red Cross to help, she thought, with marketing its services and creating a communication plan—projects that would be nice to add to her resume. In truth, she finds herself managing its social media efforts. But that's not all bad. Whether she realized or not, she learned a lot about social media just using it day to day. She has a good sense of what will fly with her audience, along with what will sound phony. And, the organization has actually started to use her marketing skills as the leaders learn to appreciate what can be done with these new channels. Whereas she once imagined pitching a viral marketing video to a boardroom of executives in a corporate environment, she is now writing, directing, and shooting a video—on a shoestring budget—for the next blood drive.

Her ten-year plan when she finished high school was to get into the right college, get a good job, work hard, move out on her own, meet someone special, get married, buy a house, and then maybe think about a family. Nothing too radical there. Now, she's thinking of starting her own social media marketing company with one of the other volunteers at the Red Cross, an out-of-work actress about Allison's age. It will be a hard slog; the books she's read about starting a business don't sugarcoat it. And those loan payments keep coming. Her parents have volunteered to pay half, and she has a new job waitressing at a restaurant near their home. Hopefully, what she makes there will not only pay the other half of her student loan payments but also help her stash a little away so she can launch the new venture.

Nick: Marking Time

It's a sweltering day in Dallas, and Nick, 24, complains there's not much you can do without money in this town. Most days he spends some time working towards his goal: getting certified to teach special education. To reach that goal, there are a number of online courses he needs to complete and tests he needs to pass. Later in the summer, he has lined up a job for a couple of weeks working as a bouncer for a friend who owns a club. For the time being, he is just marking time, and, in many ways, wishing he were still in college— or even high school. Adulthood and all it entails just doesn't seem all that appealing, especially in this economy. He's got friends he's been tight with since elementary school. They hang out together some nights, and if one of them has the cash to buy beer, they go downtown to one of the clubs.

Nick knows his mom is proud of him, the first person in his family to ever finish college—but he knows, too, she's holding her breath, waiting for him to step up to the plate and think, act, earn, and behave like an adult. She works in a department store, and it's always been all she could do to pay the rent and buy groceries. He is living with her for now—and it reminds them both of old times. It's always just been the two of them.

In high school, Nick worked as a student assistant in the special ed classroom, where the kids adored him. The girls thought he was handsome, and the boys loved his huge personality and admired his feats on the football field—and his clever sense of humor kept them rolling in the aisles. In college he thought, in the back of his mind, that if he couldn't be a coach, he would be a teacher. But he was too busy pursuing his athletic goals to spend much time focusing on the coursework required to get his certification. When he picked up his diploma on that June day three years ago, it listed his degree as *Exercise Science.* He was well aware that wouldn't get him far, but he simply preferred to not think about it.

Nick graduated from college three years ago, and he'd be the first to admit his "degree in football" hasn't gotten him far. His all-star performance in high school earned him a college scholarship where he played defensive end all four years. He worked hard—in the gym and on the practice field—to become a conference all star, and he thrived in the competitive environment of team sports. Nick still believes a team with a strong leader can accomplish most anything—and he misses the single-minded intensity he felt in those days on the gridiron.

The first year out of college, he worked as an aide to a high school girl in a wheelchair, escorting her from class to class—and doing what he could to help her finish her freshman year. It was grueling work and he only earned minimum wage, but he was good at it, and he was working. The next year he thought he had found a great job, although it was in an elementary school, and he really wanted to be teaching high school. But it turned out that, without his certification, he wasn't qualified to have his own classroom. So he tutored kids who were struggling in math and English. It wasn't hard, and it earned him a little money. The first thing he did when he got a paycheck was to buy himself an iPhone—he really didn't know how he could continue to get by without one. When his mom found out and he saw the look of disappointment on her face, he decided to spend less on clothes and nonessentials. He's been giving his mom a little cash to help with groceries.

Nick is upbeat and positive, even though he has another year of online courses ahead of him before he gets his certification. He can use his tutoring experience at the elementary school for his student teaching —and an experienced special ed teacher has taken him under her wing. She's an excellent mentor who thinks the world of him and is excited about his future.

Allison and Nick in the Workplace

This new wave of workers is both optimistic about the future and realistic about the present. They actually believe that hard work and goal setting is the ticket to achieving their dreams. They combine the teamwork

THE MILLENNIALS

On the Job

Assets

- Collective action
- Optimism
- Tenacity
- Heroic spirit
- Multitasking capabilities
- Technological savvy
- Adept at change

Liabilities

- Need for supervision and structure
- Demand for constant feedback
- Helicopter parents
- Family events trump work

ethic of the Boomers with the can-do attitude of the Traditionalist generation and the technological savvy of the Xers. At first glance, and even at second glance, Millennials may be the ideal workforce—and also ideal citizens and generally the kind of young people you'd want dating your son or daughter.

Their Work Expectations

They expect to work more than 40 hours a week to achieve the lifestyle they want. Whereas Gen Xers have never seen the point of working beyond the standard nine to five day, Millennials expect to go above and beyond. They believe they will have had seven jobs by the time they're 26.[18] And, they are surprisingly realistic about salaries. "For a generation characterized by a high sense of self-worth," says a white paper from CareerRookie, an offshoot of CareerBuilding for collegiate job seekers, "their expectations fall in line with reality."[19]

Managing Millennials

It's all about engaging them. You've heard the term. We talk about *engaging* the public in the political process, *engaging* the community in conversations about critical issues, *engaging* students in their learning, and *engaging* employees in their work.

Engagement is far more than simply communicating effectively. Engaged employees are those who are fully involved in their work. They are committed to their own growth and growth in their jobs. Engagement requires that employees have choices so that they act in ways that further their own organization's interests. Engaged employees work smarter. They're willing to put in extra time to get the job done. They recommend the organization's services and products to family and friends. In the workplace, collaboration, personal involvement, and trust are critical to creating engagement. For employees to be engaged, they must share a sense of belonging and of being part of something important. They need to trust that management is focused on the best interests of the organization and those who work there. Consider the following rules of engagement for your Millennial workers and how to put them into practice. Your youngest employees will be more productive, effective, and stay with you longer if they:

1. See themselves as connected to, and part of, the organization.
2. Are given opportunities to problem solve with their colleagues.
3. Connect their individual contributions with their own and the company's goals.
4. Feel valued, respected, and rewarded for their contributions.
5. Develop social and professional relationships within the organization.

Some Key Principles

In recent years we've listened intently to Millennials—in an extensive set of interviews, in focus groups, in company offices, and in college classrooms. When we've asked what they want from their supervisors, colleagues, and managers, they have responded with a consistency that has surprised us. Here are their nine most frequent requests:

- Help us learn.
- Believe in us.
- Tune in to our technology.
- Connect us.
- Let us make it our own.
- Tell us how we're doing.
- Be approachable.
- Plug in to our parents.
- Be someone we can believe in.

It's not an unreasonable list, yet it's a set of expectations that Millennials tell us is rarely met. Every day, Millennials walk through the doors of workplaces that have cultures based on the styles and preferences of Baby Boomers and Traditionalists. Managers from older generations, even Gen Xers, assume that what attracted them to the job and

---

THE MILLENNIALS

Markings	Bright color, pink is the new black, big brands
Spending Style	A new emphasis on saving and getting out of debt—especially college loans
What They Read	Series: *Harry Potter, Twilight, Hunger Games*
Their Humor	Memes on YouTube, Glee, CollegeHumor.com, FunnyorDie.com

---

motivated them to stay and succeed will attract and motivate today's young workers. But, as we've described, Millennials have their own unique characteristics—and a distinctly different work style.

The way work gets done in most organizations is counter to the natural instincts of Millennials. Work cultures remain hierarchical; Millennials thrive when work is carried out in more collaborative ways. Most managers practice line-of-sight supervision—"If I can't see you, you must not be working." Millennials perform better in a more flexible environment, where the result and impact of their work are given more weight than the time they spend tied to their desks. The role work plays in people's lives has shifted. The way we get things done is changing. The workplace practices Millennials prefer and ask for will be the hallmarks of the future workplace:

1. Help them learn.

For Millennials just entering the workforce, the purpose of a job is to learn, gain experience, and position themselves for the next step. In her first job after graduating from college, 21-year-old Lauren explains, "I really wanted a job where I felt like people saw a lot of potential in me, as well as a company where I was going to learn and I wasn't going to feel like I knew everything already. I wanted a job where I had no idea what I was doing so I could learn a new skill set that builds on what I originally had." Lauren will thrive in her new job if someone educates her about the organization: how to get things done, where to get information, and who to go to with ideas. A good manager will help Lauren uncover her personal goals and help her figure out how to reach them. And, while learning for Xers and Boomers often means learning by trial and error, eating mistakes, and celebrating successes, Millennials don't think that way. They feel a lot of pressure to get it right the first time. They don't have time for trial and error. So answering their litany of questions about a project won't just get you what you want—the job done correctly on the first try—it will also reduce the stress on your Millennial colleagues.

> ## THE MILLENNIALS
>
> **Messages That Motivate**
>
> - "You can make a difference here."
> - "You will have a clear career path so you can keep moving ahead."
> - "You will work on a team with other bright, creative people."
> - "You can be a hero here."

Talking about learning in her first job, Dana, 23, says, "That was something I was really looking for. Something that I struggled with was the training because it's all self led. I was really frustrated. I was like, seriously, no one's going to sit down and tell me how to do this? I had a 'learning to learn' curve there."

2. Believe in them.

Millennials have been told they're special, with unlimited potential. They've set goals—and, in many cases, met them—all their lives. They want to prove their worth. They're willing to work hard, as long as they sense that someone believes in them and that their hard work will pay off. But here's the catch: their style of working hard might not look familiar to older managers.

A manager's belief in a young employee can make all the difference. Time and again, research has demonstrated that our assumptions shape the outcome. In a well-known experiment in a public elementary school, Robert Rosenthal and Lenore Jacobson gave teachers the names of students who, they said, could be expected to perform extraordinarily well during the school year. In fact, the names had been chosen at random. Sure enough, those students they identified as "academic spurters"

showed an average 12-point increase on their IQ scores at the end of the
school year.

3. Tune in to their technology.

In his new book *Grown Up Digital,* Don Tapscott advises that organizations resist banning *Facebook* and other social networks. Instead, he
says, they should figure out how to harness them. Nothing distinguishes
the Millennial generation more than their lifelong immersion in digital
technology. They are innovators who want the latest tech devices and
want to work for companies where they can be creative with the help of
podcasts, blogs, social networking sites, and online applications.

Just when you may have been feeling proficient—finally—at email,
we're sorry to report that email usage is declining among Millennials.
For today, at least, the best way to connect with Millennial colleagues,
particularly when they're away from work, is via text messaging. Savvy
managers communicate with their Millennial employees in their preferred style. In a recent interview, Dana told us how her manager adapted to his younger employees: "He said, 'Yeah, you guys started texting
me, so I had to learn how to text.' We didn't even realize that was something he didn't normally do. He just went on and texted us back. He realized that was going to be the best way to communicate with us on certain matters. So be adaptable, willing to catch up with the times when
you need to."

One caution about Millennials and their grasp of technology: some
Millennials are faster with their thumbs than on a keyboard! Yet some
older managers assume that Millennial workers are proficient in Microsoft
Word and can put together PowerPoint presentations. "Just because I'm
21 years old," says Lauren "that doesn't mean I'm brilliant with computers. While I can navigate a computer, I can't necessarily fix a problem if
Windows crashes!" It turns out that, for many Millennials, there's a big
gap between the technologies they use and the computer skills we expect them to have. Many of our younger workers need help learning the
computer skills they need to be effective in the workplace. We found this
to be an issue in college settings as well, where students are often sty-

mied by course management software programs and online learning technologies.

4. Connect them.

Given the opportunity, young workers like Janessa, a 22-year-old director of a national nonprofit organization, will create a social network with colleagues. "People might think my life is 5 percent social and 95 percent work," she says. "But the two are hard to separate. I like it like that!" Millennials worked on teams all the way through school. Many are skilled team members who know how to identify team roles, plan responsibilities and timetables, and even to negotiate with poor performers. "I'm used to there being team leadership, committees, group decisions," adds 23-year-old Hilary, who just started in an entry-level job at a Fortune 500 company. "The more people my age enter the work force, the more we're going to bring that collaborative thought process to what we do."

Create networking opportunities for them. They want to get to know each other. They want to get to know senior leaders. For the Millennial generation, it's all about the circle of connections. Business is conducted through social networking, both online and in person. They influence each other's thinking through blogs, tweeting, multiuser video games, and sharing files.

5. Let them make it their own.

Hilary complains that her coworkers mock her for sitting on an exercise ball instead of a chair and for decorating her cubicle. Millennials expect to be seen and treated as individuals. They are used to flexibility. They like to co-create. They modify products—from their *Facebook* pages to their screensavers to the ringtone on their cellphone—to reflect who they are.

"They want freedom in everything they do," says Don Tapscott, "from freedom of choice to freedom of expression." Millennials take it for granted that they'll be able to make choices on the job. They know how to cull through for what they want. They want to choose how to fit their job into their lives. They are comfortable with complexity and problem solving.

Let them find their own way and create their own solutions. Let them personalize—the project, their workspace. Explain what needs to be done, give them a deadline, and let them *pick their own process* for doing the work.

Just as we have to change our thinking in education that more "seat time" equals more learning, we need to let go of the notion that everyone needs to work in the same way to achieve good results. If your Millennial employee is sometimes more productive working from home, so be it. If she can crank out tons of work in an hour, then needs to take a Starbucks break to regenerate her brain cells, why not? As long as individual work styles don't get in the way of others' productivity, give people the freedom to do their best work in the ways they work best.

6. Tell them how they're doing.

All their lives, Millennials have gotten constant praise, attention, and feedback from parents, coaches, and other adults. On the job, they need frequent, specific feedback. For Millennials, a lack of feedback translates, "You're doing something wrong." Elizabeth tell us, "We don't want time to go by when we are messing up and no one is telling us." She prefers "ongoing feedback" as opposed to a "touch base meeting."

Yet Millennials we interviewed were quick to admit they take criticism personally. "I am the kind of person," says Lauren, "who will assume that whatever mistake I made is ten times bigger than it might really be." Millennials are quickly finding it to their detriment that they've been raised without a tolerance for hurt feelings.

This puts extra pressure on you, our reader. If you want to tap into the power of Millennials at work, you have to become a masterful coach. "A good manager should know how to tell you you did something wrong without making you feel bad," says Lauren.

One Millennial who runs a nonprofit organization staffed by his generational peers says, "I can't even use the word 'deficient' in my office. Nobody likes it. But if I tell them, 'You're really great. You're really strong in English,' then they are a little more willing to hear, 'Your math kind of stinks, though.' "

Patrick, 22, doesn't respond well when he feels the only interaction he receives is criticism. "Sometimes the only thing you hear through the course of the day, other than some quick hellos and some perfunctory small talk, is when you get some little criticism from a boss. It wouldn't be as bad if it were balanced out by more conversation or positives throughout the day. But when that's all I hear, that makes me cranky."

"Give me something I can work with," says Kara, 25. "Give me something I can actually walk away with and know, 'This is how I'm going to do this better or differently.' " Patrick sums it up. "I think that recognizing failure and mistakes is important to building self esteem. Withholding that information isn't building self esteem. I don't think that people in older generations should continually boost our self esteem, because honestly, I would like to know if I'm not doing very well at something. I don't want someone to not tell me or skirt around the issue because it might hurt my feelings. But they also have to recognize that we grew up with that."

7. Be approachable.
Millennials tell us they become uncomfortable if they see a dividing line between managers and employees. In order for Millennials to feel more comfortable on the job, Hilary says "opening the lines of communication" is essential. Robbie suggests to managers, "Leave yourself open if issues arise." He says he likes the way his current manager has communicated "that 'if something happens, you can come to me, let me know.' Have an open door," he says "so they don't feel that something bad happened and they can't go to a manager with it. Everyone should be able to bring it forward and not feel intimidated or bad about bringing it to a manager. Create an environment where it's not so much fear, but you're teammates, you're working together." Dana says she likes to talk with her managers "in a relaxed way."

8. Plug in to parents.

Millennials were raised by active, involved parents who often interceded on their behalf. Parents challenged poor grades and negotiated with the soccer coach. The Higher Education Research Institute reports that increasingly more college students consult with their parents about which school to attend. Parents even go along to Army recruiting centers.

At work, eight in ten Millennials talk to their parents every day according to a 2006 survey conducted by the Pew Research Center for the People and the Press. We can complain about parents. We can try to change their role in the lives of their teen and twentysomething children. Or we can find the positive side of this strong bond between parents and their Millennial children and tap into the power of this other set of mentors and coaches. We might even offer to give them a tour of the office!

9. Be someone to believe in.

Millennials learned to smell a fishy email offer before they were ten. They've been sold to more than any generation, and they're savvy consumers. They know how to sniff out false promises and misinformation, and when they feel they've been burned, they can broadcast their displeasure with one click of the mouse.

They'll check out a company carefully before going to work there in search of integrity, openness, community service, greenness. Promote your organization's values and reputation. Millennials want to be proud of the organization they work for, what it does, how it makes a difference.

Be squeaky clean yourself—ethical, open, able to withstand scrutiny. If you offered something in an interview, follow through on it. If you promise to do something, do it as soon as you can. Your younger colleagues are looking to you as a role model, coach, and mentor. There's a great opportunity for you here. Years from now, you just may be the person some Millennial tracks down to say, "Thank you for what you did, the faith you placed in me, the difference you made."

Recruiting

1. Meet Millennials on their own turf. They search the net looking for jobs. Recruit prospective employees on *Facebook*. Use the company website.

2. Pitch the job. Get them excited about what your organization has to offer.

3. Use the power of peers. Tap an outstanding Millennial employee to talk to prospective employees. Your young recruiters will have fresh information about what it's like to join your organization—and they often can relate more effectively to young prospects than Baby Boomers in suits.

4. Use leading edge technology and graphics in your recruiting presentations and materials. Young prospects might consider a traditional "death by PowerPoint" presentation a signal that your company is out of touch.

5. Put your application process on-line. Millennials prefer an anonymous, paper-free digital interface where they can fill out their applications on their own time, wherever they are, dressed in their jeans and flip-flops.

6. Show them the technology in your workplace so they can see you're up to date. (A new White House staffer recently described the transition to the White House as going from Xbox to Atari. Translation: young people accustomed to the latest technologies often face out-of-date technological tools in the workplace.)

7. Offer flexible options to accommodate family and personal life. Work/life balance is extremely important to Millennials.

8. Pitch your organization's philanthropy efforts and let them know you will support the projects they are already involved in.

9. Include parents in recruiting efforts. Millennials respect their parents, and they often seek parents' advice on important decisions like choosing a job or career path. Some parents get directly involved in the hiring process—meeting a recruiter or attending an orientation, for example.

10. Remember that customers often make great employees.

Orienting

Here are the words of four Millennials speaking about what makes them feel welcome in a new job.

1. "Everybody came in and welcomed us. They told us, 'Stop by my office. I'm here to help you.' So immediately they established this environment where it was okay to ask questions. And they said, 'Here's what I can help you with. It's my job to do that, so please take advantage of it.' And they didn't just say it once."

2. "There were no inside jokes. They had two teachers come in and make a presentation about this tradition they have with teachers and flamingos during homecoming. It was silly and a little cheesy. But I had been wondering what it was all about, and now I understood. They gave us t-shirts with pink flamingos, and said, 'We want you to wear these.' So in several different ways they brought us into the tradition instead of leaving it a mystery."

3. "They build collaboration into the infrastructure of the whole environment. On Tuesdays, there's a special schedule and you start half an hour later, so it builds in an hour of collaborative meeting times for each team. It's not that they're telling us to collaborate on our own time. They are saying, 'This hour is blocked out for your collaboration time.' "

4. "The department chair explicitly said, 'I want you to contribute your ideas. I hired you because I want to hear from you. So when we're in meetings and you're hearing from experienced people, I want you to know I'm *expecting* to hear from you, not just *hoping* for your input.'"

Training

Of course, each has his or her own learning style, but Millennials—more than any other generation—learn by multitasking, playing games, collaborating, and interacting.

1. Video games will be the next big trend in corporate training. Game designer Jane McGonigal says video games teach skills—like identify-

ing opportunities and staying engaged even when things get difficult —that are essential to business.

2. Millennials, because of their upbringing, are more safety conscious than other generations. Update training programs on workplace safety.

Retaining

1. Allow them to choose their own technology devices. A recent survey by Cisco Connected World Technology showed that 40 percent of Millennials would accept a lower paying job if it offered them more of that kind of flexibility. They also think that company-issued devices should be allowed for play as well as work.[20]

2. Help them learn and keep them challenged while they are learning. Millennials leave their jobs in search of the next exciting challenge.

3. Pair them with older mentors who can teach them your business and invite them to coach colleagues who are less technologically savvy.

4. Help them learn interpersonal skills for the workplace. Many Millennials are more comfortable communicating through technology than in person and need to learn how to verbalize their ideas and work with colleagues.

5. Provide consistent and *constructive* feedback. Millennials need to hear regularly how they are doing in their jobs and need clear direction on how to improve their performance. Many take negative feedback personally and have a low tolerance for working through their mistakes.

6. Reward performance and productivity instead of, or in addition to, years spent on the job. A good Pay for Performance system encourages and rewards productivity without regard for age or seniority.

7. Offer flexible scheduling, such as flex-time, part-time, compressed scheduling (for example, a 4-day work week comprised of 10 hour days), job sharing, and options for telecommuting.

8. Offer opportunities to change jobs without changing employers. Workers can move laterally to build their skills and strengthen their resumes. "You might not always get to move up, but moving sideways can help you move along and learn more."

Giving Feedback

In interviews and focus groups Millennials consistently tell us they need and want feedback—constant, specific, constructive feedback. They say they need to know when their performance needs improvement. They say they need coaching on their work efforts so they can achieve their goals. Yet they're the first to admit they are sensitive to criticism; many were raised with constant praise. All this translates into the need for managers and mentors who are masterful at giving feedback, who can talk to coworkers about efforts that need improvement without making them feel discouraged or defensive. Always remember that your purpose in providing feedback is better results.

1. Give small doses of feedback often. If you deliver feedback just once or twice a year, it becomes a big deal. The more often you coach people on their performance, the easier it will be.
2. Meet in private.
3. Speak face to face.
4. Get right to it. Talk as soon as possible after the performance incident.
5. If you're frustrated or angry, wait to meet until you can speak calmly and respectfully, focused on improvement.
6. Be specific and concrete. Talk only about observable behavior. ("The report you turned in yesterday was a day late and had 12 errors that spell check could have caught.")

THE MILLENNIALS

The Work Environment in Most Organizations	The Work Environment That Engages Millennials
• Bureaucracy	• Ease and speed
• Straight lines	• Web-like
• One size fits all	• Can be customized
• Tenured leaders	• Competent, trustworthy leaders
• Yearly reviews	• Weekly, even daily, feedback
• Security, privacy	• Open flow of information

7. Reaffirm your faith in the person. ("I know how much you care about customers, so I know you will want to find a way to be more patient next time we've got a frustrated guest at the reception desk.")

8. Together, define steps for improvement and decide on specific actions to start or stop.

9. Watch for good performance and offer praise in specific terms. (Saying, "Oscar, you processed those nine claims in half the normal time, and every one was accurate" is far more effective than simply saying, "Great job!"

10. Move on. Get over it. Focus on results.

The Future

"There's a social role available to Millennials," Bill Strauss told us in a 1999 interview "because the Veteran generation is dying. That creates a yearning on the part of society for a return to what is missing . . . for someone to fill the vacuum. Since there's a dearth of heroes in our society right now, this generation will create new ones within their cohort

---

THE MILLENNIALS

What Other Generations Say About Them

Traditionalists say...

- "They need to toughen up."
- "They can figure out how to work the remote."
- "They don't respect tradition."

Baby Boomers say...

- "They're tethered to their cell phones."
- "They're inexperienced."
- "Can they set up my *Facebook* page for me?"

Gen Xers say...

- "Neo Boomers."
- "They're unrealistic."
- "Here we go again. Another generation of spoiled brats."

FACT AND FICTION ABOUT MILLENNIALS

Myths	Facts
They're selfish. They just don't care.	Volunteerism is on the rise. "An estimated three-quarters of high school students do some volunteering and the rapidly growing number of college students who volunteer is estimated at about 3.3 million."[21]
They're passive. They expect to be entertained and told what to do.	They are active learners and consumers. In a recent NPR interview, cyber guru Don Tapscott talked about how differently Millennials interact with TV. The Boomers, he said, watched 24 hours of TV a week. Millennials watch far less TV. "When they come home," he says, "they turn on their computer and they're in three different windows and chatting on their phones or texting, and they're listening to MP3 files with three magazines open, and, oh, yeah, they're doing their homework at the same time. The television is sort of in the background. They're thinking and learning and collaborating, and this actually affects their brain development."[22]
Kids these days are no darn good.	The Child Trends Data Bank tracks national trends on over 100 key indicators of child and youth well-being. They report reduced rates of binge drinking, violence, tobacco and marijuana use, and teen pregnancy for the last two decades.

as well as anointing them in older ones." We titled this chapter *Be Careful What You Ask For* because this generation is precisely what employers have been asking for since, well, the Traditionalist Generation dominated the workforce. They are hard working, have an old fashioned work ethic, value family and education, trust authority, and live by the rules. We are learning about Millennials as quickly as we can absorb the information. They are poised to step into the spotlight the Boomers have occupied since the 1950s, becoming media darlings and a much-anticipated receptacle of hope for the future. We know for certain they will influence the 21st century every bit as much—and probably more—than the Boomers did the 20th. They just may become the most powerful U.S. generation yet. The size of their cohort accounts for part of that power. Their civic engagement is one of their most underestimated strengths. Add in their technological sophistication, positive expectations, and bent for collective action, and you have the formula for greatness.

CHAPTER 6

The Global Workforce

Generations Around the World

"In India the term 'Generation X' is used for the younger generation of people who present a hip image. They are westernized, upwardly mobile, and against the old Indian traditions of their parents."
—Rabab Naqvi[1]

Values are our deeply held beliefs about how things *should* be—our beliefs, attitudes, and perspectives on what is good or bad, right or wrong, appropriate or inappropriate, important or trivial. According to sociologist Morris Massey, we are *programmed* in three developmental stages:

1. Imprinting. From birth to about seven years, children are like sponges, absorbing everything around them without evaluation.
2. Modeling. From 7 through 13, children look at the world around them, choosing heroes and deciding which values to embrace. At about age 10, the most crucial values development takes place—influenced greatly by world events, the economy, media, innovations, influential people, and the parenting style of the era.
3. Socialization. Ages 14 through 20 and beyond is a time of questioning, challenging, experimenting with, and adjusting values.[2]

Individual Values

During our formative years, we are each shaped by our own unique circumstances—the family we grow up in, our religious upbringing, the friends we meet, the teachers we learn and don't learn from, the clubs we join, the sports we play, and a whole collection of other personal coming-of-age experiences. All of these program us in certain ways and, as a result, we each have a unique set of individual values.

Generational Values

Each of us—whether we like it or not—is also part of a generation: the group of people who grew up at the same time we did. And we are products of that time. We are shaped by the events and trends of the era we are programmed in—the headlines and heroes, the music and mood, the newest technology, the prevailing parenting style. Because generations share a place in history, they tend to develop a set of defining characteristics. Broadly speaking, a generation covers approximately two decades, but the years dividing generations are blurry and the generations tend to overlap. Most people who are born in the early or late years of each generation actually identify with a couple of generations, sharing some characteristics and similarities in how they view their world.

Of course, the generational model is intended to be used as a framework, not an ironclad description of every individual born within the years of each generation. The model deals in generalizations and, as with all models, it has a bell curve of distribution. In other words, there are many individuals on the ends of each generation who don't fit tidily into the generalizations about their group. So we shouldn't use the model to try to predict an individual's behavior based on year of birth. As colleagues, we will do everyone a disservice if we say to ourselves, "Here comes a Gen Xer. I'm sure she will think and act in a typical Gen X way."

The model does, however, provide a general framework—a framework that is valuable for encouraging dialogue and understanding. South African Researcher Graeme Codrington offers an analogy. "Each tree in a forest is unique," he says "with its own colour, height, growth rate and health. To know how a specific tree will grow, you need to analyse that specific tree. However, you can take a group of trees together in a certain part of the forest and make general comments about them.

They will receive the same rainfall, grow in the same soil, and receive similar amounts of sunshine." Generational theory, Codrington says, helps us to look for defining characteristics within groups of people.

Here, There, and Everywhere

In the previous five chapters, we've explored the four unique generations currently working in the United States. We've outlined the major events and trends of their formative years—from imprinting to modeling to socialization—and sketched out their resulting generational values and characteristics. The logical next question, then, becomes, *Do the characteristics apply to generations in countries other than the United States?* The simple answer: it depends. It depends on whether you grew up in an urban or rural area, in a developed or undeveloped country, and if you're older or younger.

Those of us who lived in urban, developed areas during our formative years shared similar experiences with other people around the world through global mass media—radio, television, newspapers and, most recently, the Internet. During World War II, young people with access to radio and newspapers were hyperconscious of the war—and deeply affected by it—whether they were in London, Tokyo, or Tripoli. This was also true in the decades following World War II in countries like the United States, Canada, New Zealand, and Australia, where economies were growing and birthrates soaring. While American Boomers marched in the Civil Rights movement in the 1960s, busloads of Australian Boomers rolled through New South Wales on the Freedom Ride, protesting discrimination against Aboriginals. Similarities to the profiles we've outlined are less apparent in people who grew up in undeveloped countries, particularly in rural and impover-

> "Over the next decade, engaging talent from multiple generations and geographies will be vitally important for business success."
>
> —Tammy Erickson, "Generations Around the Globe," HBR Blog Network, *Harvard Business Review*, April 4, 2011

ished areas where there was limited exposure to global influences such as TV and the Internet.

Growing Up Digital

The younger a person is—thus exposed to global media—the more likely he or she is to fit the generational profiles we've outlined. In our increasingly connected world, much of our coding crosses political and geographic boundaries. If you're a Millennial, whether the Asian tsunami in 2004 or Hurricane Katrina in 2005 hit closer to your home, both influenced your relationship with your world. Millennials have shared many formative experiences through *Facebook, Twitter,* the Internet and global television news and, therefore, have some common characteristics regardless of the country in which they grew up.

Your Own Country

Since different countries have experienced similar influences at slightly different times, birth years for the generations vary somewhat, depending on country-specific political and economic events. For example, Graeme Codrington extends the birth years for the Baby Boomers into the early 1970s based on the date of the National Party's ascent to power. He suggests the South African Boomers made abolishing Apartheid a cause in much the way the U.S. Boomers embraced the Civil Rights movement.[3]

Then, too, each country has a unique history that causes its own generations to be similar or different from others around the world. "Because formative events differ over time and by geography," says thought leader Tamara Erickson, "it's logical that each generation in each geographic area will form its own unique impressions and, to some extent, think and behave based on a different set of rules."[4] For example, the one-child policy has shaped a new generation—some call it a syndrome—in the People's Republic of China. The term *Little Emperors* describes a generation of lonely, primarily "only" children who are the doted-upon center of their parents' lives. Parents and grandparents do whatever it takes so that their children can experience the benefits they feel they were denied. The entire family devotes itself to the all-encompassing years-long preparation for the national college entrance exam. Taylor Clark, a Portland-based author, writes, "With such high stakes, families dedicate themselves to their child's test prep virtually from infancy."[5]

Depending on the country where you came of age, the characteristics of the generations, as we've described them, may be strikingly similar or starkly different. Understanding each country's unique economic, cultural, political, and historical background is key to understanding the generations that reside there.

International Study of Generational Differences

The study of generational differences has been going on in the United States for nearly 50 years. Dozens of books have been written about marketing to and managing the different generations. In 2000, demographer David Foot analyzed the generations in Canada and reported on his work in the best-selling *Boom, Bust and Echo.* That same year, the

"Let me start by saying thank you for your book. You made sense of something I have been living with at work but was clueless as to how to cope with. I am from the island of Trinidad, and even though most of the literature I have read on intergenerational conflict seems to focus within the U.S., with one research paper saying it may not apply cross-culturally, I think it does. We may not have the first-hand experience of your history, but the world is a small place, and most of the Western hemisphere has been touched by your major events and influencial people. From my research among my peers, we share many characteristics with our American cohorts. Even though generational clashes occur every day, most people don't even realize that there is a name for the condition. When I explain that it is intergenerational conflict, I am usually greeted with "intergener who???" until I explain what it is."

—Vidia Rampersand, Trinidad, West Indies[6]

Japanese Ministry of Education funded a research project on Japan's changing generations. At about the same time, South African Graeme Codrington began studying the generations in New Zealand, Mauritius, England, Russia, and South Africa.

In 2010, Tamara Erickson and research analyst Timothy Bevins conducted extensive research about generations in eight countries around the world. Erickson is a McKinsey Award-winning author who was named one of the 50 most influential management thinkers in the world by Thinkers50. Erickson and Bevins studied generations in Brazil, Russia, India, and China—some of the most important markets for talent over the next decade. They also chose two European countries, the United Kingdom and Germany, because they each represent one of the opposing sides in World War II. And they chose one country, Saudi Arabia, from the Middle East.

Erickson and Bevins have developed a chart that depicts generational values for four cohorts in those eight countries (see Table 6.1). Their model uses slightly different sets of birth years than ours, but the models are generally similar. Erickson and Bevins researched the events that occurred in each of the eight countries during the time the four cohort groups would have been in Massey's *modeling* and *socialization* stages—their pre-teens and teens. We offer their chart as the best summary we've found of generational similarities and differences around the globe.

TABLE 6.1 Key Characteristics Of Each Generation In Eight Major Countries

	Traditionalists Born 1928 to 1945	Boomers Born 1946 to 1960	Generation X Born 1961 to 1979	Generation Y Born 1980 to 1995
Brazil	Modest Respectful Risk-averse	Materialistic consumers Politically cautious Idealistic	Self-reliant Wary Family-centric	Immediate Optimistic Digital natives Financially driven
China	Hard-working Idealistic regarding Communism Relationship-oriented	Rigid and authoritarian Loyal to the Party Viewing work as service to country	Educated Sacrificing for common good Committed to their children	Immediate High self-esteem Digital natives Materialistic
Germany	Disoriented and disillusioned Disinterested in politics Hard-working	Competitive Psychologically responsible for relieving guilt Activists	Career-oriented Focused on self and family Cautious about national identity	Immediate Financially pressured Digital natives Green
India	Respectful of tradition Relationship oriented Conservative	Committed to education Tied to family and tradition Dissatisfied with leadership	Career-oriented Cynical regarding politicians Eager consumers Excited about opportunities	Immediate Seeking to have impact Digital natives Steeped in democracy

Russia	Fatalistic and enduring Hard-working Respectful of authority	Competitive Patriotic Educated men Possessive mothers	Self-reliant Hyperresponsible for parents and children Short-term	Immediate Proud of country Digital natives Driven for financial success
Saudi Arabia	Tied to tribal customs Loyal to family Work to provide for family	Proud of country's progress Grateful to leaders Unsettled by oil money, religion dichotomy	Disillusioned National identity Conflicted by tradition/ modernity	Conservative National identity Mistrustful of institutions Digital natives
United Kingdom	Loyal joiners Respectful Frugal	Competitive Anti-authoritarian Idealistic	Self-reliant Mistrustful Dedicated parents	Immediate Optimistic Digital natives Family-centric
United States	Loyal joiners Respectful Fiscally conservative	Competitive Anti-authoritarian Idealistic	Self-reliant Mistrustful Dedicated parents	Immediate Optimistic Digital natives Family-centric

Reprinted with permission from Tamara J. Erickson and Timothy Bevins, "Generations and Geography: Understanding the Diversity of Generations Around the Globe," Moxie Insight, 2011, p. 5

PART 2

Where Mixed Generations Work Well Together

CHAPTER 7

The ACORN Imperatives and
Three Companies That Bridge the Gaps

Not all generationally mixed workplaces are awash with strife and tension. More than a few organizations are tapping into the positive potential of their generationally diverse workforces. They are harnessing the power in the convergence of diverse viewpoints, passions, and talents.

There are two keys to creating a successful intergenerational workforce: *aggressive communication* and *difference deployment*.

In *aggressive communication*, potential generational conflicts are anticipated and surfaced. Generational differences are based primarily on assumptions and unconscious criteria; therefore, surfacing them takes a giant step toward resolving them. The energy of behind-the-back complaining, passive–aggressive behavior, and open hostility is rechanneled to projects that can profit from different points of view, particularly the fresh perspectives of the young and the wisdom of experience. In the best and brightest intergenerational companies, overcommunication is the rule. These organizations are rife with ad hoc small group discussions, generationally integrated staff meetings, email messages, and water cooler chats, conversation rich with talk about differing viewpoints and perspectives on vital issues of the day. And there's as much listening going on as there is talking. Unfortunately, many organizations continue to stagger along amidst the wreckage of intergenerational warfare with constant passive–aggressive verbal attacks and veiled accusations, management just hoping the problems will somehow take care of themselves. But smart companies address generational issues head-on, and validate the differing points of view. They take the time to talk openly about what the different cohorts and the individuals within them are looking for on the job:

- What makes work rewarding?
- Which environments are most productive?
- What types of work load, schedules, and policies contribute to an attractive workplace?
- What will attract and retain people of differing needs, viewpoints, and expectations?

Difference deployment is, simply, the tactical use of employees with different backgrounds, experiences, skills, and viewpoints to strengthen project teams. In generationally "blind" organizations, managers and human resource departments labor mightily to homogenize employees; to fit them to a single template of the "good employee"; to make employees as alike and easily predictable as possible. But as the head of employee selection research at a large computer manufacturer put the problem for us: "We spent years and millions learning to hire people just like the people who were already here. We never bothered to ask whether the people who could best fit in today would be able to help us survive tomorrow… until it was almost too late." It is an approach, a system, whose time is well past.

Generationally savvy organizations value the differences between people and look at differences as strengths. Generationally balanced workgroups—balanced not in the arithmetic, but in a psychic sense—respect and learn from yesterday's experiences, understand today's pressures, dilemmas, and needs, and believe that tomorrow will be different still. They are comfortable with the relative rather than absolute nature of a situation, knowledge, skill, value, and, most of all, solutions to problems.

In generationally dysfunctional organizations, where generational uniqueness—as well as other important, individual differences—is subjugated by a desire to create one culture that requires individuals to "fit-in," the result is pasteurization and placation. Though pasteurized organizations think of themselves as harmoniously diverse, they are paying

The Way They See the World				
	Traditionalist Generation	Baby Boomers	Gen Xers	Millennials
Outlook	Practical	Optimistic	Skeptical	Hopeful
Work Ethic	Dedicated	Driven	Balanced	Determined
View of Authority	Respectful	Love/hate	Unimpressed	Polite
Leadership by	Hierarchy	Consensus	Competence	Pulling together
Relationships	Personal sacrifice	Personal gratification	Reluctant to commit	Inclusive
Turn-offs	Vulgarity	Political incorrectness	Cliché, hype	Promiscuity

a premium in stagnant thinking, lost creativity, and an absence of diverse opinions. Pasteurized organizations may look harmonious and productive in an outside-in snapshot, but the "glue" of that harmony is an expensive adhesive. It is based on strong adherence to peace and harmony over the outcome and the necessary innovative demands of the contemporary marketplace. Friction-free interpersonal relations are more immediately important than present and future productivity potential. Typically, younger workers are squirreled away in front-line departments, new product and design groups, and the call center. Although on some level individuals feel they are cared for and "accepted," they are usually on the lookout for a workplace where they can fit in unconditionally and where their uniqueness will be seen as valid and acceptable, not simply as tolerable oddities.

The ACORN Imperatives

As we've gotten to know the organizations featured in this chapter and other successful cross-generational friendly organizations, we've been struck by five specific similarities or common approaches to making their environments generationally comfortable and focusing their people's energies on the business of the business. We've come to think of these as the ACORN imperatives, five potent precepts or operating ideas that nurture and grow oak-strong organizations.

As you peruse the profiles, be aware of why these organizations accommodate differences, build nontraditional workplaces, exhibit flexibility, emphasize respectful relations, and focus on retaining talented and gifted associates. More specifically, be on the lookout for the variety of ways these organizations:

1. Accommodate employee differences.

With employee retention at or near the top of the list of corporate "must meet" measures, the most generationally friendly of companies treat their employees as they do their customers. They learn all they can about them, work to meet their specific needs, and serve them according to their unique preferences. They have painstakingly figured out what their employees' preferences are and have done everything they can to create a friendlier workplace in tangible and symbolic ways. There

---

What We Have in Common

In a multigenerational organization, our differences come to light when there is tension within the ranks. However, there are actually more similarities than differences among the generations at work. In the Randstad 2008 World of Work survey, employees across the generations identified the attributes they value. Regardless of their generation, employees said they want to work for a company whose leaders:

- Respect employees and recognize the value each brings to the organization.
- Care about their employees as much as their customers.
- Value employees' honest input on business issues.
- Encourage employees to be innovative thinkers.
- Encourage employees to continually develop their skills.
- Encourage a collaborative work environment.
- Focus more on employees' strengths than on weaknesses.
- Foster good relationships between supervisors and employees.[2]

is real, not hypothetical, effort to accommodate personal scheduling needs, work-life balance issues, and nontraditional lifestyles. Each generation's icons, language, and precepts are acknowledged, and language is used that reflects generations other than those "at the top."

> "The best problem solvers tend to be similar; therefore a collection of the best problem solvers performs little better than any one of them individually. A collection of random, but intelligent, problem solvers tends to be diverse. This diversity allows them to be collectively better."
>
> —Scott Page, *The Difference*

2. Create choices.

The popularity of *Mad Men* is a testament to our fascination with corporate environments of the 1950s and 1960s, where everything was predictable and regimented from the executive boardroom to the way secretaries greeted executives in the morning to the standard memo format. The companies profiled here are a far cry from that. Generationally friendly companies allow the workplace to shape itself around the work being done, the customers being served, and the people who work there. They recognize that people from a mix of generations have differing needs and preferences, and they design their human resources strategies to meet varied employee needs. They offer a variety of benefits, flexible schedules, and an array of opportunities for professional growth and advancement. Dress policies tend to be casual. The height and width of the chain of command are foreshortened, and decreased bureaucracy is taken on as a clear goal. "Change" is not so much the name of a training seminar or a core value listed somewhere in their mission statement as it is an assumed way of living and working. In all these companies, the atmosphere could be described as relaxed and informal— and there's an element of humor and playfulness about most of their endeavors.

3. Operate from a sophisticated management style.

Good managers are a bit more polished than the norm; they operate with a certain finesse. They tend to be more direct. Generationally friendly managers don't have much time for circumlocution, "B.S.," as one put it to us, although they are tactful. They give those who report to them the big picture, with specific goals and measures, and then they turn their people loose—giving them feedback, rewards, and recognition as appropriate. Seven attributes characterize these excellent managers:

1. Their supervisory style is not fixed. How closely they monitor and manage, for instance, is a product of each individual's track record and personal preferences. Control and autonomy are a continuum, not solitary options.
2. Their leadership style is situationally varied. Some decisions are made consensually; others are made by the manager, but with input and consultation.
3. They depend less on positional than on personal power.
4. They know when and how to make personal policy exceptions, without causing a team riot.
5. They are thoughtful when matching individuals to a team or a team or individual to an assignment.
6. They balance concern for tasks and concern for people. They are neither slave drivers nor country club managers.
7. They understand the elements of trust, and work to gain it from their employees. They are perceived as fair, inclusive, good communicators and competent in their own right.

4. Respect competence and initiative.

The old "manufacturing mode" of business was based on the precept that people are inherently "sliders" who are not all that interested in putting their best efforts forward without close supervision and monitoring. The organizations profiled here are very much a part of the knowledge and service economy. They assume the best of people. They treat everyone, from the newest recruit to the most seasoned employee, as if they have great things to offer and are motivated to do their best. It is an attitude that can become a self-fulfilling prophecy. These companies hire carefully and do much to assure a good match between people and work. But they seem never to forget that they hired the best possible people for a reason—so that they will endeavor to do the best possible job.

5. Nourish initiative.

Many organizations expect employees to bend to the company's will and to adapt to meet the demands of the company culture. Then their executives complain about high turnover, the difficulty of finding good people, and the skyrocketing costs of replacing those who've left. Generationally friendly companies are concerned and focused, on a daily basis, with making their workplaces magnets for excellence. They know that keeping their people is every bit as important in today's economy as finding and retaining customers. Therefore, they offer lots of training, from one-on-one coaching opportunities to interactive online training to an extensive and varied menu of classroom courses. Not only do they encourage regular lateral movement within their organizations, but they have broadened assignments. No longer do insurance claims adjusters, for example, process only a small part of the claim. Today they take it from the initial call to the settlement check, which provides variety and challenge—and allows employees to develop a range of skills.

> "Diversity as a goal has become the default, in part as a matter of simple fairness, but in part because our culture has long accepted that a diversity of beliefs leads us to better, stronger, more grounded ideas."
>
> —Dave Weinberger,
> *Too Big to Know*

You may notice something else unusual: these organizations market internally. In other words, they spend time learning how to become the employer of choice in their industry and region, and they continually "sell the benefits" to retain the best and brightest of their employees. Not a disingenuous internal public relations program, but a clear, conscious effort to remind employees of the good things the company offers.

Scripps Health: A Leader in Developing a Generations-Friendly Culture

By the end of 2001, Scripps Health in San Diego was facing significant challenges. Operating losses coupled with a downturn in the stock market loomed as dark clouds on the financial horizon. Turnover was high among the 10,000 plus employees, especially among those who had been hired within the past year. A tight labor market had made it increasingly difficult to replace those who left. To survive in such gnarly times, Scripps needed to create a place where people would enjoy coming to work. They decided they would have to create an environment centered around keeping quality employees satisfied.

Scripps launched what became an amazing turnaround, in large part by using a generational lens. The company began by setting aggressive goals:

- To reduce turnover to 15 percent among first year employees, where the churn was most dramatic
- To limit turnover among all employees to 6 percent or less
- To achieve a score of 85 on the Trust Index©, an employee survey developed by the Great Place to Work® Institute.

Then they launched an aggressive campaign to get to know their employees. In focus groups, surveys, and interviews, says Vic Buzachero, Senior Vice President for Human Resources, "We listened, really listened. We wanted to understand our employees—the whole person, inside and outside of work," he says, "and find better ways to support them." In the process, it became clear that Scripps managers had been thinking of their people in sort of a "one-size-fits-all" way. Their development programs, their benefits, their recruitment strategies were designed for a "typical employee." They quickly discovered there is no such thing.

Scripps Health

Headquarters: San Diego, California

The not-for-profit health system serves the San Diego area through four acute-care hospitals on five campuses. Together the health system is home to 1,400 beds and a network of out-patient clinics.

13,445 employees

Scripps managers realized that employees of different generations and in different stages of their lives have very different ways of evaluating the workplace, measuring their own satisfaction,

> The Great Place to Work® Institute recognizes a great workplace as one where employees "trust the people they work for, have pride in what they do, and enjoy the people they work with."

and deciding whether to stay or leave. They found that, while some of their people needed more time with their families, others were putting kids through college; while some were struggling to care for aging parents, others were working on plans for their own retirement. They began an intensive study of generations and generational differences. After analyzing the generational composition of their workforce, they conducted training for all leaders. Topics included communication styles for each of the generations, workplace motivators and de-motivators, and specific leadership strategies.

They found ways to increase options for employees. Based on employee feedback, Scripps instituted the Life Cycle Employee program. It helps employees at all stages of life and work to fill their individual needs via a wide variety of innovative benefits. The program caters to workers of all generations and includes "a few personal perks that help contribute to a fun, rewarding and appreciative work environment." New choices for employees included on-site day care, entertainment discounts, tuition reimbursement, adoption benefits, massage therapy, a concierge program, staged retirement, free biometric screening, an on-line wellness assessment, and retiree health insurance.

The next step was to market the new program to employees. A multifaceted communication program included a 4-page color newsletter, mailings to employees at their homes, and email messages.

At the urging of some of their younger employees, Scripps found new ways of offering employees opportunities that would tap into personal beliefs and aspirations. Bruce Grendell, a 20-year Scripps employee and the administrative director of clinical services at Scripps Memorial Hospital La Jolla, used Scripps' tuition reimbursement to earn his master's degree in nursing and advance in his career. "One of the things I value most about Scripps,"

> "We knew they were healthcare professionals, but we discovered they were also mothers, do-it-yourselfers, gardeners, animal lovers, students, and writers."
>
> —Vic Buzachero, Senior VP for Human Resources, Scripps Health

he told *San Diego Magazine,* "is that I've been able to accomplish my personal and professional goals while working for the same employer." The company also granted him a leave so he could perform volunteer relief work in Thailand, Uganda, and Argentina.

The results of Scripps efforts are tantalizing. By 2006, revenues had increased by $130 million. Turnover decreased. Among first-year employees, turnover dropped 8.5 percent. Great Place to Work® scores increased from 58 in 2001 to 82 in 2006. "Health care," says Buzachero, "is all about the care, comfort and service our employees provide to our patients and their families. By helping our employees through the various cycles of their life— early career, mid-career, or late career—we allow them to grow within Scripps in a position that fits their specific needs. In the end, our patients benefit through the care and compassion of our happy employees." Recently Scripps has received a number of awards for being a good place to work. The groups that have recognized them—from *Working Mother Magazine* to AARP— reflect how well the company is doing at appealing to workers across the spectrum of generations.

Ameriprise Financial: Leveraging the Unique Perspectives of the Generations

A multigeneration workforce adds value to a company when employee differences are cultivated with some guidance and awareness. To help foster collaboration and innovation in a generationally diverse company, Ameriprise Financial has established specific programs and opportunities to ensure that members of all generations feel their unique perspectives are recognized at work, and that members of different generations appreciate and can identify with one another.

The Young Professionals Network, one of 15 employee networks, offers social, civic, and career development opportunities that help Millennials grow their leadership and networking skills, and to learn from one another. YPN chapters exist in each of Ameriprise Financial's corporate locations— Minneapolis, Boston, Providence, and Green Bay—and offer a variety of different programs in which network members can participate. One such program, called peer learning groups, allows YPN members to meet regularly with a small group of young professionals from around the company to discuss ideas and experiences that contribute to their professional development. The peer learning groups also give participants a chance to learn from one another about how to manage workplace opportunities and challenges that they may encounter during their first experience in a professional environment.

In Green Bay, where 25 percent of Ameriprise employees are Millennials, the YPN chapter has been a driver of the company's mentorship program, where participants have the opportunity to learn from others in the company with more leadership experience. Since many of those working at the Green Bay location are insurance professionals, their YPN chapter has also established a designation program that helps young professionals achieve their career goals by offering support in completing certifications to achieve specific insurance designations. Leaders of the YPN chapters schedule regular networking opportunities, plan community service events, and partner with other employee networks to host employee events.

> **Ameriprise Financial, Inc.**
> Headquarters: Minneapolis, Minnesota
>
> A leading provider of financial advice, Ameriprise offers financial planning, products, and services to individual and institutional investors.
>
> 11,000 employees

One participant says, "YPN offers a great sense of community, similar to what I experienced in college activities I was involved in. It's always a good feeling to be involved in groups that have a common goal and interest. In a company as large as Ameriprise, it's also handy to know so many people in different parts of the company so I can connect the dots when I'm working on a cross-functional project." One of her favorite aspects of YPN is hearing from senior leaders. "Senior leaders recognize the drive and ambition that members of YPN have, and it reminds them of when they began their own careers," she says. "As a young professional, it's valuable to hear from them about their individual career paths and professional development advice."

Being a generationally friendly company requires educating people about generational differences. Ameriprise Financial offers two levels of gen-

> "Young professionals add a sense of energy and innovation to a company that makes them as individuals, and as a group, invaluable. Members of Generation Y are motivated by knowing how the work they do and the ideas they have add value to the company. As an organization, we aim to make sure that these young professionals recognize how they add to the company's bottom line."
>
> —VP of Talent Acquisition, Ameriprise Financial

erations training for employees about the differing perspectives and experiences of various generations. The introductory session, "Level 1: Understanding Generations," helps attendees understand the ways that members of each generation might prefer to communicate and the style in which they prefer to work. "Level 2: Managing Generations" dives deeper into the ways in which leaders can leverage the unique perspectives of different generations to increase business value.

Another highly successful Ameriprise program is LDP, the Leadership Development Program. In this full-time rotational program, trainees are placed in different lines of business based on their area of expertise. The program consists of three six-month rotations in various positions and on different teams within the line of business, allowing trainees to find their niche, and choose where they'd like to take a permanent position upon completion. As part of the program, trainees are given a learning plan that includes training and development workshops, exposure to senior leaders, seminars and other leadership development opportunities.

One participant in the LDP program who studied marketing says she appreciates the ability to learn what it's like to work on teams within the marketing department where there are different areas of focus. "It's hard to know exactly what you're good at and what you want to do with your career when you graduate from college," she says. "I like the rotating between different groups so I can learn about my own strengths and what it's like to work for different leaders and colleagues. I've learned a lot about my own leadership style and about how I work best with others because I've had the opportunity to meet and work closely with so many people." She also admits she likes being able to meet with her peers in the program on a regular basis to discuss projects they're working on, professional development, and current financial news. "Building close relationships with those I work with is important to me and I like being able to meet up with others in the LDP program outside of work, too."

The internship program at Ameriprise offers college students a chance to learn on the job and helps usher them into a career in business. Interns with diverse interests and areas of focus work together to complete a capstone project and get the opportunity to present solutions that may impact real business work. They also get the chance to meet and learn about the career paths and experiences of corporate executive leaders, and work with the members of YPN to participate in community service and networking opportunities.

Ernst & Young: Putting People First

Retaining employees from all generations is especially important for the well-known accounting firm Ernst & Young because of its bill-per-hour environment; the longer people have worked there, the more the company can bill per hour. The firm has been a consistent leader in work/life issues globally. Its People First environment is based on the belief that when individuals achieve their best, clients benefit and business prospers.

> **Ernst & Young**
> Headquarters: New York, New York
>
> Professional firm Ernst & Young provides assurance, tax, transactions, and advisory services to public and private companies in a wide variety of industries from about 80 offices throughout the US, including Puerto Rico.
>
> 152,000 employees

Recently, the company has launched a variety of innovative strategies for recruiting younger employees. One example is a recruiting page on *Facebook* to meet Millennials "on their own turf." And, instead of brochures, recruiters give out flash drives, schedule meetings with candidates via text messages, and give video cameras to interns to create blogs for the Ernst & Young website.

Orientation for the summer internship program—geared mostly for Millennials—includes a PowerPoint presentation called "Hello. WU?!"—text message for *What's up?* Included are strategies for connecting with Baby Boomers. And while trainers are teaching Millennials how to show respect for partners, they are also teaching partners how to send text messages.

E&Y's efforts aren't focused solely on Millennials. An alumni program stays in touch with 32,000 registered former employees in the U.S. The alumni participate in workshops, volunteer events, and networking sessions—and comprise a rich pool of possible re-hires. Last year, 26 percent of those hired for management positions were alumni.

> "Our research has shown that the right environment is what creates business results—not the other way around. With that in mind, we continuously seek new ways to foster an inclusive and flexible work environment that supports our people both personally and professionally."
>
> —Jim Freer, Vice Chair of People in the Americas, Ernst & Young[1]

To promote their flexibility programs, the company has built an internal website where participants can share their experiences. Ten percent of Ernst & Young employees enjoy flexible work arrangements. According to Gregg Slager, Senior Partner of Mergers and Acquisitions, the group of flex workers includes 100 partners along with employees who have received promotions while working flexible hours. This is encouraging for those who might fear that taking time off or working flex-time might endanger their career advancement. The company has reportedly saved $10 million each year through the improved retention its flexibility programs have created. Even when the firm loses employees, they keep in touch and work hard to bring them back. Of all who've left Ernst & Young, 28 percent have returned.

CHAPTER 8

Company Best Practices
and Other Great Ideas

Organizations that are finding success in engaging people from all generations are implementing the Acorn Imperatives to develop an array of strategies. To stimulate your thinking, we've collected about three dozen best practices and great ideas from a wide representation of different organizations and industries. We hear about a smart new strategy every week; this is just a snapshot of hundreds of thousands of activities going on in today's workplace. We encourage you to look within your own organization to identify best policies and strategies—and to zero in on areas for improvement.

- Booz Allen Hamilton's many community groups and employee forums build community among employees with common interests. While some participate in the firm's kickball team, others connect with a group that helps elderly people maintain their homes. The firm supports these efforts, sometimes monetarily. Any employee can start a new group.
- PepsiCo's global corporate volunteerism program, PepsiCorps, was initiated from the ground up by a group of employees who sought to bring PepsiCo's Performance with Purpose mission to life. The program deploys employees on month-long assignments to tackle global challenges. It's a great experience for employees, a boon to local communities, and a contributor to business objectives. Moreover, it helps with talent development, retention, and recruitment.
- Mercy Health System in Janesville, Wisconsin, has developed an employee-friendly workplace culture based on "Servant Leadership."

This philosophy says that to best serve patients, employee partners must treat each other with respect, like family members.

- Acknowledging that many Millennials have close ties to parents, Enterprise Rent-a-Car asks prospective employees if they would like a packet of information mailed to parents. Most accept the offer. Enterprise also trains new employees in cell phone etiquette. As part of their orientation, they teach new hires that if they are with a customer, they don't answer their cell.

- Laurel J. Richie, president of the Women's National Basketball Association, has an if-you-really-want-it-come-back-three-times policy. She says she tells people she knows she can seem controlling. "I always tell people to come back three times if they really believe in their point of view," she says. The first time she may defend her own conviction. The second, she's likely to acknowledge that she's listening—but holding to her original decision. "If they still feel strongly," she says, "they should come back and say, 'Remember when you said come back the third time? This is the third time.'"[1]

- The MITRE Corporation in Bedford, MA, allows employees to "change jobs without changing employers." This initiative encourages internal transfers and encourages managers to offer 8 to 10 percent of staff an opportunity to transfer to a new job inside the company each year. Workers of all ages move laterally and gain broader experience.

- Baptist Health South Florida in Coral Gables, Florida, offers financial incentives to senior nursing staff who provide guidance to assigned junior colleagues.

- Adecco Employment Services matches mature and experienced branch managers with new branch managers to counsel them on strategies and tactics for success.

- KPMG has a website dedicated to mentoring. Every manager has a protégé, every young worker is expected to have a mentor, and people in the middle often have both. Social activities like lunches, softball games, and happy hours are advertised on the mentoring website to encourage informal networking. KPMG also gives time off for community service. These practices have helped reduce turnover from 25 to 18 percent in the last five years.

- A new company called YourEncore employs retired (experienced) scientists, engineers and product developers and places them in assignments with companies like Boeing and Procter & Gamble.

- Randstad USA offers training for leaders on how to communicate more effectively with younger generations. They report that this training has resulted in a reduction of first-year turnover from 50 percent to 30 percent.

- Volkswagen of America, Inc, in Auburn Hills, Michigan, provides in-house classroom training and use of mentoring programs to ensure that critical skills sets and job knowledge are transferred to employees. Through the national resume database comprised of individuals who have been laid off from other companies, Volkswagen can tap experienced workers who possess highly sought-after skills that keep Volkswagen competitive.

- Lee Memorial Health System in Fort Meyers, Florida, has created an unusual perk called the Seasonal Months Off Program. It allows "snow birds" to take time off up to six months during the slow season while maintaining their full health benefits and life/long-term care insurance at the same rate.

- Centegra Health System, in Woodstock, Illinois, offers the Wellness for Life program which provides annual free health risk assessments to employees—and a one-on-one consultation with a dietician, fitness expert, or registered nurse as a follow-up to the assessment.

- At Booz Allen Hamilton, employees are encouraged to learn about and discuss generational differences. "Talk about it. Don't pretend it's not happening," says Adrienne Alberts, head of university recruiting. "When you have the conversation and people come to some understanding, people find a way to do productive work together."

- Massachusetts General Hospital offers a "Be Fit" 10-week program that helps participants to be fit, eat right, and live healthy.

- To boost recruitment efforts, PepsiCo recently released "Possibilities," an iPad app. Prospective candidates can watch for openings, view videos from current employees, read executive blogs, and have conversations with hiring managers.

- Each year, Infosys Technologies Ltd. in Bangalore selects nine top-performing young workers to participate in its eight annual senior management council meetings. As part of the Voices of Youth program, the young workers discuss their ideas with the top leadership team. The company's CEO says, "If an organization becomes too hierarchical, ideas that bubble up from younger people aren't going to be heard."

- BrainStorc, a company in Biel, Switzerland that works on products and ad campaigns for companies like Nestlé and the Swiss Railway and calls itself "an idea factory," hires teenagers to solve problems. Cofounder Markus Mettler says that, to succeed, BrainStorc needs "crazy ideas." He believes that teens "don't let their thinking get in the way." Mettler's co-founder, Nadja Schnetzler, adds, "we blend the professionalism of experts with the unbridled enthusiasm of kids. By mixing the ideas of experts and novices, of young and old, we increase the diversity of solutions that can be generated for clients."

- After every seven years of full-time employment, Intel offers a paid sabbatical—an extra eight weeks of paid vacation.

- Global HR services company Hewitt Associates analyzes Fortune's 100 Best Companies to Work For each year. They've found that the three characteristics the companies have in common are:

  - They do more to engage employees.
  - Their work environments are supportive and inclusive.
  - They give great consideration to employee quality of life.

- The U.S. Army has rewritten its training doctrine, recommending that drill sergeants switch from intimidation and command and control to leadership by example. The negative atmosphere that instilled fear in recruits just a generation ago has proven less effective for a new generation of soldiers who often see action within six months of enlisting. The best starting point, according to Jim Schwitters, commanding general at the U.S. Army Training Center in Fort Jackson, South Carolina, is to make young soldiers feel empowered. The first challenge new soldiers face is an obstacle course designed to build confidence; it's tough but not overwhelming. Drill sergeants mentor and act as role models—and do virtually everything their soldiers do, marching with heavy packs, demonstrating the proper handling of weapons, and navigating obstacle courses. The approach has worked. Retention has increased 50 percent. Young soldiers report that they are inspired by their drill sergeants. One Millennial told Schwitters, "The drill sergeant cared about me and did everything he asked me to do."

- Satellite television company DIRECTV relies on call center employees when it rolls out new products like its 2006 Sports Package. To reach sales goals, employees needed to learn the "NFL Sunday Ticket" inside and out, and they needed to sharpen sales and customer service skills. With the help of Visual Purple, DIRECTV instituted its first ever simulation based training tool. Training simulations put employees in true to life sales scenarios where they faced tough customer questions. Through engaging play, they learned to recognize key phrases and buying cues. The simulations included quizzes and a motivating score system. The simulation won the *Chief Learning Officer Magazine's* Silver Award.

- Elton Ndoma-Ogar, a diversity recruiter for Merrill Lynch, decided he needed to market his company to parents of potential recruits. Parents of prospective employees, he says, were hearing horror stories about long hours and tough demands. His recruiting efforts weren't as effective as they might be, he realized, because he wasn't reducing parents' concerns. So he instituted a Parents' Day for mothers and fathers of a group of summer analysts he hoped to attract for permanent employment. During the special event, parents learned about the company and its benefits, the way business is done, the ways employees are supported. Of the students whose parents attended, only one didn't accept the firm's job offer.

- Deloitte has career coaches who help employees transfer within the company. People respond well when they know they can remain with the organization for a long time without getting stuck in just one job. Working with the career coaches, they uncover new challenges, opportunities, and experiences available within the company. Deloitte also trains managers to adapt to employees' preferred work schedules rather than trying to change people. Stan Smith, a national director specializing in human resources issues, says a partner called him, furious with his young associates because they had told him they were "busy" on a weekend he expected them to work. After hearing similar complaints from other partners, Smith developed an educational brochure about generational changes in the workplace. The brochure is used widely by managers throughout the company.

- Lockheed Martin noticed generational differences in learning styles when Baby Boomers were asked to pass on their expertise to Millennials. When the Boomers used PowerPoint presentations, the Millennials told them they could learn better from more interactive methods. As a result, Lockheed offers workshops for managers on generational diversity, emphasizing the ways learning styles differ between generations.

- "In the Results-Only Work Environment (ROWE) at Best Buy's corporate office, employees are trusted to manage their lives and their work without being judged or micromanaged. ROWE means that employees are rewarded for outcomes, not activities, and leaders get to focus on the things that truly drive business results. According to the company's website, ROWE has resulted in:

  - Increased productivity.
  - Reduced voluntary employee turnover.
  - Increased levels of engagement.

- Andrew Ajello says he "sees plenty of potential for generational conflict." A regional sales executive for Novo Nordisk, the Danish diabetes drug maker, Andrew heads up a group of 650 Boomers, Xers, and Millennials. He has applied his knowledge about generational differences in a variety of ways. After younger sales reps complained about "driving boring beige Buicks," he persuaded executives to add Jeeps to the fleet. With his sales group, he emphasizes team results rather than individual performance because his Millennial salespeople prefer that he reward them for collaborating. At sales meetings, he urges managers to discuss generational differences.

More Great Ideas

- Reward performance and productivity instead of, or in addition to, years spent on the job. A good Pay-for-Performance system encourages and rewards productivity without regard for age or seniority. A Flex-for-Performance system might help with the growing demand for flex time.
- Offer training and professional development—including generations and diversity training—in a variety of formats—classroom style, on-line, experiential, interactive, and in staff meetings.
- Offer mentoring programs, along with training programs on how to mentor.
- Offer reverse mentoring programs in which younger employees help older ones adapt to new technologies.
- Study the generational composition of your workforce and use that information to guide HR strategies.
- Match the generational composition of your workforce to the generational composition of your customer base.
- Publicize career opportunities internally so that employees with varying work schedules have access to information about open positions.
- Offer flexible scheduling, such as flex-time, part-time, compressed scheduling (for example, a 4-day work week comprised of 10 hour days), job-sharing, and options for telecommuting.
- Taking steps to build a strong workforce doesn't have to wait until a new employee joins the company. More and more companies are

creating internships for college and even high school students that
offer training, mentoring, opportunities to shadow employees, research projects, and creative approaches to connecting interns with
a wide range of colleagues.

- Offer flexible benefits, such as auto and homeowner's insurance,
adoption benefits, child care, elder care, life insurance, paid time
off, dependent loan scholarships, dental and vision plans, long-term
care insurance, a retiree health plan, retirement planning tools and
phased retirement programs.

- Offer health and wellness programs with options that meet needs of
different age groups.

- Include representatives from all generations on organizational boards
and committees.

- Offer two-way mentoring programs. Young workers give lessons on
using web tools like portals, blogs, and wikis and demonstrate better
ways to use technology to take orders, track shipping, or capture
customer feedback; senior-level employees teach about the business.

- Create a common area where folks can take breaks from their cubicles and work together in an open environment. Supply the area
with a few computers. Add a table and some chairs so people will
feel free to gather for a meeting or lunch.

- Reward managers for retaining the people who report to them.
Managers are rewarded by the organization for many things, but
usually not for employee retention.

PART 3

The Interviews

In the first edition, we fired a series of generationally charged questions at a panel of experts. This time, after talking to our readers, we decided to take a different approach. We interviewed three people who are working at the top levels of their organizations and are well versed in generational issues, and we spoke directly to ten people who are typical members of their generations. We asked all our interviewees how work is going and how life is treating them. Their responses are fascinating and offer insights galore.

We call the first set of interviews "From the CEO's Perspective." In these interviews, you will hear how three organizations and their executives are dealing with the generational mix. The second set we call "From the Trenches." They include real talk from real people, but we have changed their names. We asked them to speak candidly about their jobs, their dreams, their frustrations—so you would get the unvarnished truth.

You could choose to read through the interviews on your own, and we're certain you would discover valuable insights—along with a plethora of business advice about how to shape a functional, progressive, and successful cross-generational workplace. But we are going to get a bit more involved than that. When we heard these individuals talk, we immediately recognized some best practices. We heard generational phrases that gave us insights and helped us diagnose what might be happening in their work situations. We will expose you to the filters we use and show you where the "aha" moments occurred for us. To accomplish that, we have adopted the Web practices of highlighting and tagging key words and phrases. In each interview, you will find a few tags with labels or explanations in the margins. You might even want to add some tags of your own.

CHAPTER 9

From the CEO's Perspective

In the following interviews we chatted with three organizational leaders, all of whom are well versed on the subject of generational differences. Here they speak about everything from technology to succession planning, from mentoring to entitlement, from training and development to leadership. One is a Boomer, one a Gen Xer, one a Millennial. As you read, notice that their leadership styles reflect their generation—as do their attitudes, approaches, challenges, and frustrations.

Glenn Horton
CEO of The Horton Group, Illinois

Glenn Horton is a Baby Boomer. The Horton Group, with seven offices in four states, provides insurance, risk management, and employee benefit solutions for a variety of industries.

How did you become interested in generations?
About 12 years ago, somebody gave me the Strauss and Howe book *The Fourth Turning,* and I found it interesting. I picked it up again five or six years later, and that's when I really got interested—probably because we were struggling with perpetuating the ownership of the business and making the generational transition. I was trying to learn and it all kind of fit together.

So you are wrestling with succession planning?
It's a big part of what we are dealing with, but not so much from a financial point of view. I think we've got the financial thing pretty well wired. But certainly from a management and continuity-of-client-relationships point of view, we're playing catch up, and we want to be successful at it.

How are you adapting to other generations in your firm?

In the way we align the work. We tend to put our Millennials on teams. We give them team assignments. With the Xers, we tend to take the opposite approach. We find that the Xers prefer to work alone. And so when we put Xers in team situations because there's just no way around it, we help management see we probably won't be able to depend on the Xers to provide continuity of relationships among the team members.

Millennials thrive on teams.

Xers tend to be loners. They were latchkey kids who learned to take care of themselves.

The way we train people has also changed. The way we train a Millennial is different than the way we train a Boomer. We've also had to adjust our mentoring relationships. We kind of assumed that Boomers would be good mentors for Millennials because of their experience. We found that most Boomers actually make horrible mentors because they want to pontificate and preach—and that's the last thing a Millennial seems to want. We've discovered that we need to have the Millennials mentor other Millennials, rather than go across generations.

Some Boomers think the only way to pass along their considerable knowledge is by lecturing.

Millennials are used to giving and receiving peer feedback.

And that works?

Yes, that works well. We find that Millennials are very good and engaged mentors.

In the movie *Cool Hand Luke,* one boss was always trying to get Luke's mind "right." Is that what you're talking about?

Yeah, that's a good one. I'll have to remember that. And of course a Millennial's mind never is right to the satisfaction of the Boomer, so we just finally faced the reality that we are not going to get mentoring out of the Boomers. Not good mentoring. They will mentor all day long. They are very willing to mentor and they want to mentor; they just don't want to mentor in a way that Millennials see any value in. Even the Xers have trouble seeing any value in it.

You seem aware of your own generational proclivities. How do you see past your own generational blinders?

I try to be self-aware. Obviously I'm seeing some of the frustrations of my Boomer partners and other people who work in the office. When you're CEO, you have to deal with the blinders. If you are at all introspective, you ask yourself, "Gee, do I look like that or sound like that or am I behaving like that? Am I presenting the same frustrations to everybody else?"

Boomers value reflection and self-awareness.

You try to turn it from a weakness to a strength. I try to be aware of generational differences in the things I read. Even with my own kids, I try to be aware of how my kids see things differently. I always ask myself, "Do I sound like that, or do I do that?" Invariably I do some of it.

What do you think of your younger workers, the Millennials?

I've got a bunch of Millennials working for me. I'm trying to accelerate that as fast as possible. I'm an enthusiastic supporter of the Millennial generation, and think we get more bang for our buck from them than from the other two. We've gotten better with the Xers. I don't personally like to work with the Xers as much as I do the Millennials, but I think we've learned to become more effective with them. As you know, Xers can be very practical, efficient, effective people. I like hanging around with Millennials more than Xers, but I'm able to recognize their value in the amount of good work we get from them.

Gen Xers' pragmatism is legendary, almost to a fault.

Xers love their independence.

They do, exactly. Insurance sales is not a business that always sits well with that. We are more and more a professional partnership in terms of ownership. Xers don't seem to have nearly the interest in being part of a professional partnership as do Millennials or Boomers.

Most Xers have not yet accepted that they really can work at one place for more than a couple of years—and actually make partner.

The Xers don't have good people skills?

It's beyond that. Ownership is a big deal. It's been very lucrative for people. But Xers just don't seem to be willing to make the short-term sacrifice to get the long-term benefits. If you are going to be part of a professional partnership, that means you're a partner. You've got to work with a lot of people. The Xers just don't seem to have a great deal of interest in that. It's like, "I'm going to come in and do my job. If I can make a low investment of energy in the business and get something for it, that's okay. But I'm not going to wake up in the morning and be driven to build the business on behalf of the company." There are exceptions to that, but generally I've found that to be the case.

Most Xers are not used to long-term thinking.

To Gen Xers, it's just a job.

Are you having any trouble hanging onto Xers? They are notoriously nomadic.

We are hanging onto Xers, but not because we are so good. The nature of our professional partnership makes it so that once they are tied to the firm, the accounts get tied to the firm. Consequently, it's hard for them to move their accounts. So they end up making a lot of money, and they have an incentive to stay. And we have noncompete agreements and things like that, so they can't just up and leave and take their accounts. They can up and leave, but then they are kind of starting from scratch. And some of these guys are making $400,000 to $500,000 a year, and they would only be worth $100,000 a year if they started from scratch. They have to really not like it to leave behind their book of clients and those relationships and start over again.

How do you motivate them?

I think by and large they are practical and they realize it's pretty good here. I don't think they feel stuck, but I don't think they think it's nirvana and the greatest place in the world they could ever work either. There's no motivation to go a lot deeper, and there's not motivation to run away. They are, "I'm going to come in and do my work. And sometimes I'll work very hard, and be very effective and very efficient, but I don't put a lot of energy into going above and beyond the work I have to do to get my job done."

With an Xer, I always say they look at the work that needs to be done in order to accomplish what they think needs to be done. They do that much and then they *Boomers are always* stop. A Boomer, or even a Millennial, will look at what needs to be *looking for more* done, accomplish that, and then say, "What else could we do and *opportunities to prove* what else could we accomplish?" That's what it seems like to me. *themselves worthy.*

You said you are getting the most bang for your buck from Millennials?

They are very effective. They go beyond just what we train them to do. We tell them, "This is what you need to do to sell something," and they come back with, "We did that, but we also did all these other things so we will sell more." They contribute a disproportionate amount of energy and work and results. If we say *Millennials are driven* we want to focus on a particular marketplace, they really get *to achieve.* around that and build a value proposition and present the next *Millennial teamwork.* level of work. It's always more than we ask them to do. Whatever we expose them to, they build something better. They do it together in a way that others don't.

So you aren't concerned about "kids these days?"

Not at all. That's the Boomers and the Xers. They think of themselves when they were twentysomething and they think the twentysomethings now are just like they *Millennial optimism* were. They don't understand the difference. There's good and bad *and confidence.* people in every generation, but my experience with Millennials is they just seem by and large more enthusiastic and more constructive. Maybe I just want to see that.

Maybe you got it right?

I think we understand them. I think we've been more effective with them. A lot of competitors and other people I know in business, they treat Millennials like they are the same as Baby Boomers. They think that's the way the Millennial twenty-somethings are, and it's so different.

Got any good stories?

What strikes me is when I get involved in something, and I have an expectation. For example, a team of Millennials will make a presentation to a potential client. I'm not really involved, but I'll sit in on the presentation. They take all the company material and they rework it and make it better and present it in a completely different better way. For example, we typically take a client a written proposal. And all of sudden I show up to the meeting, and the Millennial team has got all kinds of media presentations and they hand out iPads. Now they're carrying around iPads with the presentation instead of booklets. Nobody asked them and nobody put it together for them. They just did it on their own. It's so impressive. They will do things like that: take on projects without anyone asking. I've seen people working 25 years in the business, and Millennials pass them up.

Maya Enista Smith
CEO, Mobilize.org, Washington DC

Maya Enista Smith is a Millennial. At 28, she is a veteran in the public service sector where she began her career eight years ago. Mobilize.org works with Millennials who are creating and implementing solutions to social problems.

You have primarily Millennials working at Mobilize.org?

Currently our employees are all Millennials, but my board of directors is an intergenerational group of leaders. One of the unique aspects of our work—and one of the reasons we are as successful as we are—is that we try to foster intergenerational dialogue in communities across the country.

So what does the board of directors bring to the table?
How do the members help?

Guidance, advice, experience. My generation tends to believe that the challenges we are facing are being faced for the first time in history. As a young CEO, the challenges I face in fund raising, in staff development—it's just such an immense benefit for me to have this cadre of experienced leaders who I can go to for mentorship, for advice, and to hear about their experiences. There is very little I'm going through

Millennials listen to older people, partly because they listen to and respect their parents.

that they haven't already experienced. That's a great learning opportunity for me. And I think conversely that they also would say that they are learning from my leadership. So it's mutually beneficial intergenerational learning that's being used to strengthen the organization.

Do you need to do much intergenerational translation between the board and your staff?

I wouldn't say that's the case with my board of directors, but more broadly, that's definitely the case. I think if my performance were measured by the number of hours I sat behind a desk at my computer and worked, people might say, "Maya slacks off a lot." But this week alone I've been in New York, San Francisco, Miami, and DC. I am extremely productive at 36,000 feet. I get fits of productivity late at night, and sometimes I just want to take a nap in the middle of the day. I'm grateful that I have a board of directors that supports that. If anything, the directors have pushed me to have more work-life balance. More broadly, my generation is pushing for a redefinition of what work looks like, of what success looks like, of what productivity looks like—and it's not the traditional 9 to 5 structure where you go to the same place every day.

Millennials will work at all times of the day and night.

An important point.

Are you working too hard?

The board thinks I am. I think I'm lucky I have a board that takes the care and feeding of their CEO very literally.

Millennials were protected as they were growing up. Do we need to protect your generation from overworking themselves?

There have been a lot of times in the last seven years that I've worked until four in the morning, and then I've tried to tell other people they shouldn't. I wasn't aware of the powerful example I was setting for organizational culture. That's something I think Millennial CEOs often don't think about: how they are viewed by their teams. It took me a long time to learn I couldn't just say, "I want you to have work–life balance, and I want you to volunteer in the community, and I want you to get out and see the sunshine." I needed to model the type of work ethic I wanted to build. That was hard for me.

What about managing Millennials?

It's so much fun. I think I've learned a lot about how to recruit and retain top Millennial talent. I think particularly this flexible work environment is key. At Mobilize. org we have virtual Tuesdays, which means on Tuesdays you can work from a coffee shop, you can work in your pajamas, you can work from noon to midnight, you can work whatever hours you want to. The idea is we need to get life done: you can go to the doctor's office, you can go to the grocery store, you can go to the post office. Work isn't usually structured that way. So we try to carve out a full day where people have that type of flexibility.

Millennials put a lot of pressure on themselves—and juggling priorities adds stress. This policy recognizes and reduces the stress.

The flexible workplace is important. Honestly, that was hard for me because if I can't see you working, then how do I know that you're working? So I've learned to trust young people—I hate to say young people because I'm a young person myself—the team of people we have here at Mobilize.org. So the flexible work environment is key.

Second, have transparent discussions about decisions and leadership structure. There are definitely times I have to walk in and say, "I know you've been working hard, but I need this grant report done in the next twelve hours because I said so."

In a Millennial workplace there's very little of that "wielding power" authority compared to the traditional workplace. It's really a team, collaborative effort and everyone understands how their piece of the puzzle contributes to the larger success of the organization. Being transparent about that is really important.

Collaboration is important, but everyone understanding how they contribute to the success of the organization is vital to Millennial motivation.

As a team, we volunteer together about once a month. So we take time out of work to go to Miriam's Kitchen, or go and work with young people in the Chavez Schools here in DC. Those are great team-building opportunities. When I've told some older people that's a decision we've made as an organization, they're concerned about the lack of productivity on that day when we're not in the office. Right? Because none of those things I mentioned tie to the mission of Mobilize per se. But I think that the team building, the bonding, the excitement about the community, and the ability to give back in tangible ways, makes us all a lot better at our jobs. So those are all things that I've learned.

Volunteering resonates with Millennials—because of their civic nature and because of service requirements for college admission.

What's hard about working with Millennials?

What's hard about us is we expect instant information. We don't want to have to wait. And I have the same expectation when I send them something. You may be working on eight different things right now, but I just sent you this email so I expect a response. I think this idea that information is so accessible to this generation—we just work so quickly—is sometimes difficult to manage.

Impatience with response time is a recurring theme. Millennials grew up playing video games—where they got 86 pieces of feedback per minute.

I think that older generations may think that the turnover of young people in the workplace is a negative thing. People at Mobilize.org have a surprisingly long tenure. I've been here seven years. The senior team has been here two plus years and then we have some newer people. I think the opportunity to switch jobs and sector hop and have different experiences is actually beneficial to Millennials as workers—and needs to be celebrated instead of viewed as a loss of talent.

How should we train Millennials?

I think if we invested in the Millennial sector more holistically, we would reap benefits. For example, my younger brother works in finance in New York City. When he was hired, all the men and women who were starting at Bear Stearns, Prudential, and Goldman Sachs came together for a six-week workshop so that they would all learn the same things. They realized in the financial sector that it would benefit the sector—and the careers of these young professionals—if they all received the same training. But for some reason in the nonprofit sector, we've only just begun to think about the collective impact of what we might teach them together.

An idea that might appeal to Boomer executives.

We hear a lot about job hopping. Would a clearer corporate ladder and a map for career advancement help organizations hold onto Millennials?

I think you are on to something, but I think that Millennials would be resistant to that across-the-board structure. One of the things we do with each staff member is we create a leadership development plan. We say, "Okay, you're currently a program associate and you want to be chief executive officer. Let's talk about how you get there, what you need to do, and where we need to see you grow." Millennials prefer an individualized learning path, and it doesn't always work to say, "You need to be a program associate, then a program manager, then a program director, then a chief operating officer, then a CEO."

A best practice for motivating Millennials.

An important point for HR folks to keep in mind.

If you look at me, at 21 years old, I was given this crazy opportunity to become COO of an organization no one had ever heard of. And to people older than me, it was a joke that I got this title. Mobilize.org was only two people and a budget of $235,000. Hopefully, today they see me as more legitimate. We have a staff of ten people and a budget of millions of dollars. If I had had to wait my turn for all the different rungs, I probably would have gone somewhere else. But our founder, the first executive director, sat me down and said, "We see potential in you. Here's the position we would like to set you up for, and here's how you're going to get there." That certainly increased the odds of me staying and it helped me work toward a career path I was excited about. I think the special sauce is somewhere in the middle. You can't create a one-size-fits-all career ladder because our lives don't work like that anymore. But we do need the support to think ahead and see the potential evolution of our careers.

Millennials are goal and achievement oriented. They thrive on long-term planning.

Do older people outside the organization have any trouble with how young you are?

I would say in very few cases they have viewed my youth negatively. There have definitely been instances where I've felt tokenized—like, "Well, we need a young woman in the room so let's call Maya."—and they didn't expect me to participate. But I think in general, each generation—and especially Millennials and our technological savvy—are viewed as experts on a number of different issues and are brought in in authentic ways. We are having important conversations around our political process and what our communication tools look like. So there are actually very few

Millennials are adept at spotting token involvement.

rooms I'm in that don't have people that look like me. There's still a ways to go in this sector, but I think my age and experience are immense assets to me and something people value. Occasionally, people say something to me like, "What do you want to be when you grow up?" I get amused more than I get upset.

What about the multigeneration workplace?

I think we are getting to a place where, with a four-generation workforce, people respect one another's contributions. Do we really know how to tap into the talents of each of those generations? I think we have a long way to go. If you look at the Boomers, for example, and the contributions they can still make, we have a long way to go before we understand how to tap into that workforce, both the ones still working and those returning to the workforce. Same with Millennials. I think right now we are viewed as mostly valuable for setting up a *Facebook* page. There's a much deeper intergenerational partnership that can happen.

How will your generation reshape the workplace?

I'm sure you know the statistic: that my parents had an average of two jobs over their lifetimes and my generation is supposed to have 17. We're going to change the definition of what work looks like. Instead of having one profession, I think we're going to have a number of careers. I'm just coming up on ten years in my nonprofit career. I envision a world in which I have a career in philanthropy and then perhaps a career in the corporate world. Our trajectories look a lot bumpier but much more exciting than those of our parents.

This concept will become increasingly important as Millennials gain the majority in the workforce.

Moreover, I probably work the 18 hours that I'm awake every day. It's really not about work–life balance anymore; it's more about the idea of work–life integration.

We also have to look at the economic realities of what Millennials are making, our high unemployment rate, the high cost of college. I know very few college students anymore who just go to school. I actually know very few college students who only have one job. And so we're taking longer to get our degrees. We're working multiple jobs. We are being more entrepreneurial than previous generations. Part of that is because we want to be. And the other part is we have to be, because of the economic times we live in.

Lots of Millennials hold multiple jobs so they can pay off college debt.

You were involved in the Occupy Wall Street Movement. What do you think we can learn from that movement?

It showed us that decentralized leadership structures are extremely strong and can be very successful. If you look at social movements of the past, you can point to one person, a group of people, or an organization at the center of the movement. With *Occupy* I was in Zucotti Park, and I saw some of their decision-making structures. I learned that simple questions like, "Who do you take your orders from?" or "Who is telling you what to do?" are the wrong questions. In fact, those are the most infuriating questions to ask anyone at *Occupy*, because the answer is, "We figure it out together."

Millennial-style leadership.

Millennials prefer consensus decision-making.

That's a powerful method of building a social movement. I'm excited to see the long-term implications and how it continues to be utilized. We aren't far enough away from Occupy yet to really reflect on the lessons we learned there, but this decentralized leadership structure is going to be at the center of what we reflect on.

Can you imagine a time where instead of one CEO, there might be a team of CEOs?

I think about this all the time. I was talking to a fellow CEO, and we were talking about why we don't have partners, why it's not like a law firm. Because there are certain parts of this job that I'm really, really good at, and there are certain parts of this job that I'm not so good at. It would be amazing for me to be the person in charge of development, and then the other person is in charge of programming. But the current hierarchical organization structure has the CEO having multiple responsibilities across the board and being holistically responsible for the organization.

This came up because I got married last year. It was like the world's biggest fire drill because Maya was leaving for three weeks. But if this were a law firm, or if we had partners, or if there were someone to share the responsibility with me, then nobody would care. It would be, "Great, Maya. Have a good time. Come back nice and tan and married." But because we don't yet have that decentralized leadership structure in nonprofit, there's still that cog at the top.

Few organizations do.

We're beginning to see that change, but we need to be creative about how it changes. The *law firm partner* example is the one that came to mind, but I don't think it's the most functional structure. It's something we haven't envisioned yet, and I think it's impressive that Occupy started to envision it.

Do you have examples of generations working well together?

There are a ton of examples at nonprofits. But I would argue that the nonprofit world actually lags behind the corporate world in how generations work together. There's definitely still that hierarchical structure in the corporate world, but the corporate world is more based on merit, your ability to produce. Then it's really not about whether you are 28 or 58; it's about how you produce, how much money you make for the company, how much sweat equity you invest. Merit is a great equalizer, although it comes with its own stresses. In the nonprofit sector, we hear a lot of, "When you get to be my age," or "When you've been doing this as long as I have." But I'm like, "I'm doing it differently. I'm never going to go on the same career trajectory as you, and you need to see value in that."

Millennials aren't afraid to challenge the status quo if it's not working.

I actually think we have a lot of lessons to learn from corporations about leadership development—from the perspective of the career ladder trajectory—and the equalizing force of profit and the intrinsic motivations in the corporate world. Take my brother for example. Nobody knows how old he is. Nobody asks him on the phone what it's like to be a young person in the finance sector. It doesn't matter that he's a young person in the finance sector. The bigger deal we make about these generational differences, the more it actually supports our divisions.

Millennials believe in a level playing field and a certain equality. Will they implement meritocracy in organizations they lead?

One of our directors asked us to make a hoodie that says, "It's not an age. It's an attitude." A lot of the characteristics of a generation need to be seen in context. I still have my calendar printed for me by my assistant. I don't have it on my Blackberry because I like my calendar on paper. If you asked me to sync my Google calendar with my phone, I'd look at you like you had ten heads.

The assumptions people make about what I should know because of how old I am—and what you should know and how you should act because of how old you are—are actually detrimental. So we need to use these guideposts about generations as just that, just things we can learn from. They're not clear lines in the sand about what makes me different from you.

Any final advice?

I've seen the potential to burn out among Millennial leaders—because of the passion we bring to our work. An important lesson I'm trying to learn—and I hope other young people in my position learn—is that work is something we're going to be doing for the rest of our lives. Taking the time necessary to reflect, to learn, to read, to write, to think is so important, because we can get on autopilot. I think work requires us to be really present if our generation is going to succeed at solving the problems we are faced with.

Rich Thau
Owner and Principal, Presentation Testing, New York

Rich Thau is a Gen Xer. Presentation Testing specializes in *testing* the effectiveness of business *presentations* and improving those *presentations* through remote devices with a dial. Rich is also the founder of Third Millennium, a nonpartisan think tank for Gen Xers.

Some folks still think Generation Xers don't work hard. Are Xers slackers?

It's typical of all of us, but especially of Gen Xers, to resist generalizations.

I'm 47. I'm at the leading edge of the Xers. I think it's hard to generalize about people's work habits. I know some people in their thirties and forties—Xers—who work phenomenally hard. And I know others who don't. I can't say that, as an overall generational trait, one generation works harder than another. I think one individual works harder than another.

Do you have kids?

I have a son who is almost eight.

We've heard that Xer fathers spend a lot of time with their kids. Does that affect their career path?

I wouldn't overgeneralize about that. I think there are plenty of Xer dads who work really, really hard. Others aren't working as hard because they want to spend more time with their kids.

Has it affected your work or career?

My wife and I only have one child, and that was a very deliberate decision, driven more by me than my wife. I was unwilling to give up a lot of work opportunities because of children. So I think your question is better put to someone who has two or three or four kids than to someone like me who very deliberately wanted to throw himself into his career. We have a child, but luckily we have a child who is pretty independent minded, who is social, and who is good at fending for himself and keeping himself occupied. And when we are together as a family, he is engaged as a family member. I think people with more kids struggle more with that conflict than I do personally.

A quality an Xer would want to pass along.

Tell me more about your work.
My company does market research. We do message testing and message refinement work. Most of our clients are trade associations in Washington, DC, and we help them with their public policy messaging.

What's the generational mix?
Ours is a small company. I'm 47. A woman who has been with me since she graduated from college is 36. She is a mid-Xer. And then I've got two Millennials working for me who are both 25.

How are the Millennials?
They're great. They are very thoughtful about stuff. I think they are appreciative they have jobs, when a lot of their friends don't—or don't have jobs they're very happy with. I think they appreciate that with me, they are getting some really good experience.

They want to make a difference?
I don't know. I would say the work has meaning. I wouldn't say it's necessarily socially redeeming, making a difference in the sense of giving back to your community. It's more intellectually stimulating. They are on the cutting edge of public opinion. They get to meet interesting people. They get to travel. And they are decently compensated, especially given their age. On balance, compared to what a lot of people in their twenties are doing, it's a good gig. They are loyal to me and dedicated. But then again, it's two people. I can't generalize about a whole generation.

Very important to Millennials.

How has your career progressed? Have you jumped around a lot like most Xers?
My career has had three stages so far. And they are not wildly out of sync with each other, but they are not completely in sync. My first job out of college was checking information on job applications to be sure it was accurate—so it was a

research job—and writing reports about what I found. I followed that with two jobs working in magazine publishing in the business trade magazine publishing world. I did that for about three and a half years. That was still research oriented. I wrote tons and tons of articles. And then I went into Third Millennium, in the nonprofit sector, from 1993 to 2001. I've been running Presentation Testing since 2001. So I'm back in the research realm again, but now I'm conducting my own empirical focus group-type research as opposed to picking up the phone and calling folks and asking them for information.

You are the founder?

Yes, I own it.

What got you started? What sparked your entrepreneurial instincts?

I had a seminal moment. I can tell you exactly what happened the day it occurred. It was June 4, 1993. I had been working for a magazine for three and half years, and the owner of the magazine had declared, three months earlier, when he had bought the magazine from a different owner, that he was going to keep it going for four years. That was in November 1992. In June of 1993, he got up from his desk on a Friday afternoon at four o'clock. He pulled the staff together and said, "This is your last day at work. You're done. The magazine is not making enough money for me to keep it going."

Xers tend to remember where they got their first layoff notice—and some of them use that moment as a catalyst to reshape their careers and lives.

Xers have a strong survival instinct.

And I had an epiphany. I was 28 years old at the time, and my epiphany was, "No one is going to look out for my best interest as well as I'm going to." And that's what launched me on my career of working for myself. It was a decision I've never regretted. I have no desire to work for anyone else. As my dad likes to say, "You have the meanest boss in the world when you work for yourself." If you're a person who is ambitious, that's absolutely true. If you're not ambitious, I would say it's less true. For someone like me, I definitely work harder and put more pressure on myself than I ever put on myself when I was working for someone else.

There's no such thing as going on vacation and not thinking about work, for example. When I went on vacation and worked for someone else, I really didn't think about work. So for the last 19 years, I've been pretty entrepreneurial and running my own operations. Third Millennium was a nonprofit, so there was a board of directors, and I was beholden to them. So it wasn't just me. But running Presentation Testing, it's definitely me in charge, not reporting to anyone.

Do you have any advice for managers about how to motivate Xers?

I'm not sure there is a secret to managing Gen Xers as opposed to managing Boomers. I would say as a general rule you want to give people flexibility. Work–life balance seems important. You want to give employees flexible hours and flexibility around where they work. That's how I work, and that's how I manage my staff. I really don't care if you are doing the job at 11 o'clock at night or doing it at 4 o'clock in the morning. As long as you are able to function when I need you, and so you don't burn yourself out.

Flexibility is specially important to Gen Xers and Millennials.

There's this Millennial guy I've got working for me. He's 25. He cranked out some report for me. He was up at all hours doing it. I said to him, "Look, it's great that you're so dedicated, and I appreciate it enormously. But because you worked so many hours to get this done and you didn't really pace yourself the way I would have liked, I am afraid you're going to get burned out. So next time ask me, 'How much time do I have to do this?' and I can call in extra help or get somebody else on the staff to help you as opposed to having you put enormous pressure on yourself to get it done." He is extremely dedicated, and I am grateful to him for his dedication. I think it worked fine.

Millennials' self-imposed pressure.

The thing I didn't want to do was discourage him from being enthusiastic, and I don't think I did. I approached it as well as I think I could have. That happened a couple of months ago, and he's still been incredibly enthusiastic. He'd been unemployed for quite a while before he got this job, and he wants to demonstrate his enthusiasm for what we are doing. Plus he really likes what he's doing.

In regard to your question about managing Xers in the workplace, it's about showing them respect, making sure you give them feedback, making sure you are constantly aware of the quality of life you are providing them. Try to give them some measure of job security. I think those are the keys to keeping people happy. If people start thinking they aren't being listened to, they start to resent the people who are making the decisions. I think that's true of all generations, not just Xers.

This is a dilemma for Gen Xers. Do they want job security so they can stop job hopping or do they want to continue job hopping and enjoy the variety?

As children, Millennials were protected, and it sounds like you help protect them from burnout.

That's interesting. I hadn't thought about it that way. I haven't seen that with my two staffers in that generation—that they crave protection. There are other things that are a lot more important to them. I think the protection side of it—and maybe I'm stretching the definition here—is that workers protect themselves when they

Here we see a combination of Xer pragmatism and the high values they place on good work over office politics.

continually show their value to the enterprise. And someone who has a job and doesn't show that they are valuable is putting their job at risk.

I've had a number of people work for me on a freelance basis over the last several years. My Millennials have heard me go on a couple of tirades about poor work quality and insufficient preparedness. They know I won't tolerate bad work. If they want to protect themselves in their jobs—and I'm not saying this in a threatening way, this is just an observation—the best way to protect themselves is to do great work and show their value continuously.

Can you clarify what you mean by great work?

I think they are pretty clear about what I want and don't want—things that are sloppily put together, things that aren't in the mold of how I would have done it. They aren't going to know exactly what I want, but some people have a better intuitive sense. The two I have now have a much better sense of it than a bunch of the others—and they weren't all Millennials. There were Xers, plenty of them. They were not producing for me the way I wanted it produced. I'm amazed by what passes for acceptable work product these days, as a general proposition. And I really don't know how some companies stay in business producing what they produce.

Do you think of yourself as demanding?

More and more Gen X managers are calling themselves "demanding." When managing Millennials, it's okay to hold them to high standards—in fact, it's good policy—but Gen X managers need to be careful that "demanding" doesn't become "dogmatic."

Gen Xers' search for the new, the edgy, the thing that sets their work apart. It's not a phase they're going through; it's a lifelong pursuit.

Yeah, I'm pretty demanding because I operate under the presumption that from my clients' perspectives, I'm only as good as my last project. I'm not going to stay in business if I produce mediocre work. My clients are extremely demanding. They aren't demanding in a nasty sense. They are demanding in an intellectual sense. And for what they pay for the work we do, they expect to learn something they didn't know before. That puts a lot of pressure, especially when you're doing projects very similar to what you've done in the past. Sometimes I wonder how I'm going to find out something that's new. I share that stress with my staff, and they know it's important that they do good work. And they will also get the point if they don't produce good work. They know it themselves if there's an issue with the quality of what they produce. If there are instances where there have been issues, they know when I'm upset about it.

Sounds like you like the challenge?

Yeah, I do. It's fascinating work and I enjoy it. But it's pressure filled. I'm dealing with people at a very senior level in organizations. They don't expect poor quality from their vendors, so if I want to stay in their good graces, I have to produce good stuff to make them look good.

Do you like managing projects or people?

Here's something I'll tell you. I don't enjoy managing people. I really don't. And one reason why I haven't grown the company to some huge size is that I haven't aspired to manage a lot of people. I don't enjoy managing. I like my staff. I like the people I work with enormously. But the act of managing I find onerous, because the more people you bring on, the more headaches you have. The more personal problems people have that they bring to work,

Many Xers find managing people a chore they're not well suited for. Find an Xer who is an exception—one who likes managing people—and she or he will go far.

the more you have to spend time dealing with their personal issues as opposed to dealing with work. And I just don't enjoy it. So I hire people who are self-starters, who can take care of themselves. People who basically come to me and say "give me my directions and let me march, and then if I get to a problem, I'll call you. But otherwise leave me alone, and I'll get the work done." So they act as almost quasi-autonomous contractors more than they do employees, though they are paid as employees. We run a semivirtual organization. Whether that's a generational trait on my part, I don't know.

It is.

But don't expect me to hold meetings for meetings' sake, to hear the sound of my own voice and do all kinds of things to build a lot of team spirit. I've done some of that, but it's really rare. They

Such meetings are anathema to the Gen X psyche.

build the team among themselves more than I do. The other thing to keep in mind is that only one of the people lives anywhere near the office. The office is in Manhattan. The other Xer is in Manhattan and the two Millennials are in New Jersey. I don't even make them come into the office unless I need to see them for some reason and I know I'm going to be there. I can go weeks literally without seeing my employees. I'll talk to them on the phone most days, but not all. I'll email them almost every day. But they're operating in a quasi-virtual organization, where I'll talk to them when I need them.

Self-directed Millennials can be rare. Did you get lucky?

I might have. There's not a lot of conflict going on. When things are good, I give them bonuses. Last year we got to do a project in Hawaii, so two staff people got to go to Hawaii. I gave them five days paid vacation and a bonus to enjoy themselves in Hawaii because that was a profitable project, and they did good work. The two of them traveled around together for five days. I wasn't there. I didn't meet them in Hawaii until their trip was over. It was great. They had a wonderful time.

Millennials thrive on positive feedback, and this reward is packed with positive feedback.

If you come to work for me, with all my warts, and you're happy—good. And if you're not, you're not. The Xer has been with me since she was 21 or 22—she was still in college when she came to work for me. We've been together for 15 years, and she's never had another boss. So I must be doing something right.

One Millennial, a woman who now works for me and who started as a summer intern, did a great job her junior and senior year. When she graduated from college, I hired her full time. I've had a lot of interns over the years and a lot of freelancers, and a lot of them have failed to impress me. If that's the case then it's, "Thanks very much, but you're done."

Have you thought about growing your business and finding someone to manage the people?

Have I thought about it? Sure. I don't think I necessarily want to do that. Our company is sort of a boutique type of shop. The clients expect me to work with them directly. And for me to grow the company would probably mean merging with another company like mine rather than growing organically. I'm not sure I'm going to find other staff people who could have relationships with clients like I have. It's a hard organization to grow.

The two other Millennials are more like associates to me. The Xer runs the company day in and day out. She answers the phone, does the mail and does a lot of the technological stuff we do. She is invaluable to me and is compensated accordingly. But I'm not sure whether bringing another person in to grow the company that way is the growth strategy I would implement.

CHAPTER 10

From the Trenches

For this set of interviews, we talked with people representing all the generations in the workplace. They live and work in cities and towns across the United States. They work in large and small companies, city and federal government, universities and hospitals. They are realtors, marketing directors, doctors, project managers, and electricians. We visited with them and discussed their jobs, their colleagues, their organizations, their bosses, their families, and the quality of their lives. We've changed their first names; other than that, these are almost verbatim transcripts of their interviews. As you read, look for ways that each is typical and atypical of his or her generation—and, more importantly, for insight and empathy into each of their situations.

Jennifer
Contract Professional, St. Paul, Minnesota
Millennial Generation

Jennifer works for the federal government. Her energy and enthusiasm have been undiminished by economic conditions.

So tell me about your job.
I love my job. I love what I do, which makes it really fun. Our agency is monstrous and I get to travel a lot. I'm making friends in regions all over the country. If I have to move, I'll know somebody. I'll have someone who says "Yeah, we want her in our region." There's always something new because we deal with regulations, and they are always changing. It's definitely an interesting place to be.

Having friends at work is vital to Millennials.

Millennials are motivated by having a wide variety of work tasks and experiences.

Are there many Millennials?

In my department, it might be close to 50/50. They hired a bunch of us as trainees, and most of us are within a couple of years of each other. There's no one on our team who has been with the agency for more than five years or in the workforce for more than seven. We're a young team, including our team leader.

Government workers are going through a series of buyouts in which older workers are offered incentives to retire early.

Our technical team has one supervisor—he just got married—I want to say he's 27. The head of the technical engineers—he's my mentor—he's maybe 35. The other management team has two guys who, if we do our buyout, could go anytime. All the rest are Millennials.

Tell me about your mentor.

He's unique. We're really good friends now. We talk about everything. In the beginning we talked about, "What do you think about the agency?

The line between work and personal is blurring as more Millennials join the workforce.

How long have you been here? What's your experience?" But now we talk about his wife, his kids, career advancement, everything. It's wonderful having him as my mentor.

What's he doing right?

Part of it was organic; we just have good rapport. We value a lot of the same things. I think that helps. As far as what's kept us going, he's very,

Millennials value good communication.

very good at communicating. He's always asking questions. He loves to know everything that's going on, and so do I. We have different backgrounds so we can pick each other's brains. We are always chatting.

So in a federal agency there must be some older employees?

Some of them on our team are absolutely wonderful, and they've taken it in stride that a bunch of us came in fresh out of school with very little work experience. They aren't bitter that there are so many of us. They also haven't checked out yet. My best friend in the world is an engineer—who was military before—so I think he has 36 years of government experience. He's one of the best people in the whole office. We all adore him. He's quirky. The older workers—those who have been in government longer—roll with the punches better than the younger ones do.

We've been hearing about older employees, and especially mentors, who lecture young employees at length. Have you seen much of that?

Millennials seem to trust elders more than the two previous generations did at the same age.

I suppose there's a few. But there is also some value there. They've been in the workforce longer, and they know so much. To me, I

can put up with a lecture because there is going to be some gold- *Millennial optimism.*
en information somewhere in the monologue.

A lot of older workers are approaching retirement. Are you worried about losing them?

A little bit. There is so much to learn. Sometimes your head hurts at the end of the day because there are all these regulations and all these things to know. Regulations, you know, change all the time. But there are some base philosophies that don't change. Some of the people—the veterans, I'll call them—of our workforce know those basics and they know the fine details. They are such great resources for information. I fear losing their expertise.

On our team, there is a big difference between those who are ready to retire and those of us who are new. The veterans, they have seen everything. They know the regulations like the back of their hands. The younger generation understands that knowing the regulations is important because we don't want to go to jail. But we need to partner and we need to collaborate and we need to find new ways to do things. I think having those two groups, those two schools of thought, together is beneficial for everybody.

Three keys to motivating Millennials: partnering, collaborating, finding new processes.

Millennials learned in school that diverse perspectives make for better decisions.

Are you getting enough feedback?

Yes, because we have to do these strange things called IDPs, individual development plans. You have to present them to your supervisor every time you have a panel. In your first year, you have to give four panels and write a lengthy paper on everything you've done that quarter. When you give your presentations to your supervisor and your service center director, they critique you. They say, "We see these great things, and we are concerned about this . . . " They tell you their concerns and they tell you what you're doing great. That's a formal thing all of us have to go through, and we also have our annual reviews. I've found that reviews are actually—and I was very surprised—quite beneficial. The feedback has been honest. If they like you, they tell you they really like what you are doing. And then they will work on the fine details of, for example, making you a good public speaker or a finely tuned contracting officer. Even if you are doing really well, they still try to find something you can take away from the conversation. I was rather surprised.

On surveys, Millennials tell us they want constant feedback

Are you saying you enjoy performance appraisals?

Mine are great. I love them. The one I had last November was right after my last panel of the first year. I had just gotten promoted, and I had been working with this lady, the head of our service center. We were working late because I was in Chicago for training, so she said, "We aren't going to get this done any other time, so

Work–life integration. let's do it right now," and we had the performance appraisal over dinner. It was superb. We had dinner, and she just said, "I think you're doing great. This is what I think will be beneficial for you. You already do these things. Focus on these other things because these are what people will be watching for." She actually retired the next month, which broke my heart, but we still talk several times a month. She is amazing. I'm really impressed, I must say, about how we do our performance reviews.

Do you run into much cynicism?

Yes, there are the curmudgeons, the ones who make our lives difficult. It's like they are bitter about everything—from any miniscule change to "our new leadership isn't going to do anything. It takes so long for change to trickle down from the top,

Cynicism is a turn off for Millennials. blah, blah, blah." I notice it comes in different forms. It comes in the exasperated kind of sarcastic form—they are kind of joking, half joking, not joking. With others you hear, "It's not going to happen. You young leaders, you don't know anything." There are only a few of them, but they make themselves heard.

Anything you've noticed about working with other Millennials?

Our agency is progressive. Our director and deputy director are obsessed with making sure we are the best of the best in the whole agency. They want us to be

They're tapping into Millennials' desire to be best.

Millennials appreciate opportunities for training and development. known for having the highest results. So they told us when we were new, "You guys are going to do a public speaking program. Every month you are going to give a presentation to the entire service center, and we are going to work on your public speaking skills. In the meantime, you are going to collaborate and find topics and work together to improve each others' skills and come up with a rating system to encourage constructive feedback to each other."

Another thing our agency has done is pair us together and make sure we get to know each other. The agency had an event in DC for new employees. They gave us an in-depth history of the organization for five days. Then they made sure

Millennials find value in mixing it up with their own cohort. we networked. They really stressed networking and knowing people in all the business lines in the different divisions. They do a good job with that. It's especially important in the regional service center because it's hard to get to know people in other regions. I have friends in every single region now. I think that's because when I got to go to DC two months ago, I saw everybody and saw what was going on. I think if a person is not pretty extroverted, they might not have quite the same answer as I do. We also get to telework. Right now we are at two days a week, and I work long days. It is superb.

Other observations about Millennials?

I've noticed a lot of us who are 35 and younger, from colleagues to friends, are planning on not having children. I have no clue where it's coming from. Even my best friend who has been married for three years tells me, "Oh, I'm never having kids." As far as I can tell it's across the board. We've spent so much on school, and now we are supposed to offer our knowledge to the world. *Generational destiny.* That's why we went to school. Why have kids? It takes away from our careers.

A lot of organizations are worried about the level of technology they will need to retain Millennial workers.

Our agency is super big into that. We've got Google mail, and we are on the cloud. Then they built this thing called Symposium. It's essentially an in-house Twitter/Facebook hybrid for professionals. There are different groups and different topics. One of the groups I'm in is contracting professionals. I can go on in the morning and read posts and learn about classes and webinars. Half of the agency has iPads and iPhones. They are getting rid of Blackberries or upgrading them. Everything is connected. They've been trying as hard as they can to adopt new technology and make it work for the agency. It's cool because it's given the younger generation, who are much more fluent in that stuff, the ability to *Reverse mentoring;* work with the older generation. It makes the two groups talk to *an idea whose time* each other, and it makes them work through things together. I *has come.* think it's been helping with communication.

Are there enough teams and collaboration?

We have a lot of teams. Not just your regular day-to-day work teams, but I'm on a team that works on our strategic vision. We are trying to create logical measures to go with the goals we are trying to achieve under the vision. So a team I'm on is called "Creating a High-Performing Workforce." It's a national team. There are all kinds of teams: commissioners of different parts of the agency, directors, *Give Millennials work* and those of us who are young leaders. We're working together to *that makes* define and establish measures so we can create a high performing *a difference.* workforce.

We're also on regional teams. When we released Google and when we released Symposium, some of us were early adopters. I was an early adopter, and then I got to become a Subject Matter Expert. Your job is to be a *A reward that* *motivates.*

representative and help anybody out with any related topic. It's cool. It gets people working together and talking to each other.

John
IT Manager, Detroit, Michigan
Generation X

John has worked for a series of Fortune 500 companies and currently works in health care. Married, with a daughter, he is trying to balance devotion to his family with the desire to move up in an organization where his skills are valued.

So tell me about what you've done for a living.
I started my career as a consultant with a large IT consulting firm. From there I went to a large auto finance company. Then a couple of years ago, I went to a health insurance company.

Three career bounces.
That's pretty indicative of my generation, even though we didn't imagine any bounces. I went to college, graduated in '83, and thought I was going to be a lawyer. But I figured out that was going to be way too much reading. I'm not a fast reader. Then I thought I would be a Poli Sci major and follow in my Dad's political footsteps, but then I decided that wasn't going to make enough money. So I went to business school—thought I would be a Wall Street type—went into finance, wound up in marketing, and somehow landed a job in IT consulting after all of that.

A lot of Xers were drawn into IT, even though it wasn't the career they had planned on—because the money and jobs were there.

The consulting company operated on a partnership model—up or out. You were expected to move from being a computer programmer to a manager of large projects to somebody who sells a lot and brings in money for the firm. So I did that for 11 years. I was fortunate to not have to travel much, which is atypical for the consulting world.

But I got an out-of-town assignment when my daughter was about one or two. That's when I decided that wasn't the life for me. I didn't want to miss my daughter growing up. It was more important for me to be around my family than it was to earn the big bucks and be on the partnership trail.

Gen X fathers don't want to miss out on their kids' childhood years. They will mommy-track themselves rather than let that happen.

Children and family have caused Gen Xers to contemplate what really matters.

We see a lot of Xer fathers making that choice.

Yes, I found that with a lot of people. They've even started to change the policies of the company around that. When I started, the official stance from the firm was, "the client comes first." Even before your own family, it was the client. When people traveled, they left on Sunday and came back Friday night, because you had to be there all five days of the week for the client. By the time I left, they had changed the company policy to flying out on Monday mornings and coming back on Thursday nights and working from home on Friday. So I think the company realized that the values of the workers were changing. But when I got married in 1992 and told my manager I was going to take a two-week honeymoon, he actually made me go get the client's approval. That really was not in line with my personal values.

Workaholic managers?

I definitely saw that kind of work ethic. But that was before email and the Internet and being able to really take your work home with you. It's funny; that story I just told you came up at work yesterday. Now I'm on the client side, and I actually have a team working for me from my former consulting company, and there's a guy who is planning his wedding. I found out yesterday he's planning on taking four weeks off. I relayed this story to other people and I said, "I've got to talk to the partner about this, because back in the day when I worked there, two weeks was asking a lot. That four weeks is going to impact my project. I need to make it the partner's problem and not mine as the client." Yeah, things have changed.

Do you think the tension between Boomers and Xers has lessened?

I think the tension has reduced. There's awareness that having better work–life balance is desirable. Boomers understand there needs to be more balance — although they have a harder time actually following through on it. But at least there is more understanding toward people who want balance.

With my second job, I wound up in the same workaholic lifestyle. Part of that might have been that it was financial services, and I was working for a Boomer boss. Now we're in the era of Blackberries and emails and being able to access all your work remotely. I used to take my one relaxing vacation of the year at a place up in northern Michigan that didn't even get cell phone reception. As soon as there was reception and I could get Internet up there, my family would be down on the beach, and my boss would be expecting me to deliver new versions of PowerPoint presentations to her. I had my daughter coming up from the beach asking, "When are you going to come play with us?" And my wife was saying, "I thought we were on vacation."

New technology, same old conflicts. Gen Xers struggle to separate these two aspects of their lives, sometimes unsuccessfully.

So there still are those conflicts and expectations, but I think companies over-all do realize that you need to be able to get away and you need to be able to separate work and family life. But the appeal of being able to contact people at all times is still there. And I think the expectations are made a little worse by technology, but I think people try to combine work and vacation at the same time to rationalize that they aren't working but they are still connected.

Since the economic collapse, have you seen Boomers retiring?

I haven't seen it. I've seen people who have retired but have decided they're bored and they are picking up their jobs again or looking for less demanding jobs in their field.

What's the work culture like where you are now?

It's completely different. They're a health insurer—a nonprofit with a social mission of being the insurer of last resort. It is the polar opposite in terms of work culture: very much more focused on people.

How have your interactions with Millennial colleagues gone?

I don't know if this is typical of their generation, but I just had a meeting with one of them. She's overdue in getting her objectives for the year. The whole company is behind on that this year. In my career, doing yearly objectives has been a mandatory administrative task. But she is very persistent in making sure she has specific objectives written down for the year. She's in an atypical position where she reports to one person day to day but to another person administratively. And she wants to know how all of that is going to work out and who is going to rate her performance. She wants to know what's expected of her, what her next steps are. I should have just told her, "Don't worry, you'll get a trophy for participation anyway." (He laughs.) Of course, I try to be sensitive to her concerns and let her know I understand that the situation is not optimal and that we owe her this type of clarity. But the real answer is you have to go with the flow and figure it out as you go along. Every time I thought I had given her enough information and ended the conversation, she wanted to know about another aspect. What about this and what about that? She was a little confused on how this all works. The more I rethink that conversation, the more it sounds exactly like the typical Millennial. The real world is not so structured, and you can't plan it all out—you have to adjust on the fly. I have had limited interactions with Millennials, but I can see they need their objectives.

Gen Xers don't like having these procedures foisted on them, especially if it seems like extra work that produces nothing.

Millennials typically need clear processes and even clearer feedback or they feel lost.

This is an Xer anthem, anathema to Millennials.

Their entire lives have been about setting and accomplishing goals.

Have you experienced their optimism?

I would definitely say they are optimistic. I chalk some of that up to just being new; it's their first job so they are excited about it. Our internship program is comprised of local college kids who can potentially continue to work even when school starts up again and eventually wind up getting hired. This one guy won "Intern of the Year" and he came back and has this full time job, and he's starting up these community-based things. So when there is diversity month, or whatever, he organizes lunch events where everybody brings a dish from their background. Nice touchy-feely stuff like that which has nothing to do with work if you ask me, but it's important to them. Yes, optimism and enthusiasm. I see it in those who are just entering the workforce now. Maybe they are just happy they found a job at all.

It's probably not a phase. We call it resilient optimism.

Gen X pragmatism can frustrate Millennials' desire to serve the community in a variety of ways.

So what are the strengths of Generation X?

In my case, it may be the ability to go with the flow and adapt to changes that are thrown my way. I found a solution to staying in the consulting company without traveling. I found a division that took me off the partner track but kept me working with clients. We had won the contract to become the IT department for a major chemical company. That was right near my home and that was great. I got to spend a lot more time with the family. But then I got bored, and I couldn't handle not moving up the ladder. I had plateaued at age 30. I didn't see a way to advance to higher levels, so that wasn't acceptable either.

Gen Xers = Survivors

A recruiter actually found me somehow and, at first, I put him off. I finally agreed to one interview, and it ended up turning into multiple interviews. I got offered the job on the same day. I had never thought about leaving. But it was an opportunity to start an IT department from scratch. So that appealed to me as a challenge. I moved there, built that up and stuck with it. I did 12 years there. At the 11- or 12-year mark I get bored with the place and the same old politics, and I start looking for new challenges.

Starting from scratch motivates Gen Xers, appealing to their DIY mentality—and when you start from scratch, there are hardly any rules.

For me, it's always about looking for new challenges, a way to make a difference. I want to help find ways to actually do things that contribute to the success of the company in a real way. I'm looking for areas to transform things, and have had positions that get us into new market segments. My IT career has been on the intersection of business and IT. When it's on the technical side, I'm more like a consultant—someone who understands the business and IT. That's been my strength, to be able to understand and think like a businessperson and then understand how technology can help achieve business goals.

My position now involves transforming the culture and improving their processes. So I've got another challenge. I'm always looking for a challenge, to do
something that's different and cutting-edge while changing the
culture and improving the overall organization performance.

Gen Xers are
risk takers.

How do you handle office politics?

My father is in politics. I've always been around it. I understand it. I'm pretty good
at knowing what people value and adapting messages based on other people's
values. So I guess you would call that politics. I'm good at building relationships
and alliances. There are people for whom the world is just black
and white, and they don't understand those nuances and why it
matters. I've seen a lot people who have had their careers derailed
because everything is just black and white logic to them and they
don't understand that sometimes the right answer isn't always the
best answer to get things done.

Gen Xers who are
comfortable with
organizational politics
have an advantage
over many of their
peers.

Xer pragmatism.

Have those skills helped you advance?

I was just having a conversation with a former coworker the other day. Called me
out of the blue. We were talking about some of our former coworkers and shaking
our heads about how some of them moved up. We were talking about me taking
my daughter around to college campus visits and wondering if the school you get
into really matters in the end. We were remembering working with some of these
people who went on to phenomenal careers. They wouldn't do anything. All they
did was network. They networked their way to better and better positions, and
you sort of scratch your head because at work we hated them because they
never did their own work.

So networking is definitely a skill and it's definitely a way to the
top, and definitely I've seen a lot of those success stories. I don't
know if that's a generational thing or not, but the people I'm thinking of are my age or a couple of years older, which puts them in
the back half of the Baby Boomers.

Boomers are
notoriously good
networkers. Gen Xers
are suspicious of
networking although
they're pragmatic
enough to recognize
its effectiveness.

Caroline
Literary Agent, New York, New York
Traditionalist Generation

Caroline, still working at 72, is a hard-nosed pragmatist who never met
a hard day's work she didn't like.

Tell me about your career.

I started out in the travel business and then switched to catering: planning parties and events and so forth. That got too physical. So about 20 years ago, I decided to become a literary agent. My father was an editor at the *New York Times* book review. We grew up knowing books from an early age, so I come by it naturally.

If you were counting, that was three professions. One of our Millennial interviewees estimates she will have 17.

So do you want to work or do you need to work?

Both. I can't imagine being retired. I don't know what people who are retired do. Fifty years ago, women who were retired served on boards and committees, and they went out to lunch. Doesn't sound very exciting, does it?

Even among older workers, there's a sense that work will be a continuing force in their lives. The "traditional" view of retirement doesn't always sit well, even with Traditionalists.

You've watched a lot of people join the workforce?

Yes, but it's difficult now. My own daughter's got an MBA, and she's having a hell of a hard time getting jobs. I don't know what's happening to the workforce except that it's shrinking. I don't know what's going to happen. I don't know if anyone does. It's scary.

Do you work with a lot of younger people?

With authors, yes, I work with authors of all ages. I pretty much do nonfiction. I work on a lot of medical books. I've worked with acupuncturists and worked on a Vitamin A book—those authors are all 50 and older. The young don't write books like that, or if they do I don't know about it.

How about workers just entering the workforce. Have you noticed any differences?

I've had young people come and help out and do filing and answering the phone on a temporary basis, but that really isn't much of a recommendation for careers. I don't know how young people start a career these days, I really don't.

Having a career, rather than a job, is important to Traditionalists.

So you think they have a good work ethic?

They aren't as good as we used to be years ago. We were hired to do a job, and we did it, and we got on with it Of course we didn't have a lot of electronic devices to distract us. I remember sending a letter to the West coast and waiting ten days for a reply, which was wonderful. You had time to think about it. Now everything is instantaneous. Kids in the workforce are constantly on the computer and sending email and who knows what else. Some of that is not really productive.

Traditionalists have a no-nonsense work ethic.

Traditionalists came of age in a workplace where productivity defined work culture and being productive was the same as being virtuous.

Talk about what it means to "have time to think about it."

I think multitasking is probably leading to Alzheimers. Nobody is focusing on anything for more than ten seconds at a time. It's a terrible way to run

That would make an interesting study.

a world, it really is. I don't know if anyone sits down to reflect and
think about life and what's going on and where they are going. It's
all act and react. But young people have to get through college, and I don't know
how they do that. They surely have to focus then.

What's a good way to motivate your generation?

I think you can call on what we already know. A lot of people I

Loyalty remains a strong part of the Traditionalist psyche. It still rankles them that employee loyalty is not reciprocated.

know are thinking about or starting to go back to work. We are
expected to give loyalty to employers—not that employers give it
back anymore. It used to be you could have one job and stick with
it forever; IBM comes to mind. It's no longer true, and hasn't been
true for a long time.

Think job security and loyalty will ever come back?

I don't know. It would be nice to know that if you give your life to some company that
the company would give back to you. I hope we can find organizations that will sup-

Traditionalists value their own skills and expect companies to value them, too.

port loyalty, because if you have someone for 15 or 20 years, why
not keep that person as long as he or she is not absolutely hope-
less. Use those skills that they have built up over the years.

Are older workers flexible?

I have to remain flexible. I don't know about other people. I work for myself and I
do what I want to. If we are not flexible, if we get into a rut, it's not going to get us
anywhere. We have to move and be flexible and take on jobs we might not think
we can do. For example, I decided to take on a new category. I used to do fiction
but then it didn't sell very well. So I switched over to nonfiction, but I have to do
various avenues of nonfiction because that's where my business is.

Do you have friends still working?

Yes, and they enjoy it. Most of them say, "We cannot imagine get-

Traditionalists were a part of world-changing events. "Inconsequential" things are negative to them.

ting up in the morning and filling our days with whatever inconsequential thing you can come up with." That's what I think it is to be
retired. I have several friends with lots and lots of money who are
retired and they're bored stiff. There probably aren't enough other
people their age to play with.

How can companies hold onto older workers?

Well, they could pay them decently. They could make life more pleasant for them. I have one strange idea. All these companies have executives who must travel a great deal and have their airfare and accommodations paid for. And they get to keep the perks. They get to keep the air miles. They get to keep the hotel points. It seems to me those air miles should go back to the company and be distributed to all the workers who don't get to travel on business. How does that grab you? I've thought that for years. These executives are getting to stay in fancy hotels and entertain on the company's budget, and they also get the perks connected with that. The workers, the drones, don't get any of it. It's all paid for by the company, so why shouldn't everyone share the wealth? It would be a nice reward. You work someplace for 50 years, and as a reward, you're going to get a month off and a free trip someplace. Wouldn't that be fun?

Traditionalists are motivated by visible perks.

This is a generation that survived the Depression and has a "we're all in this together" mentality.

Do you know people who've been laid off?

Companies are shutting down whole divisions. I've got several friends, including a couple of women in their forties, who have been working at a place 10 to 15 years and all of sudden their divisions are closed, and they are looking for work. I don't know what they are going to do with the division. I suppose they will reorganize and call it something else. That's a way of getting rid of people. Companies get rid of people who have been with them for 20 or 30 years because they can hire younger people for less salary—but then they are not trained so it doesn't really benefit the company.

Being a trained worker was a ticket to the middle class when they entered the workforce. We now stress experience, but Traditionalists put a high value on training.

I think they lose money on that.

But they do it anyway, don't they, all the time?

Yes, but that's short-term thinking.

See. There you are, short-term thinking versus long-term thinking. They really should look down the road. You know you get someone at 50, and they can work until they are 70 or 75 if there's no mandatory retirement age. Use them well and treat them well.

What are keys to long-term thinking? Why is your generation so good at it?

With our generation, we were trying to formulate a life plan—whether we were doctors or lawyers or business people. And we expected to stay in our chosen career, probably at the same company, so we tried to plan our careers because that's the way it worked. And those people who didn't plan kind of fell by the wayside. You took a role in a brokerage firm or a law firm, and you expected to be a partner in 30 years. I don't know if people think that way anymore.

The next generation is pretty good at long-term planning, but I'm not sure the current employment situation rewards that.

Well, that's right, and we are going to have to change. My nephew, who is 43, says, "Sometimes you have to take a job across the street to get more money

because your old company is not going to do anything for you." Corporations have this attitude that people are expendable, and you can put someone in who has less experience and you can pay them less money. I think, as you say, they lose out that way.

What are your plans?

As long as I can work, I want to work. I love books. I started reading when I was three. I've loved books my entire life. That's what I do: I read books and tell you what I think of them and then try to sell them. I find it very enjoyable.

Sounds like a great job.

Well, I invented myself. I was trying to sell a book of my own, and I went through three agents and I said, "I know more than all of these people put together." So I

decided to be one, too. I did that about 27 years ago. That was my second—no, my third—career move. If you can't find a job someone will pay you for, invent a job you like and pay yourself. Not everybody can do that. But some can. I always say you either have a boss or you have clients, one or the other. You can't get away with having nobody to account to.

How would you define your work ethic?

I'm very fast. I think fast, I react fast, and I work very hard, and my people get value for their money. When I give them my unvarnished opinion, usually it's pretty good. People think I'm a good editor and a good critic.

Any advice for young people?

That's a good question. I wish I could give them some sage advice that if you do this, it will work for you. But I don't see anything working. A lot of it isn't working at all.

Any final thoughts?

Yes, the world's a mess, and I hope your book will straighten things out.

Caroline's generation is becoming increasingly vocal about their frustration. They worry that all their sacrifice on behalf of the country is being thrown away.

Jim
Facility Manager, Scottsdale, Arizona
Baby Boom Generation

Jim has worked for the city for four-and-a-half years, managing 3 million square feet of space and supervising a staff of 60. His wife, a high school counselor, will retire this month.

Sounds like a lot of responsibility. Tell us more about the job.

I manage buildings like city hall and the municipal courts, all the city facilities. Anything with infrastructure—grounds, elevators, lighting. That's my job. If things break, my staff gets them back in operation quickly. But we do a lot of preventive maintenance to try to head off emergencies.

What do you like about it?

I like feeling needed. I really like the unknown. In the world I'm in, I never know what the day will hold. I schedule things, but the schedule more often than not flies out the window. It's not just operations issues that change things. It's also people; I meet people's needs—whether it's my internal customer or an employee.

I like being a manager. No, I love being a manager. I love the responsibility. It feeds my ego, makes me feel I've accomplished something. Employees need things. They need to feel valued. They need my validation and support. They need someone to defend them, to go to bat for them. Sometimes it's a family issue. Or time off. Or they need to leave on short notice. I'm a human face versus what the policy says. I'm not a policy wonk. I like to do what I think is right.

Managing others taps into Boomers' desire to prove themselves.

Boomers think the rules are often wrongly conceived and aren't questioned enough.

I enjoy having the ability to meet my customers' needs. Or not. Not to be a wise guy, but sometimes I have to say, "Gee, that can't happen." It comes with the turf. For example, somebody might ask for unique lighting. If they can't demonstrate that there's a medical need for it, I probably won't address it. I run across people who just want to push the envelope. I don't like going overboard to accommodate someone who's taking advantage of the system.

What's it like working in the public sector?

The majority of people who work here work very, very hard—harder than I would have thought as a private sector person. I might've thought city workers were lazy, that they came in at nine and left at three. But the majority work very hard. Every place has slackers, but there aren't many here. These people are not paid that well, but they really care and they get the work done. They are there when somebody needs their help; when there's a sick child, they donate money or time or their own vacation time. They're giving people. It's not about the money. It's much more about security and satisfaction. I've been pleasantly surprised at the work ethic in the public sector. They're innovative, they take risks, they deliver, they see the task through completely.

A list of attributes that are important to Boomers—characteristics of people reaching for their full potential.

Another thing I like about the public sector is the benefits. The pension is so lucrative that a high school dropout can do well. You may not make a fortune, but after 20 years you will have earned a pension that will sustain you. I worked in the private sector in the computer industry for 32 years. My 401K was hit hard by the stock market. It's only come back by about 80 percent. I'd have to have $2 or $3 million in the bank to have the incomes that people enjoy after working 20 to 30 years in the public sector. There's a lot more security in the public sector. People sacrifice for their future. I'll suck it up because I know in the end I can retire and I'll have a reasonable income.

How about city politics?

Boomers characteristically use chain of command as a negative descriptor. They inherited a hierarchical workplace from Traditionalists, who learned organization management from the armed forces.

A sense of equality is embedded in the Boomer psyche. It was what drove Boomer involvement in the civil rights movement.

I call it the *Tin God Syndrome*. A few of those who are in authority demand that everyone follow the chain of command. I was in the military and I understand the need for it there, but I don't understand not being able to talk to someone in the hallway who is at a higher level. When I had been working here for three months, I talked to the City Treasurer. He wanted an ATM onsite. Someone saw me talking to him and said, "I'm going to write you up." You've got to be kidding me. That kind of thinking marginalizes people.

Who was your best boss?

His name was Ira. It was my first job in the public sector. When I was a young guy, I hadn't figured out who I was. Ira was 25 years older, a father figure. I wasn't sure about my career path. He guided me with a gentle hand. He was firm, but he never discouraged me with negativity. He understood my strengths and weaknesses. Treated me like a son. I'll be eternally grateful. He taught me an awful lot formally and informally through his behavior and actions. Because of him, I stayed in the facilities realm. I've lost track of him now. I think he lives in Maryland. He probably doesn't know how much of an influence he had on me.

Specifically, I was a hothead. I tended to get angry easily. I had a bad habit of *fire, ready, aim*. He would say, "What the hell are you doing?" He was a retired coastguard commander from the South. Very direct. He would say, "Why would you say that? Why would you get upset over nothing? Why do you think it's all about you?" It shocked me because it was true. He did it in a fatherly way. He was upset with me. I didn't always like what he said, but I couldn't argue. He showed me the logic or the lack of logic over getting upset about petty things. He helped me look at the big picture and see where my behavior was going to get me.

Sounds like a constructive intergenerational relationship: the tough, rational, logical Traditionalist tapping into what's important to a young Boomer.

And your worst boss?

Unfortunately, that one stands out as much as the great boss. She was actually someone who sought me out and worked hard to see that I was hired here. We had a good relationship for a couple of years. I don't know what went wrong, but it got nasty. Toxic. She did things in an underhanded way. She made accusations that were unfounded. She said, "I heard that you told someone in the hallway that I was a bitch." This is in the city environment! The culture here is so politically correct. I would never have talked that way to someone in the hall. I just wouldn't have done that. I lost 14 pounds on a 160-pound frame. She tried to load me up with enough work that it would be impossible for me to succeed if I worked 15 hours a day.

She got a reputation for doing things like that. It takes a lot to get in hot water here, but eventually they do circle the wagons. She ended up being removed from her position and moved to another area. It was a lateral but career-changing move. Her career is done. I think she was insecure in her own skin. I met her husband once by chance. He didn't treat her with respect at all. I think she was second or third fiddle in that family. Her only power and recognition came from work. I don't think her self-esteem was high, so she had to compensate by bullying.

Boomers strive to understand the underlying motivations of people, no matter how ill treated they've been. They are psychologically astute.

They also care about others' self-esteem. Most Boomers have high EQs.

How do you define work ethic?

I have a strong work ethic. I had a paper route when I was a kid. I've always

Work is hard wired into Boomers' self-esteem.

worked. I usually have four or five things going on at once. I own property that I manage. I do my own yard work. I maintain my own pool because I'm a tightwad. I take pleasure in working, even if it's mindless. Work is a nice escape that I get fulfillment from.

Like a lot of people in my generation, I'm defined by my job. I try to demonstrate that I care by delivering on my tasks. If I say I'll do something, I try to do it really well so that the people on the receiving end know I care about it. I want it to be professional: cross the T's and dot the I's. I want people to respect what I do. They see me as the guy with the most keys on his hip. Well, yes, but I'm also managing a budget of $14 million. I always try to demonstrate that facilities management is a profession, not a trade. It's something I take pride in. I speak like a professional, behave and dress like a professional versus a tradesman. I'm not

Boomers' identity is tied to work.

taking away from tradesmen; I couldn't do the work they do. My work ethic is critical. My work ethic defines me.

What's the work ethic at City Hall?

The city hosts lots of special events. I've had situations where we've had major pieces of equipment fail. They have to be operational 24/7. If they don't operate, the city can't do its business. I've seen people interrupt their din-

Low value on clock punchers. High value on those who take pride in their work.

High value on team players.

ner and time with their families to come down and work until the job gets done. They don't ask me what they're going to get paid or if there will be overtime. They just want to make sure we're back in operation. You can't put a price tag on that. These people may not even like each other during the day, but they rally and get the job done. They don't like a lot of visibility. They don't brag about themselves. They're tradespeople.

We had a guy who had a braided ponytail. His name was Randy. He made a bet with his son. He said, "If you'll give me a grandson, I'll cut my hair." He donated his hair to Locks of Love. These are very giving, humble people. It's not about the pay. The pay is okay. It's not enough to get fat on, not enough to take a vacation to Tahiti on. But it puts food on the table and takes care of the basics. These are salt-of-the-earth people.

How does retirement look?

When I reflect on my life, I feel incredibly lucky. I made good decisions that have played out well. When my wife says this is the last quarter of our lives, I'm resisting. I don't want to hear it. I want to take on more responsibility. The people in my peer group ask why I am all excited. They're downshifting, but I love to work. My father came from Greece just before the Depression. They had nine kids, some born in Greece and some in the U.S. My siblings grew up during the Depression. It marked them. Those bad experiences stuck with them. My parents instilled a strong work ethic in us because they saw what could happen. They taught us to work hard. To save money. Not to get silly with finances. All that was instilled in me early on.

Work is deeply integrated into his personality.

My wife is retiring three weeks from now. She'll be a free lady. I'm happy about it. She's worked 30 years in her field. She's ready. I'm not ready to stop working. I'll watch her and see what she does because I don't want to wake up and find it's too late—that I don't have my health and I've worked until I dropped. I'll take pleasure in watching her do whatever she wants, like go back East and visit family and not worry about whether she'll be back on time. She's got an income to fall back on, so that's great. She'll probably travel and get involved in something in the community. She'll expand her jewelry making. We bought her a fiddle and she'll probably play it. I think the options for her are wide open. Maybe she'll write a book. (He chuckles.) I'd like her to get her PhD. She's close. I don't think she'd ever do it, but it wouldn't take her long.

Boomers will transform retirement, just as they've transformed every other phase of their lives.

Adam
Licensed Electrician, Boston, Massachusetts
Millennial Generation

Adam is out of work, skilled, willing to work hard, and driven to succeed.

So how is work going?
Currently I'm unemployed. Laid off. The company is recovering from some growing pains: customers falling through and things like that. I'm a licensed electrician. The last four years I've been doing solar and solar voltaic installations—everything from roof work to wiring and other electrical stuff—some high-end telecommunications stuff and some big battery work. The battery work was in telecommunications: big buildings full of computers that are the Internet, and they all have big battery backups. It's specialized work.

Do you think the layoff is temporary?
I'm not sure. The company I worked for is small. It was started about six years ago, and I started four years ago. I was the only employee. Then we grew to about

four of us. Now he can't keep us busy enough. We had all our eggs in one basket —one customer selling one kind of product. A couple of very slow months and now there is no money to pay us, to keep us on the clock.

What's the process of getting licensed as an electrician?
In Massachusetts, it's a four-year apprenticeship with a licensed electrician plus 600 hours of schooling. I took a more nontraditional route and took a full year at a trade school. Most will take a helper position and get the schooling in while they work. I went the other way and did the education first so I was able to start at a little higher rate. Then I began working full time after I got my license.

What was the age spread in your company?
I'm 28. The second guy is 22. The other licensed electrician is 28 also. The boss is in his late forties.

So he's a Gen Xer. What was it like to work for him?
This guy was an interesting character. He wasn't the greatest manager. He looked at us like children. He didn't look at us as peers. It felt like we were the kids that worked for him, so his feedback was not ideal. It was really about doing it his way, even if he didn't understand it. It was very difficult to change his mind.

So how was it working with people your own age?
That part was great. In fact, one of them was a guy I went to school with, so we were pretty good friends. Working with him was great. He was a real hard worker. He was understanding, and he accepted guidance and help. Then when we hired the other guy, he was my age.

I understand that you've been involved in the Occupy Movement?
I went to Zucotti Park when I was in New York City back in October. I hung out and went to some stuff. I wasn't an active participant in the movement. I was just interested in it, in some of the things it was trying to accomplish.

What do you think Occupy can teach older generations about Millennials?
I saw a willingness to work in a more cooperative fashion, less of top down structure. There was more of a one-worker, one-vote

Millennials expect to be heard, to be involved in decision-making.

He felt marginalized by his boss.

It is difficult for Gen Xers to admit they don't understand something, especially since they've prided themselves on being the smartest person in the room about technology.

Gen Xers can be dogmatic managers.

Millennials tell us they want to work with people who are also friends.

Millennials respond well to peer mentoring.

Millennials have a strong team ethic. Read their references to cooperation with a capital C.

mentality. People were saying "let's bring back the fact that we are equals." It was more of a real democracy, a real equality. There wasn't much top-down "I'm the boss. I'm in charge. You do what I say."

Millennials will bring new meaning to equality in the workplace.

Do you think some of that will migrate to the workforce? Will it create a new kind of leader?

What kind of leaders will it create? I guess the kind who are more interested in sharing power, more interested in sharing information, and more willing to hear from and learn from other people. Leaders who are more open to everyone's opinions. For example, it was hard to convince my former boss of anything other than what he already knows.

When managing Millennials, look for opportunities for cooperative decision-making.

What's the best way to manage your generation?

Listening to people works for everyone, not just my generation. I think everyone's opinions should be valued. It's not just a Millennial thing. And I think that means valuing the input of others, rather just handing you a task and making you do it.

What motivates your generation?

For me and the guys I worked with, it's important to be challenged and given a task that is not clear cut. Being an installation company, there's a lot that's not in the manual. There's a lot that has to be figured out, solutions you come up with on our own. Having that challenge is a good thing. To be able to say to the guys, "Here's the task. Here's what has to get done. Now let's figure out how to make it happen." That is always a good motivator—something that pushes us beyond our known abilities.

He needs less structure and guidance than Millennials typically do.

He would make a good team leader, training his peers to be more self-directed.

We've been hearing from some Millennials that it's important to get a task done right the first time. Does that sound right?

For me, in my work, that was very important. A lot of the stuff I did was actually dangerous. There were serious risks. A dropped tool could set off an explosion. I don't know how much of a generational thing that was.

Was it important to you to be working on sustainable energy projects like solar power?

At first it wasn't important. I just wanted to go to work for this guy. It definitely matters to me now, having done it for four years. I'm a big believer. I've worked with

Millennials face environmental issues that will be part of their generational destiny. Their task will be, as Tom Friedman says, akin to reaching the moon in the 1960s.

it, seen it, and that proved to me that it works. In my life, it's something I value—that energy be renewable and sustainable.

How was your transition from school to work?

It was an interesting transition, because at the time I was working in a grocery store almost full time. Out of high school I worked that job for a number of years. I had a typical attitude of not really going anywhere, no big plans. I spent most of my time partying and enjoying life rather than worrying about a career. And then I went to trade school, and it was a big transition to working full time. Getting up at 5:00 in the morning. But for me it was the right transition, the right thing to do. I feel better now that I'm doing it. I look back on what I was doing and it feels silly.

It's weird to say, but I enjoy getting up early, going to work and working hard —coming home tired. I can't say I really have significant goals. I

Millennial work ethic.

know I'm going to keep doing electrical work, being a licensed electrician. I don't want to be slapping on a tool belt in 30 years, but I want to still be in the field.

If you were a manager, how might you approach that?

I actually have some experience already. I was the first guy in at the company, so when the other guys started, I was given a lot of responsibility. I decided which guys went to which jobs, so I was a manager of sorts. It wasn't necessarily easy for me at first. I tried not to be too authoritative. Over time, I came up with the right balance. We had other people come in as temporary help. I worked with one guy

A good call for managing his peers. He might need to be more directive with Gen Xers and Traditionalists.

who was in his sixties.

Did he listen to you?

Yes, he was an electrician his whole life, and he had retired. The stuff he was helping me out on was not too different than what he had done in his career, but different enough that he listened. He was definitely easy to work with. He had no problem taking direction from a much younger guy. That was not an issue for him.

Any thoughts about starting your own company?

No time soon. There's a lot to be said about being an employee. I clearly enjoy the ability to have days off, to call in sick, to not have to worry about running the business. I'm happy with just doing the work. I do enjoy having more responsibility than just having to turn a screwdriver. But I don't want the responsibility of running a business, doing the books, signing the work, finding the customers, paying the taxes, all that stuff. That's more than I'm interested in at this point.

You don't sound like someone who wants to be in a cube all day.

I'm definitely not the kind of person who could do that. I love going to a different place every week, going to a different job site every other day. Even though I'm doing the same thing—installing solar panels—I get to go to a new place. It's more interesting like that for me.

This desire for having a variety of interesting tasks shows up in numerous studies of Millennial work preferences.

Barbara
Realtor, Denver, Colorado
Baby Boom Generation

Barbara has worked with a small independent real estate company for the last 15 years. She and her husband live alone, with adult children and their families living nearby.

You've mentioned your current work overload.

I came back from vacation 60 days ago to an unexpected, unplanned workload. In the month I had been gone, the market had picked up and suddenly I had listings, contracts, and closings—and a plethora of related large and small tasks. It's more work than I have experienced at any one time in the 15 years I've done real estate, like going from zero to a hundred in a day or two. So right now I'm processing the work that's on the plate in front of me, and I wish I could complete it sooner. I see a three- or four-month horizon. It probably has been a really good experience in terms of clarifying that this isn't what I want to do anymore.

A lot of Boomers are winding down toward retirement, taking time to smell the roses—and spending time with grandchildren.

Are there retirement decisions on the horizon?

I'm committed to finish and not take on that level of work again. It has no appeal for me. I've been weighing the timing of my retirement. I know I'll want to work part time first, then ultimately stop working. But I ask myself when the best time is, how I can retire in a non-abrupt transition that feels comfortable to me. Will I have the financial stability or resources to have a comfortable semi-retirement and comfortable retirement? Can I create an environment or structure for myself that feeds different parts of my intellectual curiosity and my need to be psychologically engaged? Can I commit to something so that I continue to feel needed?

This is a challenge for Boomers since many nest eggs were destroyed in the crash of 2008.

Boomers will continue working towards becoming complete, self-actualized persons.

I get some of that from my work, so I want to make sure to replace it. I want to walk away from and leave behind the amount of stress I feel when the work I love just gets to be too much and it then becomes work I don't love. I want to retire gradually, with a component of transition. I don't want to retire too soon, then realize I don't have adequate resources. I want to dip my toe into the experience and pull back if I find it isn't the right time for me.

Boomers' relationship with work has always been intense and emotional. For Gen Xers, not so much.

There are a number of reasons I'd like to retire now. I'd like to travel more than my current schedule allows. I want to spend more time with my grandchildren. Perhaps more than anything else, I want to do the ordinary things in my life more slowly, at a different pace. All my life, I've felt the need to rush. I rush to the grocery store and rush home to put things away. I rush doing the laundry and putting it away. So I speed through my chores mindlessly to get them done and move on to something else. In the last year or two, when the market had slowed and I had a little less work than in the past, I just relished going to the grocery store and taking an hour or two . . . or folding the clothes and laundry for my husband and myself and smoothing them out . . . sitting on my deck and watching the squirrels and birds . . . slowing down and luxuriating in that.

Eat, pray, love, and slow down.

Are you changing your approach?

I've already taken the first steps on the trajectory by announcing to my colleagues and the managing broker that I would be changing my work role and my pace. I gave up my private office and let people know I wouldn't be writing a business plan. By telling them, I reduced expectations. I also declared to myself that I can't be Susie Realtor. I'm less and less interested in generating the enthusiasm and external attitude of sales and competing, finishing your business plan and attracting more clients. These things don't have meaning for me anymore. I can't and don't want to try to force that or pretend that it's important to me. I want a slower pace and a smaller scale. In the future when unsolicited work comes in, I'll select a small amount to keep for myself and gratefully refer the rest to colleagues I have mentored along the way.

Seeking self-actualization away from work.

Boomers enjoy mentoring.

Talk about the sales culture.

Once a week there's a sales meeting at which we get new information about legal, market, and financial issues that will keep us up to date. But in addition to the information component, which is really helpful, there is a cheerleading component or a motivational piece—like sharing tips on how to attract clients or writing notes to a certain number of clients each week in order to yield a lot of new clients. It's a bounciness, an enthusiasm, that has lost its appeal—if it ever appealed to me. It seems disingenuous to me now and it's hard for me to sit in the room with it. I extricated myself from having to attend those meetings. I don't want to write any more business plans.

Here's a word you never want to hear from a Boomer. Authenticity is important to them. Holden Caulfield's harshest criticism was reserved for phonies.

What is the generational mix?

It's an office of about 60 realtors. I'd say there are probably ten my age or older. Probably half the people are between 40 and 60. The remainder are in their late twenties and thirties. So I'm in the older 15 percent. As I have watched some of my colleagues who are my age or older, I see some actual errors they make and the risk for potential errors that would be expensive and serious. I still believe attention to detail is critical. I want to make sure I leave while I'm still competent, effective, and at the top of my game. I want to leave before I decline in the kind of service I provide: my competence, my creativity, my carefulness.

A big fear for Boomers is being less competent than their idealized self imagines them to be.

Tell us about a high-performing colleague.

My most successful colleague is a typical midcareer realtor. She has a fire in her belly. She's 42, high-energy level, intellectually very bright, master's degree, two young children. She's the breadwinner in the family. She taught school many years. She's now making probably 12 to 15 times the money she made then. She's well suited for the work because she's service oriented, client centered, willing to make a lot of sacrifices of her own time to do the work. She works easily 60 hours a week. She's technologically very advanced with social media, with electronic professional support. She has boundless energy and enthusiasm. Certainly she's motivated by money—growing college and retirement funds, but she's also motivated because she needs a lot of stimulation and she thrives on the demands on her time and energy.

Sounds like a Gen Xer.

Talk about what you bring to the table at this point in your career.

My clients are all people I've worked with before. They've had a positive experience with me. I've been an ongoing resource for them before and after real estate transactions. They call me if they have a tax or market question, if they're making a purchase decision, if they're curious about the value of their property, if they're thinking of investing in an apartment, buying a second home, or deciding whether to buy or rent. They count on my expertise and experience and the relationships we have with the trust, familiarity, and track record.

Is your age an asset?

Many of my clients are the age of my children of younger, so the gray hair factor has been a huge asset for me. Buying a home is a big financial decision, sometimes the biggest of their life, and I think it's a comfort to them to talk to someone and be advised by someone who might be the age of their parents or a trusted aunt.

In some ways, a realtor is like a therapist. The realtor learns almost everything about a client—their financial issues, their relationship issues. The realtor is with them during a vulnerable time in their lives when they're making decisions that are stressful for them. The realtor knows a lot about the client, and the client knows very little about the realtor's personal or financial life. I feel honored to be in that role and I feel like I can respond to that vulnerability and exposure with respect. That includes respecting their privacy and respecting the confidentiality of their information. So my listening and response skills are really a help in that aspect of working with clients.

Most Boomers value their EQ as much as their IQ. They are people persons.

How are you with teams and rules?

Boomers challenge the status quo and the rules.

This is atypical of Boomers. Most enjoy teams and the relationships they engender.

Like most realtors, I'm basically self-employed. As I've gotten older, I've become more of an independent operator. With more confidence, it has become easier to strike out on my own. I often have an atypical, nonconventional approach that's about two degrees off of normal. I don't need the affirmation of a team much.

What about giving back?

Boomers trust their intuition and are good at connecting with others.

She is looking for ways to stretch herself as work fades in importance. We will see a lot more of that in the next couple of decades.

One thing I haven't talked about is creating time to give back. I've been volunteering for five or six years at a school where I teach English to adults. I had never taught in any setting before and didn't know if I could do it. Since I hadn't had teacher training, I relied more on my intuition and on making a connection with my students as a vehicle to teach them. I don't teach in a conventional fashion but my classes are effective. My students learn what they came to learn. Mine is the most popular class in the school. I'm funny with them and it relaxes them. So that little classroom becomes an opportunity twice a week to extend myself.

What about building community?

Retirement for Boomers will include more time to think and reflect and less time playing golf than for their parents' generation.

When I look to the future with work occupying a smaller percentage of my time, I want to travel, spend time with family, and do things at a more mindful pace. But I also want to share something inside me—information, but not just information. I want to create an atmosphere where people want to learn English and feel welcomed, befriended, and respected. I love the diversity of this assignment. My class is comprised of Asians and Latinos from six or seven different countries—Koreans, Vietnamese, Chinese, Guatemalans, Mexicans, Hondurans. The Spanish speakers sit together. The Asian students sit together. In the beginning, they're suspicious of each other. I build a community, a safe place where we can sit together, laugh at our mistakes, mimic each other's accents, help each other out. I'll see a Korean sitting next to a Guatemalan, both trying to figure out how to pronounce *refrigerator,* and nobody even has a recognizable semblance, but they're working together and helping each other out, and on break they show each other pictures of their kids and bring in food. We get together and talk about customs, like a miniature UN.

It takes a village plus a Boomer. They believe that getting people together can make a difference.

When I turned 45, I went on an Outward Bound trip. There were only two women and I was the oldest. At the end, everybody said I had been the glue that held them together. They told me I picked everyone up like they were on a knitting needle and pulled them all together. This teaching experience reminds me of that.

Political engagement?

Along with volunteerism, I want to stay politically active, certainly aware and informed. We don't get to sit that out. It would feel almost criminal to be in this society and take a walk on political engagement. At the very least, we need to care about and support what we believe.

Boomers are retiring and moving into a stage of life where they will have a strong influence on politics.

Any final issues?

I don't much feel an end-of-life need to pack a lot of stuff in. I don't feel, for example, that I haven't traveled enough. It isn't like that. I do feel the clock ticking. I probably won't be able to travel in 5 or 15 years as easily as I can right now. But I don't have a big bucket list.

Jessi
Emergency Room Doctor, Albany, New York
Millennial Generation

Jessi has just finished medical school and will begin her residency in June.

So why did you choose emergency medicine?

During the third and fourth years of med school, we go on short rotations—usually four to six weeks—where we assist residents in a particular specialty such as pediatrics, surgery, psychiatry, and internal medicine. These rotations help students get a sense for some of the specialties. Early in my third year, I decided I wanted to be a family doctor, but when I did a rotation in the emergency department, I completely changed my mind. I knew the ER was where I wanted to be. I like the pace, demand, intensity, and lack of agenda. It was only after emergency shifts that I would leave, just gleaming, wanting to tell anyone who would listen about the amazing things I had seen and learned.

It's important to Millennials to make a difference.

How do you decide where you'll end up?

We've just had Match Day, the event where all fourth-year medical students across the country find out where they will be working after they graduate. It's a highly charged ceremony in a big auditorium where the students and their families gather to get the match news. It's the end of a long, intense process. I interviewed at nine programs in different parts of the U.S. After all the interviews, the candidates rank the programs in order of where they would most like to work down to their last choice of a place to work. At the same time, the programs rank order the medical students from their top choices down to the least desirable ones. Then a computer takes all the lists from all the students and all the residency programs, and matches them up.

Older generations worry that Millennials don't handle disappointments well. But they do bounce back.

I got my second choice. At first I was stunned; I had my heart set on the program I ranked number one. But it only took about five minutes for me to remember how much I liked the people and the program I matched with, and I'm honestly thrilled and excited to be going to New York for my residency.

Millennials don't jump into decisions. They set long-term goals and do their research before they step through the door of a potential employer.

Before I started the interview process, I had a list of priorities in mind for the programs and places I would be rating. Being somewhere near good rock climbing, biking, hiking, and skiing was high on my list of priorities. Another, of course, was the reputation of the program. But after going to the interviews, having spent some time away from my home state, I scaled down my priorities. I thought about the "bike-ability" of the cities, the opportunities to have a house with a yard for my dog, and how well I related to the program director. Maybe you could say my priorities just became more specific. In the end I ranked them based on: location, program director, the enthusiasm of the residents (although this was hard to judge after spending only about five minutes with them), the clinical strength of the program (which was also difficult to judge), and the length of the program. One of the programs where I interviewed was four years. The rest were three years. I was more attracted to the shorter programs.

High-achieving Millennials became accustomed to accelerated programs in high school and college.

The program I rated number one was in an amazing location—dozens of ski areas nearby, great mountain roads for biking. It had an incredible program director—she had spiky pink hair—and very enthusiastic, intelligent residents with lots of interests outside of medicine.

Millennials want lives outside of work every bit as much—maybe more—than Gen Xers.

It's sort of wild how we are expected to make an informed decision about where to go. Each program has a website with statistics like patient volume, how many weeks patients spend in intensive care, and the percentage of the patient population that has children. There is a dinner with a few of the residents and then the interview the next day. That's it. Then you choose the place where you will be living and working for the next three or more years of your life.

Here's an indication of how carefully Millennials weigh decisions. This process might have seemed adequate to older generations.

But I'm incredibly glad to be going to New York. When I was there to interview, I was lucky enough to sit next to a resident at dinner the first night who kept talking about the great climbing and skiing nearby. It was just luck, but it helped with my decision.

You say the director had you at *hiker?*

The next day, the program coordinator—the emergency medicine physician in charge of the residency program—really won me over. She started off by telling everyone that "hiker/biker/climber types" liked the program. Since those are things I love to do, I knew I was in the right place. She knew all of our names, and she remembered that my birthday was coming up in a few days. She remembered from my application that I do yoga, and she told me I could find great yoga studios near the hospital. She talked to me about things that are important to me—like a farmer's market, easy access to the outdoors and wilderness areas, a new Trader Joe's. She even remembered I'd be bringing my dog. I thought to myself that if she took the time to know all this about me—I was one of a hundred interviewees—I couldn't even imagine how helpful and great she would be during residency.

Millennials value mentors and people they can bounce ideas off of.

In my interview with her, I felt, for one of the first times during the interview process, that she had actually read my application and was trying to point out strengths of the program—like wilderness and international medicine—that were particularly suited to me. In most of the interviews, I felt like I was constantly trying to convince *them* that I should be ranked high on their list. But she was selling the program to *me*, convincing me that they were good for me. She wasn't necessarily telling me what she thought was strong about the program from her perspective, but what she thought *I would think* was strong. It's a fine but important distinction.

The traditional approach to the interview process.

The program director was following the Titanium Rule: Do unto others keeping their preferences in mind.

It is nice to know that the match really works by matching applicants with programs they want, but also with programs that want them. It's important to have that fit. I think this will be a great adventure for me.

What are your challenges?

Millennials are generally unaccustomed to dealing with angry people and difficult situations.

Certainly I'm young, maybe even naive. Without a lot of life experience, it is sometimes hard for me to relate to and understand patients' living situations and extenuating circumstances. I'd also say I'm "intimidate-able." This isn't good when you have to be the one in charge, but I'm working on it. I still concern myself with making sure other people think I'm smart. I consider that a weakness because having a sensitive ego can get in the way of focusing on the patient's issues.

And your assets?

This may be atypical of Millennials who have become so accustomed to multitasking that they have a hard time staying focused on one task.

Interesting addition. Safety is a big concern for Millennials, but not so much for older generations.

I really enjoy emergency medicine and it always helps to like your job. One of my strengths is the ability to focus and generally stay on task while at work. My ability to establish rapport with patients is an asset. When we only have a few short minutes to get to know them, it is important to be able to establish trust quickly. I'm nice, pleasant and polite—generally speaking. And I'm not arrogant. This can be a weakness, too when it comes to not having confidence in the decisions one makes and confidence in one's knowledge. I'm committed to patient care and safety. I study and stay up to date on current treatments. My parents weren't physicians, and I think that's an asset because I come from a different background than many of my colleagues.

How do you define work ethic?

Older generations are often surprised at Millennials' strong work ethic.

Millennials typically need more structure than this.

I had a lot of different jobs in high school and college. I was a cook in a Mexican restaurant in a ski town in Colorado. I worked as a barista in a coffee shop near my college campus. I delivered pizza—after I made the dough and hand tossed the pies. I worked hard in all those jobs. I enjoy working hard. It's something I thrive on. It's hard to fake a good work ethic, at least for long. To me, a good work ethic means being self-driven, not needing to be told or asked what to do. During my first trauma as a med student, I knew I wasn't going to get to help do something like put in a chest tube, but I was ready with my trauma shears so at least I could help with something. I think if you have a strong work ethic, you have the ability to shift into work mode, in the sense that you don't take your bad day out on your patients or colleagues. Work ethic is really a matter of integrity, being honest with yourself, colleagues, and patients, asking yourself, "Would I treat my mother, brother, or child this way?"

Ethics is a serious subject for Millennials, who expect it to receive more than lip service.

What does the future look like?

Last weekend, my dad and I flew to Albany so we could get more familiar with the city and the surrounding areas and so we could check out the house I'll be renting. We found a great coffee shop just a block from the house and a grocery store that will be perfect. It's a locally owned natural foods coop. The visit made me excited for my new job and new location, but it also scared me. It made me realize that it's all real, and it will be happening in just a month.

Parents will remain in the picture well into Millennials' adult lives.

M.J.

Project Manager, Denver, Colorado
Generation X

M.J., who works in a federal agency, discusses the challenges his generation faces as they negotiate the departure of the Boomers and the arrival of the Millennials.

You work with Millennials. Any observations?

They seem aloof and at the same time they want direction. You can't just give them something and let them go when you are assigning a project. A girl I work with now comes back and wants to ask questions about what I thought we had covered. I've already said, "Do this and do that." You have to be real specific about what you want—what the output is supposed to be. I'm not directly managing anyone right now. I'm doing project management.

A continuing source of friction between Millennials and Gen Xers.

Xers tend to be just the opposite, preferring to work with little or no direction.

Gen Xers typically prefer project management to people management.

Are you losing a lot of Boomers?

There's definitely a lot of knowledge walking out the door. A big focus here in the research program is trying to figure out how we mitigate this loss of institutional knowledge. It's funny because we will get—I've heard anecdotally anyway—proposals for projects and then we will have some guys in their fifties or sixties say,

Gen X pragmatism. "Yeah we already looked at that—30 years ago." It creates ineffi- ciencies and gaps in knowledge. With these people walking out the door, we're losing a lot—not just in knowledge. We are going to be reinventing the wheel on a lot of stuff. You don't know what you don't know.

Unfortunately, leadership—the people who should be strategizing around knowledge management—haven't caught on to the importance of funding those activities and technologies and creating solid strategies. They don't see it from my perspective. I'm in my mid-thirties, and I'm sitting here wondering what we're going to do. I'm not in leadership, and so my priorities aren't always funded and implemented, or even taken seriously.

Few organizations have their middle managers working on succession planning. Yet they're more motivated than any other group to save organizational knowledge.

When our research managers leave here in the next five years, and I ask questions, I'm not going to get the same answers. We're going to have to go back to square one because not only will they not be there, but the information system won't exist to retrieve that information. It's just not being handled on a strategic basis.

Gen Xers dreamed of the days when the Boomers would move on and management positions would open up.

That's the funny thing. That's not happening. They are focusing on cutting and consolidating things like IT services and knowledge management. More focus on saving money and generalizing services. I think they are going in the wrong direc- tion. They are always asking, "How do we make ourselves look like we're saving dollars?" Then they throw in that "this will be more efficient," but they don't really prove it. I think the lack of strategy around knowl- edge management and transition planning is going to hurt.

Gen Xers are wary of lip service.

You've been in a lot of organizations over the years. What are you noticing lately?

I was a late bloomer because I dropped out of high school and then I went to col- lege late. I've done all kinds of jobs, everything from blue collar to white collar. What I've noticed is that everything is freaking exponentially complicated these days. There's just so much information out there. It feels like we're making progress because there's all this information flying around, but I don't think we're really getting anywhere. We spend a lot of time answering email and trading information, but I don't know that that translates to real results. I'm a proponent of social media, but I just don't think we're using it in a strategic way.

Add "spinning your wheels" to the list of phrases Gen Xers use to describe less than optimal situations.

Xer pragmatism again.

Some of the generational differences contribute to that. A lot of leaders—whether it's legislators or senior leadership in your organization—don't grasp what the technology does or how it should be deployed or funded. I still hear from people, "Oh, *Facebook* is just a flash in the pan." These tools—*Facebook* and *Google*—have such a massive impact on the way people communicate and the way the world works. Information can be moved around in a more efficient and transparent way.

Gen Xers have traditionally been frustrated by those who don't understand technology or what it can do.

Talk about strategy.

It's like when I was at a different organization and fighting to get social media implemented. The public relations and old-school journalism folks—not the IT folks—are in charge of the web. The agency is spread out across many states, with diverse stakeholders and projects and responsibilities in all of these different places, and they still think we should have one *Facebook* account and one *Twitter* feed. The people in charge are in a different generation. Sometimes I look at them and think, "You're not getting this because…you're old." I don't mean that as an insult because I'll be old someday, too. Maybe when I'm old, I'll feel the same way about the cybernetic brain implants all the kids are getting.

We hear a lot about young people and entitlement. You seeing any of that?

Yes, they are entitled. No question. Part of it is how they were raised. I see entitlement when it comes to smartphones. A lot of the kids think you should be able to pick up the phone and use it whenever you want. They structure their time around the smartphone. It's not like this is a block of time to sit down and work. When the phone rings, that's what dictates what's going to occur. It doesn't even ring anymore. It beeps and there's a text or there's an email or *Words with Friends* or *Angry Birds* and I'm sure there are other things—hipper games—that I don't have a clue about. Incorporating those games into the day is just part of the routine. The fact that you should always have your phone on, that you should answer it whenever it buzzes, that's a definite issue I see.

It's funny because sometimes I see the "adults" or the leaders annoyed by that, but they are the same people who will be Crackberry-ing in a meeting. I've given presentations where I've seen people sit there and be on their Blackberry the whole time. And I know they see it differently because they think they are "multitasking" and "doing business." I'm wondering if that is any

An underlying point here is that Gen Xers hate meetings. They think that, if you're going to drag them into one, you darn well better be paying attention and not doing three other things.

different. If you are answering email not related to what's going on in the room, is that any different than some kid who is fresh out of college playing *Angry Birds* on his phone while I'm talking? I don't know. Maybe. Maybe not.

How is this generation different?

Their idea of rebellion is different than my idea of rebellion when I was younger. When I was young, it was cool to do drugs, be antisocial, and things like that.

Millennial-style rebellion. Today's kids are rebellious but in socially acceptable ways. Like getting tattoos. My cousin will say, "I'm going to get a lot of tattoos, but I'm going to make sure I can cover them up so I can get a job. I won't get something I can't cover with my collar or my sleeve." It's like they think rebelliously but in a way that they can still get what they want.

A more controlled rebellion?

It's weird. We Xers went so far. We said, "Pump up the volume, pump up the volume, pump up the volume." We've already turned the volume up to 11, so where

Obligatory Spinal Tap reference.

Two generations pushed the envelope. The pendulum has started back the other way.

is there to go? Is this regression what has to happen? We've had extreme Doritos and Mountain Dew. We had all these things that were extreme and in your face with neon colors and rock music. Maybe you have to have a generation where they still need to rebel—because they're kids and that's the way their brains work— but at the same time, maybe they have to become more conservative because the pendulum has to swing back. I don't know how much further it could go without degrading into anarchy.

You think they are less extreme than Xers?

I don't know if people get that impression, especially when you see all those YouTube videos, and they always record themselves doing dumb stuff. I think we did a lot of dumb stuff too. We just didn't record it. Would there have been just as many dumb videos in our day? There probably would have been if we hadn't had to carry around that 20-pound Betamax camcorder.

An honest assessment of one of the core issues that creates generational conflict. What defines work ethic? Often, we don't have the discussion and instead rely on our own, "I'll know it when I see it" preconceptions.

Do they work hard?

No, they don't. I don't think they have the same idea about what work is. When I went to school, when you had to write a research paper, you would go in and the teacher would give you the assignment, and you'd check out books, and you'd read the books, and you'd incorporate the quotes and themes of the books into the paper. And then you'd write a bibliography. Now when you give people an assignment, what's the first thing they do? I'm guilty of it too. Now you go and *Google* it. That's the fallback. Instead of putting together original thoughts from disparate sources, people are relying on the first ten links on *Google*.

And like we talked about before, they want explicit direction. For example, I was working on a brochure with a kid, and I just kind of gave him the general parameters. That was just not working. While I thought it was pretty clear what I wanted, it just wasn't happening. So we had to sit down and detail out, "This goes in this panel, and this goes in this panel, and this goes in this panel, and this goes in this panel."

I was thinking if I was him, I would have been thrilled to get a creative assignment where someone said, "Here's the general approach of what I want and go ahead and do it." But I think he wanted to do exactly what I wanted him to do. A lot of times I don't approach things that way. I don't really know what I want, so therefore I don't give people explicit direction because I expect them to come up with something innovative and then show it to me, and we riff off that. That's contrary to coming up with a concrete plan where the details are all mapped out before we go ahead and do it.

> We hear from Millennials that they want to get it right the first time, mostly because they feel so much pressure to achieve.
>
> Xers like to fly by the seat of their pants when it comes to work.

Did you feel like you should have just done it yourself?

Yes. You hire people so they can make independent judgments. You can then multiply your efficiency. If he is away working on the brochure, then I can be doing something else. If we have to do it together, then why is he here? It's one thing with student workers, but it's another when you've actually hired someone and are paying them to do the job. I wonder if five years down the road that person will become more independent. Is he this way because he doesn't have the confidence or is he always going to be this way?

> This is a question almost all managers will need to answer. Can independence be learned? Will organizations need to spell out all their processes explicitly so everyone knows what to do?

That's what worries me. It's one thing to say, "I don't have experience and I need to learn." It's another thing if people have had all their independence and creativity and decision-making processes baked out of them. If we have a generation of kids where every little piece of their life is dictated—whether it's in school or by their parents—are they going to be able to be creative and innovative and flexible? That's where I think we are going to be in trouble in the global marketplace. If that's the case, I don't think we are going to be any better than our counterparts overseas. If we are competing in that market, and we lose that one edge we have in America—freedom, creativity, innovation—that would concern me.

Fouad
Marketing Director, Detroit, Michigan
Baby Boom Generation

Fouad grew up in Lebanon. He is the manager of ethnic marketing for a large utility company where he has worked for the past 14 years.

What is ethnic marketing?

In some companies, the work I do is called *community relations;* in others it's called *diversity marketing.* I believe it is a mixture of both. In our service territory there are lots of ethnic groups—African American, Hispanic, Chaldean, Asian, Arabic, and others. In order for us to build loyalty among those customers, we need to understand their needs, their drivers. The company established the ethnic marketing department to build relationships with ethnic communities, especially with their institutions and organizations.

The stats show we have lots of segments in our market. For example, there are approximately 100,000 Chaldeans and about 400,000 Arab Americans in metropolitan Detroit. Chaldeans are from Iraq. They're non-Arab Christians who have their own language, their own culture, and their own dishes. Their values are different. They are a business community unto themselves. They own many of the gas stations, hotels, and department stores. Our job is to go out and build relationships with those customers.

Boomers excel at networking and community development. Look for more of that as they cross the retirement line.

We focus not on individual customers but on organizations such as Chamber of Commerce groups, trade associations, political and social organizations. We feel that, by building relationship with a chamber, for example, we are building relationship with a larger number of our customers.

Tell us about coming to America in the 1970s.

I came to the U.S. from Lebanon in 1971. I was 20 years old, and I had been accepted into a college in the U.S. While attending college, I was also learning English. It was very difficult for the first two or three months. I had moved from a big city in Lebanon to a small town in the Midwest. Nothing ever happened there after 5:00 P.M. It was snowy and cold. Then I moved to a larger city and things changed a bit. I met people and made friends and stayed there five or six years.

When I left Lebanon, it was at its best politically and economically. The late 1960s and early 1970s were the best time in Lebanon. Then in 1972-1973, civil war broke out. It tore the country to pieces. I didn't witness any of the destruction, but all my family was still there. I couldn't reach them to find out how they were doing; I could just see pictures on TV and in magazines. It was an ugly war. Two or three hundred thousand people were killed. It was a painful experience for me.

The 1970s in the U.S. was a beautiful time. There was freedom everywhere—free spirits, free people. It was the post-Vietnam War hippie period. I made a lot of friends in the mainstream. I was fascinated with the U.S., with the school system. I was really impressed with supermarkets and highways even though I had come from a very sophisticated city with sophisticated banking, food, and clothing industries. Here everyone was wearing jeans. Over there, people dressed in Italian suits. In Lebanon, there were all kinds of restaurants. Here at the time it was just lots of fast food.

Baby Boomers were still riding high from the 1960s and the political and cultural changes they had been part of.

But what fascinated me from a business point of view was the franchise system. You could go to one and it would be the same as all the others. If you went to one grocery store in the chain, in the same aisle were the same colors and the same products in the same aisles. I thought, boy, this is smart. They're saving a lot of money since one improvement in one store can be duplicated in every other one.

A remnant of the one-size-fits-all mentality of Traditionalists.

I witnessed the oil embargo and how people were waiting in line for gas. I witnessed all of this, and I will never in my life forget it.

What are the plusses and minuses of your job?

I'm at the executive level, between middle management and vice president. What I like best about my job is that it gives me opportunities to build relationships with community leaders and people from different cultures. When there's a function or event or annual meeting, we get invited. It gives me a great opportunity to meet influential people, the leaders in my community. I'm a people person. I love to introduce myself to people and represent the company in a professional way. I'm a good ambassador for the com-

Most Boomers are. Natural born networker.

pany's mission and I am a good messenger from the community to my company and other corporations. I like talking to people. Over the years, I've accumulated a large and highly respectable network in my business. I also really enjoy learning about other cultures, which is something I get to do all the time in this job. The people we meet are respectable. They're loyal. I've accumulated a lot of good friends over the years.

In every business and profession, there are some disadvantages. In this job, they're minor. But I have found with a few organizations that I deal with, because I've attended their banquets and other functions, they assume they're entitled to special benefits. Our company is a good corporate citizen. It's a great company, but like all corporations in the last few years we have faced some challenges. We have had to review our funding process and reduce the amount of funding in some cases. There have been some unpleasant conversations about the reductions. Some people understand, but others take it personally. That's one of the things I have to deal with and sometimes it's challenging.

Tell us about the company.

Honestly, I feel blessed to be working. They've given me the support I need, and the tools and opportunities to excel. On a personal level, the company has been

Helping him reach his full potential.

of great emotional and social support to me and understanding of my personal situation. My wife struggled with cancer for three years. She was in and out of the hospital, and I was back and forth between the hospital and work. She passed away in 2004. But I will never forget the leadership of the company from my director, the president, and the CEO. They regularly asked how she was and if they could do anything to help. It made me feel like I was working for a company with heart, one that genuinely cares about their employees. I felt lucky to be part of the team, the company.

On the professional level, the company has supported my requests and respected my professional opinion over the years. My goal, as I've said, is to build

Boomers resonate with organizational vision.

Core values: also important to Boomers.

relationships with organizations. I'm on the board of directors for about ten organizations. So I go to events and functions constantly and attend high level board meetings. They give me a free hand to do whatever I want to do. The company vision and messages filter down through me to our customers. It's a great company with great core values and a classy culture. I would recommend it to anybody. I feel blessed.

How have your values been affected by your Lebanese background?

My foundation is different than others in my generation. My upbringing was a little different. When I came here, I was a young man with different values and views. In the Middle East, we understood things like the Vietnam War. Here, people were busy doing their own thing. Young 19-year-old men in Lebanon were knowledgeable about world economic and political issues and world affairs. Unfortunately, 19-year olds here seemed narrow minded, like they didn't know what was going on. They were busy with their own little circle. I felt like I knew what was going on around the world. Young people here just didn't know about world affairs, geography, and history. Somebody asked me once where I was from. I said Lebanon. Then he said, "Oh. Is that near Chicago?"

Young people in the U.S. listened to the media, and since the media here is very powerful, whatever they heard in the news, they didn't argue with. They didn't question. They didn't analyze, investigate. Whatever they read, they just took it and walked with it. In Lebanon, we questioned and we didn't take a *yes* or *no* for an answer. We needed to ask the five why's.

In Lebanon, there is a lot of emphasis on core values such as respect, dignity, honor. For example, I would never tell someone, "You're a liar." Or not accepting what my father or mother tells me to do. Another thing that really bothers me is the loss of family values and family ties. Family back home is an integral part of our lives. Our decisions are made with our families.

Boomers questioned their parents to the point of distraction.

Talk about being a Boomer.

I know that Baby Boomers are devoted to the company mission, that they are good team players, and that they are hard workers. Yes, it's true. We value work. I worked with General Motors when I finished college. You had to wear a white, beige, or blue shirt with a necktie. We stuck to that culture. We came on time and left on time. We welcomed all that. It is a part of me. I'm a lawful person. I follow rules. I follow guidelines, company policy, and procedures. When it comes to family ties and values, I feel like a Boomer.

And sometimes it goes beyond valuing work so that work becomes an integral part of their sense of self.

Forty years ago, the workplace was strict. Now it is more open. There is more freedom—not freedom in a negative sense. It is better somehow. There is more balance between home and life and work. There are opportunities and options. You can work from home. You can work here. You can work from a different station. In the past, it was rather strict, but it has changed over time. I think it's a double-edged sword. Things are more open and free, but some people misuse it. As a manager, I see people misusing the opportunities we are getting. Some stick to the values and don't misuse the system. I feel the younger generation is smart, aggressive, and knowledgeable. This is probably due to technological advancements such as the Internet. It brought people closer, especially social networks. In the past, if we needed to do some compilations, we used a slide rule. After that came the calculator. Now you can do everything on your phone! People connect via the net. On the other hand, they are far from each other physically. This era is causing people to be alone and to be isolated, causing them to lose the human touch.

Mostly due to Boomers reshaping the workplace to flatten out hierarchies.

A common Boomer complaint about younger workers.

How do you define work ethic?

I judge someone's work ethic on the quality of reports they prepare and how well they produce, the way they handle conversations, the goals they are trying to achieve. I can detect an ethical person from the first conversation by the way they carry the conversation, the way they conduct a meeting, how they treat everybody else.

Who was your best boss?

The best boss I ever had was one I learned from. He was someone who brought out the best in me, who listened, and communicated. I learned whenever we were in a meeting, whenever we talked. He was very demanding, but I learned a lot from him. I gained from him. I'll always be thankful to him for that. He was tough. He was hard—firm, but fair. But he contributed to my development. Some bosses drain you. They don't add to your skills and knowledge. They don't add to your abilities. But some bring something new to the table in terms of ideas and ways of managing things. This man came up with something to teach in every interaction. He gave advice and direction— about the organization, about time management, about questioning, about saying the right thing and doing the right thing. He would say, "Never accept 'no' for an answer. Seek to understand. Ask more questions. Be straightforward with people. Say exactly what you want and say it in a clear way." The more demanding he was, the more polished, skilled, and sharp I became. I put in a lot of hours, and I always learned something new.

Boomers appreciate mentors who push them to be the best they can be.

What do you do with your free time?

There are two or three things I love to do. I like to read. I enjoy visiting family and friends. I am very involved in the community. I believe in volunteerism. I volunteer in my community and others. I attend events and functions and try to assist. Community involvement is very dear to my heart. I'm on the board of one of the local colleges, on the board of one of the community hospitals. I'm involved in the chambers of commerce. That keeps me busy, active, and alive. I love it.

Qualities Boomers will seek in retirement.

Michael
Career Counselor, Kansas City, Missouri
Gen X/Millennial Generation

Michael, who works in higher education, is on the cusp of two generations. His insight into the Millennial generation comes from working with scores of them every day.

Your current job puts you in touch with Millennials.

I'm in student employment. My job is to counsel students on soft skills for employment, working on resume skills, helping them choose majors. Sometimes I think I'm helping them identify who they are. My belief is that it's unusually cruel to make an 18-year-old choose what they want to do for the rest of their life. I also work with businesses and employers trying to get them to recruit the students.

Empathizing with the pressure Millennials feel.

So are you a Millennial or a Gen Xer?

I don't know. I feel like I'm riding the fence. I don't understand some of the younger Millennials but some of the older Xers I don't identify with either. I'm probably in the middle. I call those of us close to the beginning or end of a generation "cuspers." When it comes to technology, I think like a Millennial. I think it's better to work smarter, not harder, and I prefer to "work to live." I work with a lot of Boomers—we all do—and they don't seem to get it that I can get my work done anywhere. I can work on it at home or I can work on it on my phone. I can do almost everything but face-to-face appointments electronically. Even that is changing. Skype, for instance, can enable virtual face-to-face meetings. But I also understand work ethic and the importance of physical proximity for certain things.

A clear Xer statement.

This is something Xers have advocated for years, and the Millennials have joined them.

Talk more about work ethic.

I was raised by Boomers. My dad worked in the grocery business in a small town with 24,000 people. That was my first job. I learned the customer is always right. But to me, work ethic is all about doing the ethical thing. What's ethical? What's right for the customer. What's right for your colleagues. Then making sure the job gets done. I don't really care how the job gets done—whether it's in a group or as an individual—it just needs to get done. Then you must constantly reevaluate it.

Xers value hitting the deadline.

So do you prefer to work in teams or on your own?

I'm an extrovert. I'm an ENFP on the Myers Briggs scale. I draw my energy from groups. I have good ideas and I'm creative, but I don't believe one mind is going to make as creative an impression as multiple diverse minds of people getting together and making decisions.

He sounds more like a Millennial here.

There is some new research about diversity and decision making that's been verified by some...

You can get too many people involved and it just becomes circular and really counterproductive. But if you get three, four, five people together with some different experiences, it just stands to reason that it will be a more well thought through process.

How would young people define work ethic?

It's funny because I have heard students say things in front of Boomers, and I thought the Boomers would have a heart attack. One young worker said that if he was supposed to go to work but he had free tickets to a Red Hot Chili Peppers concert at the same time, he just wouldn't go to work. He would go to the concert and deal with the consequences later, because the Chili Peppers concert would be a once in a lifetime thing where work is every day. It was funny to watch the Boomers gasp when they heard that. But I don't think this is typical of Millennials. I think there are many students who understand the importance of work ethic. But their values are different. They think that you don't live to work, you work to live. That's how I personally view things. My family comes first. Your job needs to be your passion, but at some point it's a means to an end. You might need to give 110% at work, but if your family needs you, then that's a real conflict. For managers of a different generation, I see that as a real difference.

This is a variation on the Harley Davidson slogan that appealed to Gen Xers.

A common denominator between Gen Xers and Millennials.

So are you one of those fathers totally dedicated to his kids?

I have a seven-year-old and a three-year-old, and if they've got a party at school, I would sacrifice an hour of vacation time or even take an hour without pay if I have to. And that becomes a source of frustration. Bosses say, "You always want to take off."

But I come from a mindset of, "We can work around it." I think the whole 8:00 to 5:00 schedule thing could easily go away and let people work until the job gets done and still meet the needs of your family. That's a motivator to me. I want to work hard, but the employer needs to understand the importance of family as well.

Your thoughts about Gen Xers and motivation?

The old stereotype of the lazy generation you mentioned in your first book? I believe that if I'm going to manage a situation in a leadership role, I have to understand each generation and what motivates them differently. To me motivation is not solely focused on the bottom line, it's more focused on the employee. I think if you take care of your employees, they will take care of you and the bottom line will follow. If I've got a 22-year-old employee, I have to say, "If you've got family and you've got things that come up, I completely understand. If you need to take off, take off and go take care of it, but you still need to plan ahead. I still need you to do—not just the minimal—but really take pride in what you do because that's a reflection of yourself. I don't think you should have to live two separate lives, your home life and your work life. I think they should work together. But you still have a job that needs to get done."

Pure Millennial-on-Millennial management wisdom.

Does that work?
I think it does. I think employees understand. I use a lot of motivation and praise. I believe we don't tell people enough "thank you for what you do" or let them know they really are impacting someone's life—what you do is important. It's not just the bottom line. The bottom line is there if you take care of the people you are supposed to take care of. I think that making people feel valued is underrated. It doesn't even have to be about money. It's just about making people feel that they are important. If you do that, the money will follow.

Millennials respond to messages about the importance of their work.

So feedback is key.
I think feedback is an ongoing conversation, but a lot of us expect an immediate response. When you text someone you expect an immediate response. Who expects a letter anymore? We always send email. I see that struggle with students, because when they see an employer, I tell them they need to follow up with a thank you letter. And they say, "Can't I just send them a thank-you email?"

I say, "You can, but you've got to remember these managers are Boomers or late Xers, and they are blown away by a candidate who sends them a thank you letter because they don't believe people care about that anymore."

I don't see this generation requiring too much feedback, but I see them wanting to be taken care of, like they need to be enabled. They come in and ask me to help them set up their class schedule. I say, "Let's look at class options. Then you get a computer and go set it up." But they want you to do it for them. There's a lot of caretaking. I even see myself doing that for my children; I see them frustrated and the first thing I want to do is jump in and do it for them. But that doesn't help them to grow. They have to learn how to handle some incredibly complex things.

An acknowledged helicopter parent.

You've studied the generations more than most. Are you able to put aside what we call generational blinders?
I don't know because I tend to misunderstand many Boomers. Many of my colleagues are Boomers. Here I am preaching to others, "You have to understand generations and the way people think, and they have to understand how you think." But I sometimes don't do that myself.

I had a great Boomer boss once. He did a really good job when he first came on board. He was wonderful. He asked, "How do you work? What are your expectations?" We sort of ironed that out ahead of time. That really helps someone like myself who looks for a lot of communication up front.

But then there's the unspoken communication. I don't know how to get the blinders off, but the more I think about it, the easier it is for me to say to myself, "Okay, instead of getting frustrated, I need to think. What's going on in *their* life? Why are *they* reacting that way?" We all, regardless of generation, need to stop having to constantly justify the things we believe. Maybe it's our generation and maybe it's just who we are. We all need to understand. And there needs to be more give and take.

We encourage people, when they see bothersome behavior, to stop and look to see if there's a generational cause.

Yeah, and if the world were all Xers, that would be better. (He laughs.) You see that in a lot of policies, too. A lot of times when businesses change things, they forget to change policy. Like flex-time policies. I think flex-time is horribly underused. For example, if you work ten hours one day, you should be able to come in later the next day. Or if you have an evening activity, work through lunch and leave early. That

Gen Xers feel strongly that work isn't about hours spent in a chair but about measured outcomes.

Boomer boss I mentioned earlier was phenomenal. He would say he didn't understand why people don't do that more often. That is something that this generation seems to be looking for in an employer, one who understands they have a life outside of the office and creates that balance for their employees.

Are you a middle manager?

Yes, I'm a middle manager. I am supervising people in one program. In the other program, I'm not doing everything. I can't fire them. I'm more responsible for coordinating and guiding each party through the process.

We hear that Gen Xers don't like to manage.

I'm kind of the same way. I don't micromanage. The problem is, the Millennials sometimes take advantage of the fact that I'm just a fair manager. They might not think I care. I do, but it's hard for me because I tend to look at the person before I look at the job. That makes it hard to fire people. I have had to, and it is never fun regardless of the generation. I think that's kind of what I like least about the management piece because I think, "Oh my gosh, they have a family," or "If they don't have a job, maybe they can't afford food this week." It's hard for me. I would rather give someone a million chances and coach and train and support them than ever let somebody go. So that's why I think some of us find management difficult. With that said, my work ethic also understands that sometimes firing someone is what is best for the team or those you are serving. That makes it easier.

You've studied systems theory?

It helps you through every situation and helps you work with every group. It helps me understand how others think. And it helps me with groups so I can identify what I call a "boundary spanner," someone who can bring me into that group and find out its optimal level of functioning. It also helps me look at a system and figure out who is the cog in the wheel that's not working.

Any parting thoughts?

I don't want to shove it down people's throats, but I think our government, our economy, our business world, would all be better off—and work together better— if each of us understood the differences in generations. We need to stop believing that people are being hard-headed or people are being lazy. I think that's a cop out. We just really need to understand each generation, the way they are, the way they were raised. If we have to work with other generations, we have to not have our blinders on and have some give and take for each generation. I think we would be a lot more successful in business.

You know the "can't we all just get along" phrase? We could if we all stopped thinking that our way is the only way, and instead of believing that, we just need to say "let's stop having all these black and white policies and understand that some of them could, in fact, be gray."

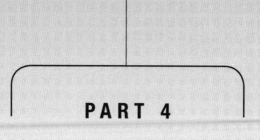

PART 4

Articles

In Part Four, you will find articles written by all of us. We've included a "classic" Ron Zemke piece, a reprint from *Training Magazine*. It was published more than a decade ago when Millennials were just kids. But it's uncanny how relevant, perceptive, and insightful it still is today. Next you will find a reprint of an article from Claire Raines' company website about older workers and younger managers. As it turns out, this configuration has become the new business normal. Claire offers practical tips and techniques for both the worker and manager. The last two articles from Bob Filipczak address important contemporary work issues: mentoring and technology. In the first, "A Field Guide to Mentoring Millennials," Bob discusses the challenges each of the generations faces when they mentor—and offers helpful advice. In "Emerging Media and the Workforce," he reviews leading-edge research about multitasking and the ways in which digital technology and the Internet are shaping the way people think and work.

CHAPTER 11

Here Come the Millennials

Ron Zemke

Reprinted from *Training Magazine*, July 2001

Ready or not here they come—the new kids on the block. No, not the bubble gum, boy band rock group, but the new and improved next generation of workplace denizens in need of your new employee, welcome to Acme Inc, here's how-you-do-your-job best. Referred to variously as Generation Y, the Nexters, Millennials, Echo Boomers and the Internet Gen, there is increasing evidence from generational researchers and on-the-ground reports that the newest group showing up at the personnel office is indeed as new and different a breed as the students of population and sociology and demographics have been prophesying it might be.

Economist/historian Neil Howe, co-author of Millennials Rising: The Next Great Generation, (Vintage Press, 2000) and co-founder of Great Falls, VA-based LifeCourse Associates has been studying the nuances of American generational differences for almost two decades. He sees a challenge ahead for the Baby Boomers and Generation Xers who by far dominate today's workplace. "The Baby Boomers, who really never got that good at managing Xers, are going to face some noteworthy problems and some real opportunities with the arrival of the Millennials." Given the history of conflicts that characterized early Boomer/Xers workplace relations (see It's Just a Job! April, 1994, *Training Magazine*) it's small wonder Howe and others who specialize in generational conflict are alert to the potential for a new set of problems as the Nexters begin their working lives.

High Expectations

Claire Raines, a Denver, CO-based consultant, and my co-author of *Generations At Work: Managing the Clash of Veterans, Boomers, Xers and Nexters in Your Workplace* (AMACOM, 2000), calls the Nexters "Basically good kids" but believes that they are showing up for work with pretty high and probably unrealistic expectations. "They see an article in the paper about this company that has a basketball court, that one with a pool table and beer in the refrigerator, and another one that gives you any day of the week off you want. They think that is just the way it is. They're in for some surprises."

Howe sees the Nexters as extremely self-confident and sure of their competence but because of the circumstances of their upbringing, expecting a more highly structured, "me" oriented environment than exists in most organizations. "These kids are used to a lot of structure in their lives. Chaperones, organizers, community coordinators. Their parents and teachers have always planned things out for them. They've had very little unplanned free time and aren't used to ambiguous situations and may not be very spontaneous." As a result, says Howe, many come into the workplace expecting employers to give clear detailed directions and to have a detailed career plan complete with a time line for raises and advancement. "Whoever is in charge is seen as 'in loco parentus' and accountable—for everything. Accountable for training, career planning and for providing a safe and risk free work environment."

Carolyn Martin, a partner at Rainmaker Thinking, Inc., (New Haven, CT) and co-author of *Managing Generation Y* (HRD Press, 2001) agrees with the high expectation thesis: "They have been micromanaged by their parents and teachers all their lives and expect that in the workplace. At the same time they don't see that as incompatible with an expectation of a $75,000 starting salary and a corner office in six months." Indeed, that attitude is already making for some surprises in the training room.

A seasoned claims adjustment trainer in a well-known property-casualty insurance firm—who would only speak with us anonymously

WHAT NEXTERS REALLY WANT

"Industry of Choice," a 1997 study of turnover in the food service industry by the Food Service Research Forum, sheds some light on the expectations of today's twenty-year olds. As working teenagers, they made clear the factors that made an acceptable workplace. The researchers divided respondent expectations into two categories: Human Resource Practices and Organizational Culture Factors. The top ten in both Categories:

Organizational Culture	Human Resource Practices
Having a boss who is fair	A regular paycheck
Having a boss who doesn't embarrass or make fun of me	A safe place to work
Having a boss who treats others like they would like to be treated	A clean place to work
Feeling like the company treats employees fairly	Competitive wage or salary
Feeling like I do my job well	The right equipment to do my job
Having a boss who I get along with	Having enough employees to handle the work load
Being treated like an adult; even when I make a mistake	Health insurance
Having a boss who is moral	Working enough hours
Feeling like the company is well managed	Paid vacation
Feeling like everybody does their part to keep things running smoothly	Worker's compensation insurance

"Industry of Choice" sponsored by the Foodservice Research Forum, sponsored by The Coca-Cola Company, January 1997.

—says he is astonished by his new college trainees' brazenness; "We spend six months training them and after a few weeks in the field the phone calls start—'Hey, when am I going to get promoted' or 'Hey, when do I get training for my next job?' They act so insulted that they are going to have to do this same job for an extended period of time; that this is the job, not just some developmental field trip."

THE FOURTEEN EXPECTATIONS OF GENERATION Y

1. Provide challenging work that really matters
2. Balance clearly delegated assignments with freedom and flexibility
3. Offer increasing responsibility as a reward for accomplishments
4. Spend time getting to know staff members and their capabilities
5. Provide ongoing training and learning opportunities
6. Establish mentoring relationships
7. Create a comfortable, low-stress environment
8. Allow some flexibility in scheduling
9. Focus on work, but be personable and have a sense of humor
10. Balance the roles of "boss" and "team player"
11. Treat Yers as colleagues, not as interns or "teenagers"
12. Be respectful, and call forth respect in return
13. Consistently provide constructive feedback
14. Reward Yers when they've done a good job.

Taken from Bruce Tulgan and Carolyn A, Martin, *Managing Generation Y* (HRD Press, 2001), page 63.

Raines isn't surprised by the scenario. "They don't value work for work's sake. Work that isn't seen as a learning experience that leads to something better—is seen as a dead end to be avoided." This attitude, says Howe, explains the trouble many organizations that traditionally employ teenagers and college students are having with staffing—and attendance. "They say it out loud with no apologies—jobs where you handle food or simply tote and carry aren't growth or learning opportunities and are to be avoided. And if they take one out of economic necessity they think nothing of not coming in for work if something better—meaning something they can learn something from—comes up."

Rainmaker Thinking's Martin agrees that attitude of performance exists, but in good trainerly fashion sees the situation itself as a learning opportunity. "Take that problem with the adjuster job as an example," she says. "That attitude 'I've mastered it. I've proven my worth. What's next?' That's an opportunity to help them stand back and look at the nuances that separate knowing the data and the procedures from being a real player in the big leagues. That's where the manager—or the trainer —can take on the role of experience enhancer, and mentor that person from tyro to master performer." Raines adds: "Mentoring really works well with this group. And it works particularly well to pair a wise old Veteran with a Nexter in a mentoring relationship. The Nexters kind of admire and respect the Veterans for what they have been through in life."

Not That Different?

Bruce Tulgan, founder of Rainmaker Thinking, and author of *Winning the Talent Wars* (W.W. Norton & Company, 2001) is well known for chronicling the work life struggles of Generation X. When he turns his attention to the Nexters, he sees more similarities than differences—and isn't convinced that the Nexters are expecting—or in need of—as much hand holding, mentoring and coaching as some observers are anticipating. "I think there are more similarities than differences. Institutions are in a state of flux. Self-reliance and independence are more possible and more important than ever. The Generation Y people are coming into the workplace during an unprecedented time of economic expansion. So, yes, they are more optimistic and positive than the Generation X people who fully believed they would end up financially worse off than their parents. So the Xers aren't just independent, but fiercely independent. The Gen Y people are much more relaxed and confident." That said, Tulgan believes that Nexters are as independent and self-reliant as their Gen X predecessors, they are just more tolerant of close supervision and somewhat more accepting of the possibilities of life in a corporate—as opposed to an entrepreneurial—world.

That sense of self-directedness, Tulgan attributes to Nexters, greatly impresses Chris Rhan (26) a department chemist at Rayovac Corp, in Madison WI. Rahn, who acts as a mentor to Nexters coming into his department was surprised by his charges' focus. "They desire a large degree of autonomy. It has worked out well to give a person a project with direction only in what we are looking for in the end result. It's nice to be able to give a person a project and not have to hold their hand." Nor has he found them to be shy and retiring, observing that when they are subject to close supervision or to following established procedures

GENERATIONS@WORK:
CAN'T TELL THE PLAYERS WITHOUT A SCORE CARD

Welcome to the new generation gap. The broadest range of age and value diverse employees in American history are being asked to work together, shoulder to shoulder, side by side, and cubical to cubical. And get along in the bargain.

A generation is defined by both demographics and the Key Life Events an age cohort experiences together. Breathes there an American Baby Boomer who doesn't remember the crowded schools, shared desks and large classes of their youth—or where they were when they heard the news that president John F. Kennedy had been assassinated?

The four generations alternately collaborating and duking it out in the workplace are:

The Veterans   Technically two groups. The GIs (1901–1924) and the Silents (1925–1943). The annealing and uniting event for Vets was World War II. Think Tom Brokaw's Greatest Generation and all the kids during World War II who came to conscious awareness during that tumultuous, anxious, yet exhilarating era. Though fast exiting the workplace, they remain connected and influential.

Baby Boomers   The postwar Baby Boomers created the largest, most positive, most doted upon generation the world had ever seen. This demographic Pig-in-the-Python claimed the world by right of inheritance and vowed to change everything for the better. They hold most of the "good" jobs, occupy most of the important posts. In 1969 *Time* magazine declared the ascendant Baby Boomer "Person of the Year." Today they are turning 50 at the rate of 11,000 a day. Birth dates vary by definer, but 1943 to 1960 covers most conceptualizations.

Generation X   Born between 1960 and 1980 and reared during the anxious days of Three Mile Island, wide spread retrenchment and the belief that they would inherit a has-been country, Gen Xers acquired a wary demeanor and a cynicism about work, business and careers. Their "It's only a job" attitude puts them in perpetual conflict with the "Let's take a meeting!" and "Thank God it's Monday!" Baby Boomers.

Generation Next   The New Kids—referred to variously as Millennials, Gen Y, Generation D, the Internet Generation and Nexters—dates, depending again on the definer—from someplace between 1977 and 1982—and continues to grow. Doted on, sheltered, helmeted, organized, and raised on the one hand like hot house flowers and wild weeds, they are only now defining themselves in the workplace and moving beyond fast food, paper route, lawn mowing and web page design part time jobs.

they speak up: "Rather than just accepting how something is done, they ask why. This has helped us change our processes and procedures to be more effective." It also fits with another Tulgan observation: "They want to be taken seriously. From the beginning. Don't treat me like a kid. Don't treat me like an intern. Treat me like a colleague."

If Kate Ward is any example, Nexters definitely don't lack in self-direction and determination. Ward (22), a class of 2000 graduate from Millikin University, Decatur, IL, went from college and a part time bartending job to a position as an e-commerce analyst with a start up, high tech, logistics management firm in El Segundo, CA. The pace was a surprise for her: "It's basically one big balancing act. You have to learn to prioritize and stay organized. The strain is mental, physical and emotional all at once. That was a big surprise." Just the same, she thinks she's mastered the art of work and credits her college experience with preparing her for the unexpected rigor, "If you are active at all in college you get a taste for what it's going to be like. They hand you a syllabus and a schedule and you have to learn to make some tradeoffs and some how get it all done. I just applied the same thing to my work."

Team Oriented

If GenXers are the epitome of You, Inc, an ethic that says "To thine own self be loyal—all others take a number," the Nexters seem to exude a collaborative "leave no one behind" value. "Team is very important to this group" observes Howe, adding, "Millennials are used to being organized as teams to get things done and being evaluated as a unit—getting a group grade for a project or assignment." Raines agrees with Howe's assessment adding, "They've been trained to think inclusively and collaboratively—and to be sure everyone is involved and that everyone does his part."

There are several important implications to that collaborative impulse. Howe believes organizations are going to have to revisit the ways people are evaluated and paid—and take care in singling individuals out for special treatment. "Millennials really resent the way Xers wheedle special little perks and deals out of the company. They don't mind the idea of being evaluated—and paid—as a group. They prefer standardization to predatory competition among colleagues. They don't think it's fair."

That impulse for fairness can have some unexpected side effects. Don't be surprised if you hear from a disappointed employee's parent, several of our experts report such occurrences. Raines recounts: "The parents seem to see it as no different than challenging a bad grade in school. A supervisor in a Florida hotel I was working with hears from the parents of 18 and 19 year olds when they think they aren't being treated fairly or didn't like something in a performance review."

Of that peculiarity Howe observes "The parents *are* Baby Boomers and their kids *are* perfect, aren't they?"

That idea of fairness and fair play in the workplace has a high valence for Nexters. Seeing peers treated better—or worse—than they themselves are treated put them on edge. "They are very uncomfortable when they see someone violating the ethical conduct code—in school they learned to avoid cheaters and shirkers—and they believe rules are rules. They expect bosses to enforce them and not bend them," says Howe.

That collaborative nature can be a little unsettling particularly to Boomers who are used to a lot of clear job focus. Nexters expect to be hooked up with colleagues on the intra and extra net, and to be in constant contact via computer and cell phone. Collaboration assumes communication --lots of communication. Says Howe, "They expect to be in constant communication with their extended network. The cell phone and beeper are natural appendages to the body. And they are as likely to be calling mom as a colleague."

Contrary to popular opinion, Nexters don't live on the Internet. They just consider it another communication medium. According to Frank Gregorsky, publisher and editor of *Love Those Millennials* newsletter (www.millennials.com), the Nexters spend about 123 hours a month of free time on the Internet. "Their T time to their web time is about 7 to 1, in favor of television," he says.

Enthusiasm for Learning

Nexters are surprisingly sensitive to and enthusiastic about situations, and assignments they see as learning opportunities. Rayovac's Rahn says, "They are a real treat to tutor and supervise. It has been a real experience for me," adding, "Opportunity for growth and learning, the ability to be innovative in their job, and the chance to work on developing new systems and processes seem very attractive to them. Salary and wages seem secondary."

Both Howe and Tulgan have picked up this learning enthusiasm and the importance learning plays in Nexters' decision making about the jobs they take and what it takes to retain them. And both advise managing Nexters as "paid volunteers." Tulgan's advice; "You have to roll up your sleeve and really get to know them and what turns them on, what they want to develop competence in, what motivates them. It also doesn't hurt if you are a little flexible—like letting them pick assignments from time to time, maybe bring their dog to the office and relax the dress code a little."

Ward makes it clear that learning opportunity was a big factor in the decision making that led to her first job. "My number one consideration was the people. I really wanted to work with people I click with. But after that, it was the amount of knowledge there is here. There is so much to learn and so many great people to learn from. I can really spend time developing areas that are of interest to me."

Still a Seller's Market

It's clear that these new kids on the block are, well, a little different from you and me. And that it is going to take some adjusting to help them fit and fit them into the always evolving organizational tapestry. Oh, and if in the back of your mind you are hoping that the most recent economic turns can save you from those adjusts—just uncross those fingers, friends. As of today the simple facts of demographics, those same demographics that have created our generational differences are negating that faint hope.

Government figures reveal that government workers are reaching retirement age at a double digit pace. The average U.S. registered nurse is 46 years old. And about half the licensed public school teachers in America are within five years of retirement. It is still and yet a sellers market for talent. And our challenge is to make the work-a-day world as comfortable and compatible as we can for every one of those talented, soon to be associates.

CHAPTER 12

Younger Boss and Older Worker

Claire Raines

Reprinted from www.generationsatwork.com,
the website of Claire Raines Associates

*"It's increasingly common in the Canadian workplace to find older,
more experienced workers reporting to significantly
younger, less experienced managers."*
—Multigenerational Workforce Management
2008 Randstad Outlook Randstad Canada

Robert, 59, believes a company with a vision can still set the world on fire, and that when there's a problem, you need to get everybody in one room and pound out a solution. "I grew up with TV dinners, Clapton on the eight-track, Alvin and the Chipmunks, and Neil Armstrong," he says. "I believe in reading the manual." He runs marathons and watches reruns of *Law and Order*.

Jeanie, 24, says she can't remember a time when she couldn't text as fast as she can talk. "I concentrate best when I'm watching TV, listening to my iPod™, and answering an IM," she says. She believes in instant gratification, frequent rewards, and life after work. "People started caring about my self esteem when I was twelve," she says "and that's when everyone started getting a trophy." She wants feedback every day on how she's doing. She grew up with Wii. Her favorite show is *The Office*, and her mom is her best friend.

Jeanie is Robert's new boss, and the two represent the new normal in today's workplace. Baby Boomers, many of whom have delayed their retirement, often find themselves working for people young enough to be their grandchildren. A survey by Harris Interactive® on behalf of CareerBuilder.com finds that 69 percent of workers 55 and older report to younger bosses.

Just a few years ago, people from different generations were separated at work by rank and status. Older employees filled executive positions, the middle-aged were in mid-management, and the youngest worked on the front lines—and because of the nature of work, people weren't likely to rub elbows on a daily basis with those in other age groups.

The older worker/younger boss configuration can create challenges. Different generations have unique perspectives on everything from workplace humor to communication style to work ethic. Baby Boomers may feel awkward taking direction from younger bosses—and younger bosses may feel awkward dishing it out. Since the generations define hard work and loyalty differently, teamwork can suffer. While Boomers tend to prefer face-to-face or even written communication, younger generations prefer text messages and IMs. The generations even hold different perspectives on what to wear to work.

In the scenario above, Robert may resent his younger manager and fear she will favor his younger, less experienced, more tech-savvy colleagues. He may think that the hours she spends in the office don't justify her title. For her part, Jeanie may hold stereotypes about older workers—that they're not adaptable and can't learn new skills, for example. She may sense that Robert feels superior even though she's the boss.

Yet the mix of generations on a work team can give it a competitive edge. The variety of perspectives and approaches can:

- Increase a team's creativity.
- Make the group more responsive to a wide range of clientele.
- Contribute to broader-based decisions.
- Simply add an element of fun.

As we emerge from recession, it's more important than ever that all employees realize their full potential, contribute their best, and work well with the team.

The Titanium Rule

It's human nature to treat people the way we want to be treated. Most of us, for example, want to be treated with respect, and so we believe we're doing the right thing by treating others with respect. However, each generation has its own ideas about what respect looks and sounds like.

Jeanie is a member of the Millennial Generation, or Generation Y. Typical of her generation, she prefers efficient, streamlined communications that respect her time, or lack of it. She likes to communicate via text messages and IMs. For his part, Robert, a Boomer, works most effectively when he is involved in designing and monitoring the group process. He wants friendly work relationships with his colleagues. He prefers to communicate face-to-face.

Robert and Jeanie will work together more successfully by following The Titanium Rule—Do unto others, keeping *their* preferences in mind. Rather than communicating in their own most natural style, they should ask themselves, "What expectations, attitudes, and behaviors does he/she bring to the workplace? How can those influence the way I communicate?"

What Robert and Jeanie Can Do

Both Robert and Jeanie need to recognize the value the other brings to the table. By understanding and accepting their differences, Robert and Jeanie can tap into each others' strengths and work together to produce solid business results.

To bring out Robert's best, Jeanie may need to adapt her style. Here are some steps to consider:

- Acknowledge his expertise. Identify Robert's skill sets and strengths, and be open to learning from him. Tap into his experience.
- Consider giving Robert a bit more face time than might be natural for her. For most Baby Boomers, relationships and business results are intertwined. Get together for a cup of coffee and get input on whatever issues are at hand.
- Give plenty of direction without micromanaging. Make certain Robert is clear on her goals and standards, and let him make his own decisions about how to reach them.
- Link her messages to organizational vision and values. Robert may have been part of the group who formulated them, and the vision and values help him see where his contribution fits.

Here are some ways Robert can follow the Titanium Rule and work effectively with his younger boss:

- Focus less on relationship and more on results. Avoid talking about his years of experience; instead, keep track of his accomplishments and keep Jeanie up to date on them.
- Identify Jeanie's strengths and respect her expertise. Be open to her ideas and approaches.
- Refrain from behaviors that drive younger generations crazy. Avoid comparing Jeanie to his daughter or granddaughter. Don't act like a know-it-all. Nip cynicism or sarcasm in the bud.
- Learn the new technology. Ask Jeanie how she prefers to stay in touch. If she tends toward text messages and Robert doesn't text, it's time to learn. Check IMs and cell phone messages regularly.
- Jump on training opportunities. Learn new software programs. Attend communication workshops. Keep his skills up to date.

Strategies for the Manager

To harness the potential of her multigeneration work team, Jeanie will need to implement intentional strategies that help people learn from one another and work together effectively. Work teams that succeed across generations use a variety of strategies to develop effective teams.

1. Initiate conversations about generations.

Okay, Baby Boomer, what do you really think about your Millennial co-worker who texts during meetings? And Gen Xer, how do you react when your World War II Generation colleague says he has to check his paper calendar that he keeps at his desk before committing to a meeting with you? We all make judgments about each other based on our own history and frame of reference. And, afraid we'll offend, we rarely talk openly about generational differences. Jeanie's team will work better together when they learn more about the backgrounds and perspectives of each of the generations.

2. Ask people about their expectations, needs, and preferences.

Out of the best intentions, we often project our preferences onto others. Creating an environment where each team member can openly share information about work style and preferences, needs, and perspectives will help Jeanie's team members find ways of working together that will satisfy all participants. As team leader, Jeanie should personalize her style and be flexible. She will need to find creative ways to meet team members' varied expectations and needs.

3. Communicate on the personal level, as well as the business level.

Jeanie should devote some time in team meetings to casual conversation and help team members get to know one another on an individual basis. In addition to strengthening their understanding of one another, team-mates will build trust and develop personal commitments to one another.

4. Pursue different perspectives.

Many work teams tolerate differences, but the mixed-generation teams that truly succeed go beyond tolerance. Jeanie should choose people with varied backgrounds and perspectives to work on projects together.

5. **Focus on the goal and play to team members' strengths in reaching that goal.**

If everyone clearly understands where the team is headed, they can bring their creativity and skills to play in designing ways to reach the destination. Jeannie should help team members identify their complementary skills and assign responsibilities accordingly. For example, Gen Xers and Millennials might bring more technological savvy to the group's efforts, while Baby Boomers like Robert might take the lead with problem-solving. Whereas some team members might work on "big picture" strategies, more detail-oriented colleagues can make sure no stone is left unturned in arriving at solutions.

What Organizations Can Do

Savvy companies with multigeneration workforces recognize that priorities, attitudes, work styles and perspectives differ with each generation. They develop intentional strategies to build understanding so that generational differences don't lead to frustration, conflict, and poor morale. Creating a climate of respect is a critical foundation for bringing out the best in everyone. Organizations that handle the generational mix especially well build upon shared values, attitudes, and behaviors while reaching out in ways that are appropriate to each generational group. They:

1. **Know their company demographics—internally and externally.**
They gather data about their current customers and target where they want to increase market share. They gather data and learn about their employees and consider how well their staff mirrors current and projected customers.

2. **Are intentional about creating and responding to generational diversity.**
They identify needed skill sets within the company and recruit new staff from across the generations. They seek out individuals from under-represented generations for work teams, boards, and advisory groups.

3. Build on strengths.

The most effective mixed-generation work teams recognize the unique strengths of each individual. Successful companies find ways to bring out those strengths and help each individual develop his or her talents so they can reach their own potential and contribute in their own ways.

4. Offer options.

They recognize that people from a mix of generations have differing needs and preferences and design their human resources strategies to meet these varied employee needs. They offer a variety of benefits, flexible schedules, and an array of opportunities for professional growth and advancement.

5. Develop an understanding of, and appreciation for, generational differences and strengths.

They find ways to learn about their employees' needs, perspectives, and interests—and share that learning across the organization. They structure opportunities for less experienced employees from each generation to learn from their more experienced and knowledgeable colleagues—and for older employees to learn from younger ones. Managers help people become more aware and accepting of generational differences. Rather than perpetuating generational stereotypes—"young people are rude, disrespectful, and ill-mannered," "older workers are stuck in the past,"—managers gather their own data and draw upon current research. The facts show that young people today are generally positive, respectful, patriotic, and goal-oriented. Surveys of older workers find they are continuing to learn and contribute. If managers start the generations conversation and offer opportunities to learn about generational differences, employees stop judging one another and find the strengths in their differences. Creativity, productivity, and morale increase.

6. Train people to communicate effectively across generations.

Communication styles and levels of comfort with varied technologies differ from one generation to the next. Successful companies recognize those differences, employ an array of communication methods and teach employees how to reach out effectively to their colleagues and ensure that their communication approaches are inclusive and welcoming. They offer training that gives people a basic understanding of the communication style and preferences of each generation.

CHAPTER 13

A Field Guide to Mentoring Millennials

Bob Filipczak

Mentoring has always been part of work, but it became formalized and popularized by Boomers. And why not? For a generation of people seeking to reach their full human potential, being a mentor was an acknowledgement of their wisdom, knowledge and experience.

Let's face it, a lot of Boomers wanted to be Jack Welch. But most organizations realized that wasn't in the cards for all Boomers, so mentoring was the next best thing. You didn't have to pay them anything extra. It felt like succession planning, and recruiting Boomers for mentoring programs was, if you'll pardon the expression, like shooting fish in a barrel. Not everyone could have an office in the C-suite, but everyone could be a mentor. Mentoring played to Boomer's strengths, and they were intrinsically motivated to guide young employees along. That was perfect for Millennials who liked their parents, admired their parents, and turned to their parents for advice. Now here was an older employee, who looked and acted like their parents, to take them under their wing and protect and guide them. To them, it was natural and comfortable.

This is probably a good time to interrupt this generational love fest to acknowledge that every generation goes through the socialization of work. The transition between school and work is a rite of passage that can be tumultuous and disruptive. Not everyone makes this transition smoothly. The skills that worked in school don't always spell success at work, and most organizations don't know how to help people through the transition. Combine that potentially volatile transition with a generation of young people who have had their lives, not to put too fine a point on it, programmed. They were told what they needed to do to get through school and into the college. They were scheduled for an array of extracurricular activities, volunteer work and AP courses that put the previous two generations to shame. And they believed us when we said they could get a good education in the college of their choice.

So as they transition into life at work, a mentoring program seems an ideal solution—match outgoing Boomers with incoming Millennials and let the wisdom transfer begin. But as we hear from Glenn Horton, the insurance company CEO, it doesn't always work. In fact, Boomers can be notoriously bad mentors. They've reached an advanced stage in their lives and careers, and they know a lot. Many become professorial. Being professorial makes them feel like they're at the top of Maslow's hierarchy, but it can turn them into lecturers rather than mentors.

Chip Bell, author of *Managers as Mentors* (third edition coming in Spring 2013) agrees. "Boomers are more into the telling mentality. They are like 'If I'm the expert, you're the novice, so listen up and I'll tell you all you need to know.'" It's important to remind Boomers that this is the workplace and not the lecture hall. Bell adds, "It needs to be a partnership. You need to think about how you get people to take risks and try and experiment. The context you create contributes to that and a telling mentality doesn't usually contribute to that kind of context. For mentoring to be effective, at any age, it has to be laced with discovery and exploration"

Megan Emme is a 20-year old Millennial running a mentoring program teaching high school students how to blog for her organization— which raises money and awareness to fight hunger across the world. She's been on both ends of the mentoring role, and she has found that lecturing doesn't go over well. "I think the main problem with that is when someone is lecturing you, you're not really learning anything because they are not giving you the space to think critically and learn those skills for yourself," she says.

The Give and Take of Mentoring

Bell has recently been consulting with oil workers, the guys out on the rigs in the middle of the North Sea, about mentoring— and he has run smack into generational issues. He quickly learned that the older engineers had to be convinced to share their considerable knowledge. What they knew wasn't the stuff you could learn in a book or elearning module or classroom. The older engineers had hands-on working knowledge that had soaked into their bones over the decades, but they saw their knowledge as the primary source of their own job security. Says Bell, "one of the challenges between generations is around security: 'do I want to share my wisdom, and will that then render me unnecessary?'"

The young guns, on the other hand wanted to learn the on-the-job wisdom that would make them more effective out on the rigs. But they didn't see why the knowledge had to go one way. They were frustrated by older engineers who didn't see value in the new techniques the younger engineers had learned in school. They felt devalued. So Bell set up what he called *upside down mentoring*, where there is a full partnership between mentor and mentee, and knowledge flows both ways. The older engineers started passing on what they knew, what they had learned during long hours out on the platform, and the younger engineers passed on the new techniques they had learned in school. This wasn't, of course, automatic. Bell says the evolution was a slow one, and after 6 months he was back out in the field monitoring progress and taking them to the next steps in the mentoring process. "I think people spend their life making a difference, making a contribution and mentoring, if properly managed, can be a venue for a lot of these who have retired, or could retire, to make a contribution that would be beneficial."

So one technique for facilitating a useful and successful mentoring relationship is to make sure both participants are open to learning. It's not a one-way transfer of knowledge. When you're recruiting senior managers to be mentors, make sure they can answer this question: what do you want or need to learn from our younger employees?

Knowledge about social media should be an easy sell for older employees if they aren't already comfortable with it (a lot of them are). That's the quid pro quo—older employees can help Millennials with office politics and company culture while the younger employees can explain why a viral YouTube video might deliver a better message to more customers than a brochure. As Bell puts it, "Why wouldn't the kid who is 23 be the mentor of the CEO who needs to know more about the cloud and how to use it?"

Another of Bell's examples comes from a premier New York hotel. The organization had set up an open mentoring environment where people could identify their strengths and volunteer to teach those strengths to others. Then they would register those abilities. The general manager noticed that one of the night supervisors was particularly good at handling people. "She saw the great diplomacy of this supervisor," says Bell. "The GM was from the not-so-diplomatic section of New York. She said to herself, 'I'd like to learn that.'" While there were a lot of organizational levels between them, that didn't matter to the general manager. "That's, to me, the epitome of a learning organization: mentoring is occurring where it needs to occur without regard to race, color, creed, sex, national origin, age or any other factor for that matter," says Bell

Mentors Can Teach Risk

Earlier, Bell commented on how mentoring can help young people take risks and experiment. We've already discussed how risk-averse Millennials can be, so can mentoring overcome that? Can mentors teach younger workers how to go out on a limb, or even when to go out on a limb, when they don't really even like the idea of climbing trees?

Bell says that you need to first teach younger, risk-averse, workers that all innovation and learning comes from measured risk. "It's all about creating a context where that risk taking will occur. The core of innovation is learning," he says. "There's no way you can go from A to Z without taking some risk." Then the mentor has to be supportive while slowly introducing some independence and self-reliance into the mentee. "The avenue for weaning them from that protectiveness is around accountability. I think there's a great place for tough love in the mentoring relationship. It's a great place for bringing about a sense of discipline," says Bell. He cites the example of the Zen master—which should appeal to Boomer mentors—who were not always gentle with those they were instructing. "That's part of the responsibility of being a mentor, to be willing to hold them accountable and set high expectations. You want to be supportive, but in the end you've got to be tough."

Enter the Generation X Mentors

At first blush, the DIY, pull yourselves up by your bootstraps Gen X mentality doesn't seem to lend itself particularly well to the mentoring model. Xers traditionally have not been drawn to mentoring. Many went through it with Boomer bosses, not because they wanted or needed it, but because they—perhaps cynically—equated mentoring with career advancement. In organizations led by Xers, you can expect mentoring programs to either be scrapped or allowed to die of attrition.

That would be a mistake. The very skills Millennials need are the ones Generation X workers excel at. Young workers need fewer lectures and more practical day-to-day guidance about how to navigate the work world. Generation X is pragmatic to a fault, and they don't give a cuss about mission statements. Their nature is to deliver exactly the kind of advice Millennials need.

Moreover, if Bell is right about risk, there are no better teachers of the joys of risk-taking that Generation X. Xers' motto is "ask forgiveness rather than permission." Good Xer mentors can show how risk—even measured risk—has been helped them be successful in their careers. And if they are in upper management or supervisory positions, nothing communicates that risk is okay/good louder to young employees than stories about risks that have paid off. Even more can be learned from the risks that didn't pay off but didn't get the risk-taker sacked either.

In terms of tough love, Generation X learned it early and knows just what it looks like. The only drawback might be they will be too tough. They are survivors and don't suffer non-survivors—or those they perceive as soft and fuzzy—gladly. The question you need an Xer to answer before you recruit them into your mentoring program is: are you willing to teach some of your survival skills, your street smarts, to younger employees and leave your cynicism at the door?

Here's what Bell has to say about cynicism. "What do you lose by being cynical about mentoring?" he asks. "What you lose is the capacity to grow people and be competitive and the capacity to attract people who want to be part of a growing organization--a learning organization that is expanding and adapting and succeeding." In the end, Bell quotes Arie de Geus, former head of Strategic Planning for Royal Dutch Shell, "Your ability to learn faster than your competition is your only sustainable competitive advantage." That should get the attention of the most cynical Xer out there.

Millennials Mentoring Millennials

We've talked about peer mentoring in the interview with Glenn Horton, so we were interested in Megan Emme's program where Millennials mentor other Millennials. It seems a bit counterintuitive, since our mental model for mentoring consists of older professionals passing on wisdom, but there's actually much to be passed along when you have people who are closer to the same age. Says Emme, "For me, I'm not that far from high school. I remember what it's like to be in high school. I remember the challenges that are part of that. And I think it's a little bit easier for the younger kids to feel understood by me."

Trust is, from Emme's experience, key to making a mentoring relationship work. "I think a lot of it actually has to do with trust. And if you are closer to them in age, there's more trust there," she says. "The ideal mentor would be first of all someone I could trust. If I don't trust the person that's mentoring me, I'm not as liable to really agree with the things they are telling me to do." Her mentoring program for high school students teaches them about blogging for her organization and consists of both a weekly conference call and individual face-to-face time with each mentee. It's important to her to make sure there is an open environment where her mentees can explore and discover and learn. "The worst thing you could have, is a mentor who is absolutely authoritarian, who is just telling you to do x, y, and z," she says. Did you hear that, Generation X mentors?

Emme also says that two-way mentoring is essential, where both participants agree to learn from each other. "I think the ability to recognize that, as a mentor, you can learn things from your mentee--I think that's huge. So as a mentor, you need to realize that you don't necessarily know everything. You need to acknowledge that there are things that mentees can teach you. That is really big."

Boomers as Mentors

- Don't lecture
- Teach them about day-to-day office skills that may seem obvious
- Teach them to slow down and think from time to time
- Listen and learn from Millennials

Gen Xers as Mentors

- Teach them about risk, about making mistakes.
- Teach them about project management and how to take a project from start to finish
- Listen to Millennials about technology, teamwork and collaboration

Millennials as Mentors

- Earn the trust of your mentees, no matter their age
- Listen to mentees and learn from them
- Learn when you can mentor virtually and when you need to do it face-to-face.

CHAPTER 14

Emerging Media and the Workforce

Bob Filipczak

One of the early concerns about Generation X was that their attention span was too short. But experts soon suggested that Xers have a new kind of attention that allows them to attend to more than one thing at a time. They can, for example, answer the phone and type an email at the same time. Soon the IT world was calling it *multitasking*. Now we take multi-tasking for granted. With two of the generations currently in the workforce—Gen Xers and Millennials—living and breathing multitasking natives, it's become the default way people work.

But the jury is out on its efficacy. Some experts say that our inability to focus on one thing at a time degrades our ability to solve serious problems and reach strong, well-founded conclusions. Others would argue that serious, focused problem solving and analysis is not required in most peoples' day-to-day work lives, and that multitasking, therefore, is fine for the majority of workers most of the time. They have a point. Many routine tasks don't require all of your brainpower, so sending an instant message to a coworker while fixing typos on your company's website makes perfect sense. But some routines, like those in manufacturing or construction, are dangerous enough that you don't want the guy swinging the crane to also be texting his girlfriend.

As we were writing this second edition, the Pew Research Center's Internet & American Life Project released a new report, *Millennials Will Benefit and Suffer Due to Their Hyperconnected Lives*. The Pew Center surveyed 1,021 Internet experts and some Internet users. So what were the major conclusions?

- Technology experts and stakeholders were about evenly split as to whether Millennials' connectedness will be an advantage or a problem for them.

- Most agreed that this generation uses the Web and their mobile connectivity as part of an external brain they can access for information. So we may see the word *multitasking* replaced by the concept of cloud consciousness.

- About 55 percent agreed that, due to their exposure to the digital world, Millennials' brains are "wired" differently than the brains of those older than 35. They concluded—or hoped—that this would not impair them cognitively and would help them find answers to deep questions using the collective intelligence of the Internet.

- A large minority (42%), however, came to the conclusion that these differently wired brains would create a population of distracted, shallow-thinking, less social people who won't function well in the real world of work.

Rather than get tangled up in experts and their predictions about the future, let's compare what we know about Millennials to what research is saying about their brains and their ability to process. In short, what do we agree on and what does it mean for the future of work?

A New Definition of Social

Millennials are social animals, especially when compared to the more independent Generation Xers. But when older generations see a dozen young people texting in a coffee shop or food court, they don't perceive what they're seeing as *social*. They think they're seeing a batch of isolated individuals cut off from society by technology. If you define *social* as purely face-to-face communication, then they aren't being social.

Older generations may be stuck in a communication mindset that can be blamed partially on email. Generally, email facilitated communication for a lot of people in a short period of time. Xers and Boomers embraced email, but few people ever thought it was much of a substitute for social communication. It worked more like a memo or letter than a genuine dialogue, though people grew more conversational with email as they got the hang of its tools. It was, after all, a great way to forward jokes to folks you liked to hang out with.

But the connectivity of Millennials is a very different way to approach sociability. To them, interacting online or through mobile devices is the same as interacting with their friends in the real world. In his manifesto in *The Atlantic,* Piotr Czerski, writes:

> We made friends and enemies online, we prepared cribs for tests online, we planned parties and studying sessions online, we fell in love and broke up online. The Web to us is not a technology which we had to learn and which we managed to get a grip of. The Web is a process, happening continuously and continuously transforming before our eyes; with us and through us. Technologies appear and then dissolve in the peripheries, websites are built, they bloom and then pass away, but the Web continues, because we are the Web; we, communicating with one another in a way that comes naturally to us, more intense and more efficient than ever before in the history of mankind.[1]

Even the term *real world* is blurry to them. While older folks accuse them of having poor social skills (especially when the Millennial is multitasking while talking to one of us), the same accusations can be leveled at us if we are not entirely comfortable using social media and mobile communication. But by choosing to narrowly define social communication, you eliminate your ability to participate fully in conversations you and your organization definitely want to be part of.

We can change our definition of what it means to be social. We can broaden our definition to include online digital communication in real time. In that case, you take the team-orientation of Millennials and the online technology they use to enhance their social reach, and you get a workforce with skills that aren't limited to their own brains, the computer in front of them, or even the boundaries of your department. We all know someone who crosses boundaries and builds connections in unlikely ways with folks all over the place. Are you ready for a whole generation like that?

But What Do We Do With Their Brains?

So if Millennials handle more information and offload some of that to an online cloud consciousness from which they can retrieve information seamlessly, how does that affect their ability to work? The first most obvious place this will show up is in meetings. Think about it. If you walk by someone's office and they are staring at a screen, you assume they're working. But if you are in a meeting and the guy next to you is tapping on his iPad or smartphone, you may assume he's otherwise occupied and not paying attention. If the guy is 27 and everyone else in the meeting is an older executive, sparks could fly.

But what if that 27-year-old employee is just accessing part of his online brain as he listens to the meeting? Left to his own devices, he may come up with a solution no one else thought of. Do you really want him to put down the iPad or iPhone? Telling younger workers to turn off their technology during meetings is tantamount to asking them to turn off their brains. Of course, we've all been in meetings where we felt we were expected to turn off our brains, but that's another matter entirely.

There's a bigger issue at hand. The experts who participated in the Pew project are evenly split on whether digital offloading to an external brain will make workers better or worse. Will the rewired consciousness make them into shallow thinkers or deep thinkers? In the Pew Research, 42% of the experts agreed with this paragraph:

In 2020, the brains of multitasking teens and young adults are "wired" differently from those over age 35 and overall it yields baleful results. They do not retain information; they spend most of their energy sharing short social messages, being entertained, and being distracted away from deep engagement with people and knowledge. They lack deep-thinking capabilities; they lack face-to-face social skills; they depend in unhealthy ways on the internet and mobile devices to function. In sum, the changes in behavior and cognition among the young are generally negative outcomes.

If it will make them into deeper thinkers who can make quick, well-informed decisions based on plenty of evidence, then there's little to worry about, right? That's what we want in a workforce, so we older workers just need to readjust our notions of the route people should travel to reach good decisions. But what if the skeptics are right, that this digital brain will leave people shallow and unable to focus the right amount of attention on a problem? You could be left with a workforce that doesn't think through problems completely, resulting in sloppy work, poor solutions and ineffective performance. If you think your organization has already reached this sad state of affairs, you probably aren't so interested in the debate as you are in how to fix it—fast.

As with a lot of generational work style issues, it's good practice to take a person's strengths and reapply them to make up for deficiencies. If Millennials aren't coming up with thoughtful, thoroughly considered decisions, you need to engage one of their other strengths.

For example, when they are working on a tough problem, tell them that the solution is important and that other stakeholders have failed to find a solution. That will force them to rethink the issue using one of their other strengths—their belief that they can fix big problems. Or, as they are researching, you could ask them to double check all the sources they draw from on the Web to make sure they are legitimate. A lot of older generations underestimate the ability of younger workers to judge the veracity of online sources; in fact, they've done it since they were tikes. We've noticed recently that Millennials are far less likely than Boomers and Traditionalists to forward those blast emails full of erroneous information and dire warnings—the kind that a quick search of snopes.com will clear up. But it doesn't hurt to have them go through the exercise of fact checking, because they will be able to do it quickly, and it might help them think about the solution in a different way. Millennials work fast, both because they are young and because their brains are wired for speed.

Two other things as we consider a workforce of distracted, shallow-thinking employees. The first relates to training. In the past, we gave time management training to people who were disorganized. We taught interpersonal skills to employees who needed better people skills. Soon we may need to offer training that helps people concentrate on difficult tasks.

Finally, don't let go of your Boomers. They may be the last generation in the workforce with the ability to singularly focus on the big issues your organization faces. We know many of them are retiring, but you may want to bring them back as consultants. They're naturals. When you've got a particularly big, important project that is going to require focused decision makers and problem solvers, you could do worse than bringing back some of your Boomers. They can do big-picture, mission-driven, focused problem solving when you need it.

Appendix

Inventory

How Cross-Generationally Friendly Is Your Work Group, Department, Business, or Organization?

Accommodating Employee Differences

1. There is no one successful "type" in this organization: managers, leaders and those in the most desirable jobs are a mix of ages, sexes, ethnicities.

1	2	3	4	5
completely false	somewhat false	somewhat true/some-what false	somewhat true	completely true

2. When a project team is put together, employees with different backgrounds, experiences, skills, and viewpoints are consciously included.

1	2	3	4	5
completely false	somewhat false	somewhat true/some-what false	somewhat true	completely true

3. Employees are treated like customers.

1	2	3	4	5
completely false	somewhat false	somewhat true/some-what false	somewhat true	completely true

4. There is lots of conversation—even some humor—about differing viewpoints and perspectives.

1	2	3	4	5
completely false	somewhat false	somewhat true/some-what false	somewhat true	completely true

5. We take time to talk openly about what different cohorts—and the individuals within them—are looking for on the job . . . what makes work rewarding...which environment is most productive . . . what types of work load, schedule and policies work best.

1	2	3	4	5
completely false	somewhat false	somewhat true/some-what false	somewhat true	completely true

Creating Workplace Choices

6. Our atmosphere and policies are based on the work being done, the customers being served, and the preferences of the people who work here.

1	2	3	4	5
completely false	somewhat false	somewhat true/some-what false	somewhat true	completely true

7. There is behind-the-back complaining, passive-aggressive behavior and open hostility among groups of employees.

1	2	3	4	5
completely false	somewhat false	somewhat true/some-what false	somewhat true	completely true

8. There is a minimum of bureaucracy and "red tape" here.

1	2	3	4	5
completely false	somewhat false	somewhat true/some-what false	somewhat true	completely true

9. The work atmosphere could be described as relaxed and informal.

1	2	3	4	5
completely false	somewhat false	somewhat true/some-what false	somewhat true	completely true

10. There's an element of fun and playfulness about most endeavors here.

1	2	3	4	5
completely false	somewhat false	somewhat true/some-what false	somewhat true	completely true

Operating from a Flexible Management Style

11. Managers here are a bit more "polished" or professional than in most companies.

1	2	3	4	5
completely false	somewhat false	somewhat true/some-what false	somewhat true	completely true

12. Managers adjust policies and procedures to fit the needs of individuals and the team.

1	2	3	4	5
completely false	somewhat false	somewhat true/some-what false	somewhat true	completely true

13. Managers here are known for being straightforward.

1	2	3	4	5
completely false	somewhat false	somewhat true/some-what false	somewhat true	completely true

14. Managers give those who report to them the big picture along with specific goals and measures.

1	2	3	4	5
completely false	somewhat false	somewhat true/some-what false	somewhat true	completely true

Respect for Competence and Initiative

15. We assume the best of and from our people; we treat everyone—from the newest recruit to the most seasoned employee—as if they have great things to offer and are motivated to do their best.

1	2	3	4	5
completely false	somewhat false	somewhat true/some-what false	somewhat true	completely true

Nourishing Retention

16. We are concerned and focused, on a daily basis, with retention.

1	2	3	4	5
completely false	somewhat false	somewhat true/some-what false	somewhat true	completely true

17. We offer lots of training—from one-on-one coaching/mentoring to a varied menu of classroom courses to elearning.

1	2	3	4	5
completely false	somewhat false	somewhat true/some-what false	somewhat true	completely true

18. We encourage regular lateral movement.

1	2	3	4	5
completely false	somewhat false	somewhat true/some-what false	somewhat true	completely true

19. Work assignments here are broad—providing variety and challenge, and allowing each employee to develop a range of skills.

1	2	3	4	5
completely false	somewhat false	somewhat true/some-what false	somewhat true	completely true

20. We market internally—"selling" the company to employees, continually looking for ways to be the employer of choice.

1	2	3	4	5
completely false	somewhat false	somewhat true/some-what false	somewhat true	completely true

If your score was:

Under 70   Your organization is in danger; the high costs of losing, recruiting, and training employees will seriously damage your bottom line, if they haven't already.

70-79   You're typical of most organizations. Though you're doing some good things, you must make major improvements to your work environment if you're going to survive and thrive in today's competitive market.

80-89   Your turnover is probably lower than the industry average; you are doing a good job, but there's room for improvement.

90-100   Congratulations! Not only is turnover lower than the average for your industry, but the work atmosphere you've created is so attractive to employees that recruiting nearly takes care of itself. Good job.

Endnotes

Introduction
The New Economic Reality and the Cross-Generational Workplace

1. "Fertility Rate Reaches 25-Year Low," Demographic Intelligence, April 18, 2012, http://www.demographicintel.com/fertility-rate-reaches-25-year-low (Retrieved July 2012).
2. Claire Raines and Arleen Arnspager, *Millennials@Work* (Colorado: Claire Raines Associates, 2009), p. 15.

Chapter 1
A New Chapter in the Cross-Generational Workplace

1. David K. Foot, *Boom, Bust & Echo* (Toronto: MacFarlane, Walters and Ross, 1996), p. 2.
2. *Ibid.*, p. 7.
3. William Strauss and Neil Howe, *Generations* (New York: Quill Publications, 1991), p. 23.

Chapter 2
The Traditionalists: What Will the Colonel
Do Now—Work? Retire? Consult?

1. Tom Brokaw, *The Greatest Generation* (New York: Random House, 1998), p. 37.
2. Alvin Toffler, *The Third Wave* (New York: Bantam Books, 1991), p. 118.
3. M. Scott Myers and Susan S. Myers, "Toward Understanding the Changing Work Ethic," *California Management Review* XXI (1974):7.
4. Kathryn Zickhur, "Generations and Their Gadgets," *Pew Internet & American Life Project*, Feb 3, 2011.
5. From Kristin Anderson and Ron Zemke, *Coaching Knock Your Socks Off Service* (New York: AMACOM, 1997), p. 110.
6. Christopher Bayer, PhD, "The *Grand* Parent Economy," The Source for Investor Empowerment, 2012, http://theshareholderactivist.com/senior-investors/seniors-money (Retrieved July 2012).

Chapter 3
The Baby Boomers: Retirement Posponed

1. The Boomer Institute, based in Cleveland, Ohio, in a study conducted on their Web site, August 22, 1998.
2. The Boomer Institute, based in Cleveland, Ohio, in a study conducted on their Web site, August 22, 1998.
3. William Strauss, Interview by Bob Filipczak, October 1998.
4. D'Vera Cohn and Paul Taylor, "Baby Boomers Approach Age 65—Glumly," Pew Research Center, December 20, 2010, http://www.pewsocialtrends.org/2010/12/20/baby-boomers-approach-65-glumly (Retrieved July 2012).
5. Susan Quilty, "How Baby Boomers are Driving the Motorcycle Trend," 55 Places. Com, http://www.55places.com/blog/baby-boomer-motorcycle-clubs, December 29, 2009 (Retrieved July 2012).
6. Arthur Delaney, "Retirement And The Recession: Savings Destroyed For One Out Of Four Older Workers, Says AARP Survey," Huffington Post, May 24, 2011, http://www.huffingtonpost.com/2011/05/24/retirement-savings-older-workers-recession_n_866109.html (Retrieved July 2012).
7. Andy Sedlak, "Senior Citizens Attracted to Campus Settings," Middletown Journal, September 26, 2011, http://www.middletownjournal.com/news/news/local/senior-citizens-attracted-to-campus-settings/nNRw5/ (Retrieved July 2012).
8. Ashley Lutz, "Here's the Real Reason Why Millennials Are the Most Stressed Generation," Business Insider, April 19, 2012, http://articles.businessinsider.com/2012-04-19/news/31365379_1_stress-in-america-survey-millennials-baby-boomers (Retrieved July 2012).

Chapter 4
The Gen Xers: Survivalists in the Workplace

1. B. Drain, *Generation X Entrepreneurial Generation* (Video), Bloomberg TV, 2011, http://www.bloomberg.com/video/75529586-generation-x-the-entrepreneurial-generation.htmlBoomberg.com (Retrieved July 2012).
2. Margot Hornblower, "Great Xpectations," *Time Magazine,* June 9, 1997.
3. Jonathan Strickland, "How the Googleplex Works," How Stuff Works, 2008, http://computer.howstuffworks.com/googleplex.htm (Retrieved July 2012).
4. Greg Felt, "Generational Differences," *The Mountain Mail,* August 9, 2012.

Chapter 5
The Millennials: Be Careful What You Ask For

1. Jon Stewart, "Jon Stewart's ('84) Commencement Address, Office of University Relations, The College of William & Mary, May 20, 2004, http://web.wm.edu/news/archive/index.php?id=3650 (Retrieved August 2012).
2. London Jones, *Great Expectations* (New York: Ballantine Press, 1980), p. 44.
3. Neil Howe and Bill Strauss, *13ᵗʰ Gen* (New York: Vintage Press, 1993), p. 63.

4. Neil Howe and Bill Strauss, *Generations* (New York: Quill Publications, 1991), p. 335.
5. Al Lewis, "Kids Get Upscale Touch," *Rocky Mountain News,* November 22, 1998.
6. Kathy Boccella, "New Baby Boom? Nope, It's a Parent Boom," *Denver Post,* March 28, 1997.
7. Matthew Scott Kuhn, "Leading Schools Through a Generational Lens," doctoral dissertation presented to the faculty of the Morgridge College of Education, University of Denver, June 8, 2012, p. 38.
8. Claire Raines and Arleen Arnsparger, *Millennials@Work: Engaging the New Generation* (Denver, CO: Claire Raines Associates, 2009), p. 28.
9. Barbara Dafoe-Whitehead, "The Girls of Gen X," *American Enterprise,* January/February 1998.
10. David Leonhardt, "Old vs. Young," *The New York Times,* June 22, 2012.
11. Transcript for "Political Implications of Today's Generation Gap," The Diane Rehm Show, National Public Radio, June 27, 2012, http://thedianerehmshow.org/shows/2012-06-27/political-implications-todays-generation-gap/transcript (Retrieved July 2012).
12. Joseph F. Coughlin, "America's New Generation Gap: Optimism," October 30, 2011, BigThink,http://bigthink.com/disruptive-demographics/americas-new-generation-gap-optimism (Retrieved July 2012).
13. Piotr Czerski, "We, the Web Kids," Pastebin, February 15, 2012, http://http://pastebin.com/0xXV8k7k (Retrieved July 2012).
14. Matthew Scott Kuhn, "Leading Schools Through a Generational Lens," doctoral dissertation presented to the faculty of the Morgridge College of Education, University of Denver, June 8, 2012, p. 38.
15. *Wall Street Journal*
16. Transcript for "Political Implications of Today's Generation Gap," The Diane Rehm Show, National Public Radio, June 27, 2012, http://thedianerehmshow.org/shows/2012-06-27/political-implications-todays-generation-gap/transcript (Retrieved July 2012).
17. Jean Twenge, Sara Konrath, Joshua D. Voster, W. Keith Campbell, and Brad J. Bushman, "Egos Inflating Over Time," *Journal of Personality* 76:4, August 2008.
18. "My Youth and Intrepid Conduct Study on Millennials and the Company of the Future," Mr. Youth, Intrepid, May 11, 2010, http://www.marketwire.com/press-release/mr-youth-and-intrepid-conduct-study-on-millennials-and-the-company-of-the-future-1258031.htm (Retrieved July 2012).
19. CareerRookie, "Millennial Job Seeker Perceptions and Behaviors," Career Rookie, 2010, http://www.careerrookie.com/CC/JobPoster/Default.aspx (Retrieved July 2012).
20. Vivian Giang, "40 Percent of Young People Would Take a Pay Cut," The Business Insider, February 14, 2012, http://articles.businessinsider.com/2012-02-14/news/31057836_1_young-adults-social-media-access-college-students, (Retrieved July 2012).
21. "Volunteerism Growing as Factor in Awarding College Scholarships" *Arizona Daily Star*, January 2, 2009.
22. "Praising a Grown Up Digital Generation," NPR News, November 3, 2008, http://m.npr.org/news/front/96503209 (Retrieved July 2012).

Chapter 6
The Global Workforce: Generations Around the World

1. Rabab Naqvi, "Generation With Aspirations?" The Hindu Magazine, February 6, 2005, http://www.hindu.com/mag/2005/02/06/stories/2005020600630800.htm (Retrieved July 2012).
2. Susan Burgess, "Your Past Experiences Will Effect Your Future, Unless You Implement a Change, Right Now," Ezine Articles, January 12, 2007, http://ezinearticles .com/?Your-Past-Experiences-will-Effect-Your-Future,-Unless-you-Implement-a-Change,-Right-Now&id=746155 (Retrueved July 2012).
3. Dr. Susan Murphy and Arleen Arnsparger, *4genR8tns: Succeeding with Colleagues, Cohorts & Customers.* (Denver, CO: Claire Raines Associates, 2008), p. 15.
4. Tamara J. Erickson and Timothy Bevins, "Generations and Geography: Understanding the Diversity of Generations Around the Globe," Moxie Insight, 2011, p. 3.
5. Taylor Clark, "Plight of the Little Emperors," Psychology Today, June 6, 2012, http:// www.psychologytoday.com/articles/200806/plight-the-little-emperors (Retrueved July 2012).
6. Claire Raines and Arleen Arnsparger, *Millennials@Work: Engaging the New Generation.* (Denver, CO: Claire Raines Associates, 2009), p. 19.

Chapter 7
The ACORN Imperatives and Three Companies That Bridge the Gaps

1. "Ernst & Young Marks Tenth Anniversary as One of Fortune's '100 Best Companies to Work For,'" Ernst & Young, January 22, 2008, http://www.ey.com/US/en/Newsroom/ News-releases/Media-Release-01-22-08DC (Retrieved August 2012).
2. Randstad, "2008 World of Work," Randstad North America, L.P. 2008, p. 17.

Chapter 8
Company Best Practices and Other Great Ideas

1. Adam Bryant, "Corner Office: Laurel J. Richie," *The New York Times,* August 5, 2012.

Chapter 14
Emerging Media and the Workforce

1. We, the Web Kids, by Alexis C. Madrigal, The Atlantic, Feb. 21, 2012. http://www .theatlantic.com/technology/archive/2012/02/we-the-web-kids/253382/

Acknowledgments

This new edition was born, became a toddler, and reached adolescence in dozens of conversations and dialogues with scores of people who are interested in, encouraging of, and enthusiastic about the concept of a workplace filled with four generations of people working through their frustrations, forging ahead, collaborating, and producing great results together *because* of their differences. We were blessed with the opinions, perspectives, and insights of hundreds of people out there working every day. It is our good fortune that they were paying close attention to the ways in which generational differences affect the way organizations get the work done. There are many people to thank for helping us with the original book and this new edition.

Many thanks go to Chip Bell, Megan Emme, Stevy Merrill, Dale Merrill, Steve Georgoulis, Nikki Moss, and Mary Pat Wilson for providing information, support, and contacts. Over the years, Neil Howe and the late Bill Strauss were generous not only with their time but with their invaluable insights into the character and conflicts of the generations. We are grateful to our AMACOM editor, Christina Parisi.

Our spouses, Amy Filipczak and Allen Alderman, were models of patience, perseverance, and support during this journey. Susan Zemke counseled and advised through every stage of the process. Thank you, thank you.

For the last fourteen years of Ron Zemke's life, Jill Applegate was his right-hand person at Performance Research Associates—and continues as its business director. She edited every chapter of this new edition with care and precision, and we are deeply grateful for her help.

We're certain we've left important contributors off this list. If you're one, please know that, as you read this, we're burning with guilt and humiliation since we remembered we forgot to include you, and that, oafish as we are, we are, nevertheless, deeply grateful for your assistance.

To each and every one of you, thank you. We hope you'll enjoy reading this new edition and finding your contributions. We're proud of what we accomplished together.

Claire Raines
Bob Filipczak

Index

Index

About the Authors

Ron Zemke (1942-2004) proudly represented the Traditionalist Generation in our first edition. Ron's award-winning writing, consulting and research with such organizations as Ford Motor Company, Roadway Express, Dayton Hudson Department Stores, Beverly Enterprises, Microsoft, Southern California Gas, the Audubon Institute, Harley-Davidson, Courtyard by Marriott, Motorola, and Wendy's International, brought him face to face with the problems and opportunities of the cross-generational workforce and marketplace. As Senior Editor of Minneapolis-based *Training* magazine and contributing editor of the Training Directors' Forum newsletter, he covered the emergence of the nation's growing service sector as well as other major issues in American business and management. Ron is the author or coauthor of 27 books, including the best selling *Knock Your Socks Off Service* series (AMACOM), and *Knock Your Socks Off Selling* (AMACOM, 1999). He is also the coauthor with Karl Albrecht of *Service America!,* the book credited with starting the U.S. customer service revolution.

Claire Raines is one of the leading experts and a pioneer in the field of generations in the workplace. Her book *Twentysomething: Managing & Motivating Today's New Work Force* was the first to address the topic of Generation X on the job and was named one of the 30 best business books of 1992. Claire has been studying generations at work for more than 25 years, and she has shared her findings in eight books, five videos, and a board game, earning national awards for her groundbreaking and practical information. In 2012, she introduced the *Values and Influence Assessment*®, a new tool based on four generational profiles that identifies an individual's values regardless of birth year. Her company, Claire Raines Associates, delivers interactive speeches and workshops that focus on better understanding the generations and creating environments that engage employees of all ages. Clients include Kellogg, PriceWaterhouseCoopers, DTE Energy, McDonald's, MasterCard, Toyota, and Coca-Cola. Claire has been featured widely in the media, including *USA Today*, *Training*, *Working Woman*, and *Personnel Journal*. She resides in Tucson, Arizona. You can visit her website at www.generations atwork.com.

Bob Filipczak is an honorary member of Generation X, though some argue that his 1962 birth date makes him too old to make the claim. He himself has no trouble grouping himself with the Xer cohort and has always identified strongly with them. He took his first plunge into writing about generational issues as staff editor for *Training* magazine. His early editorial "Working for Boomers" was followed by a cover story entitled "It's Just a Job: Generation X in the Workplace" in April 1994. That was so well-received, especially by Xers, that he started talking to Ron Zemke about the book you now have in front of you. After journalism, Bob became the nomadic Xer, bouncing from job to job—and not always voluntarily. He works in social media and video, and also gets up in front of audiences to present on the topic of generations. Bob currently does presentations on "Communicating across Generations," "Marketing across Generations," and "Managing across Generations." Ask him your generational workplace questions on Facebook at Generations at Work and on Twitter.